WITHDRAWN

Illinois Central College
Learning Resource Center

BASIC STORY TECHNIQUES

BASIC STORY TECHNIQUES

by Helen (Reagan) Smith

University of Oklahoma Press

Norman

BY HELEN REAGAN SMITH

If My People (Dallas, 1944)
Basic Story Techniques (Norman, 1964)

Library of Congress Catalog Card Number: 64-13590

To that dean of teachers, Foster—Harris
who showed us how

SO YOU WANT TO WRITE . . .

A QUARTER OF A CENTURY ago the late Professor Walter S. Campbell and I launched a modest writing program at the University of Oklahoma, based on the thesis that competent writing, either fact or fiction, is a learnable, teachable skill, and not, as some loons insisted, a peculiar and unknowable gift, awarded only to God's pets.

Twenty-five years later I get some quiet satisfaction out of the record: more than three hundred published books by students and graduates, including a number 1 national best seller, book-club selections, scholarly works, histories, biographies, travel books, religious books, juveniles, westerns, books in foreign languages from Japanese to the Scandinavian—in brief, the range.

And there have been many, many sales of shorter material, to more than one thousand periodicals—again, all over the world. Sales have been made also to the motion pictures, to television, to radio. Yes, it can be done.

Certainly we enjoyed no unending invasion of potential geniuses to spark this continuous parade of sales. These writers were just people, like yourself. They had simply learned the secret, available to anybody willing to accept it.

The secret of successful writing is the secret of all human communication. First the human spirit, the sincere emotion of the author, must reach out and evoke a response from the reader. The broadcasting station must find a receiver turned on and tuned in.

Then, by a simple and learnable technique called "reversal," you can communicate practically anything. The reversal itself is the most important learning of all.

Here is a fair sampling of the works of writers who have learned something of this reversal in classes over the years. We are proud of these authors, and equally proud of many others whose stories could not be included. After all, Mrs. Smith had limits to observe: one book, not a whole library! I think you will find that she has here done a thoroughly competent job of explaining, with impressive examples, just what good fiction is.

We have never tried to put on any gaudy, self-serving show, Mrs. Smith, Professor Swain, and I. (That's all the Professional Writing staff there is!) But there is one article of faith, sometimes ironic, in which we believe: "A good writer sells others, but he gives himself away."

FOSTER-HARRIS

PREFACE

A NUMBER OF VOLUMES have been written to aid the would-be-
writer. My reason for adding this one to that number is to prove
that, indeed, professional writing can be taught and learned. The
stories which I have used as illustrations in this book were all
written by professionals who got their training in the University
of Oklahoma.

A word of explanation concerning my arrangement of this
book may be in order here. The first chapters are an introduction
to the basic techniques of story-writing. Then, after Chapter 4,
each chapter of the book is followed by a complete story. This
seemed to me an ideal—and interesting—way of illustrating the
points made in each chapter.

All of the stories here have been published before in top-flight
markets. The writers included are by no means all the best prod-
ucts of our professional-writing classes—it would be impossible
to include so many. But here you will find a sampling of what has
been learned—and written.

The authors include Cliff Adams ("Reconnaissance Patrol,"
Saturday Evening Post, October 8, 1949), who has published
nearly thirty books, and Helene Carpenter ("Violets from Portugal," *This Week,* February 28, 1943), who has published in many
of the top magazines, including *Cosmopolitan.* Death claimed
Mary Agnes Thompson ("Stubborn Bride," *Saturday Evening
Post,* November 9, 1957) when she was working on her first book,
but she supported herself for years with her stories and had sold
more than a dozen of them to the *Saturday Evening Post, Good
Housekeeping, Cosmopolitan,* and other magazines.

Alberta Wilson Constant ("The Preacher's Confession," *Saturday Evening Post*, May 3, 1963) is a housewife. Ennen Reaves Hall ("Heaven Knows," *Christian Herald*, November, 1948) was a grandmother when she began her studies and has lived from her writings since selling her early westerns. Fred Grove ("Comanche Son," *Boy's Life*, September, 1961) won three awards for his novel *Comanche Captives*. Ed Montgomery ("The Most Important Man in Town," *Saturday Evening Post*, June 23, 1956) makes his living as a newspaperman. The *Saturday Evening Post* has purchased every story that he has written.

Al Dewlen ("Showdown at San Saba," *Saturday Evening Post*, September 18, 1954) won the $10,000 fiction award from McGraw-Hill for his *Twilight of Honor*, which was a Book-of-the-Month Club selection. William R. Scott ("Real Gone Guy," *The American Magazine*, March, 1956) is the author of the best seller *Onionhead*, and will have two books published this year. "Real Gone Guy" is his last short story.

I am grateful to the above writers for granting me permission to use their work. I want also to express my appreciation to my students, Ann Jensen, Helen McNair, Bea Zeeck, Betty Bain, and Margaret Uri, for allowing me to quote from their lessons.

Struggling alone in the dark is not easy for one who wants to be a writer. There are few means of finding those road signs which point away from failure and toward success, although it is gratifying to note that more and more universities are adding training in professional writing to their curriculums.

For years in the University of Oklahoma, Foster-Harris, later ably assisted by Dwight V. Swain, has demonstrated that writing can be taught and learned. Countless books have been dedicated to Foster-Harris, saying: "To Foster—who showed me how." Enough cannot be said for this man who has paused from his own success to point the way for others.

In my own experience I have discovered that it is a delight beyond measure to lead a student from his first struggling efforts to the printed page. My work with my colleagues, and with my own correspondence and extension students, has been a great joy. In writing this book, I hope that I have been able to pass the joy along to you.

HELEN REAGAN SMITH

Norman, Oklahoma
March 13, 1964

CONTENTS

So You Want To Write . . .
    by Foster-Harris   vii

Preface   ix

PART ONE, THE STUDY OF SOURCE MATERIAL FOR YOUR WRITING

ONE, Basic Needs of a Writer   3

TWO, Aim for the Heart   10

THREE, Develop Your Perception   18

PART TWO, TEACHING YOURSELF PROFESSIONAL HABITS

FOUR, Your Character Tells the Story   27

    "Reconnaissance Patrol" by Clifton Adams   30

FIVE, Time Moves Forward   47

    "Violets from Portugal"
    by Helene Carpenter   51, 75

SIX, Establish Your Writing Habits   87

    "Stubborn Bride" by Mary Agnes Thompson   93

PART THREE, THE STUDY OF TECHNIQUE

SEVEN, See with Scenes   111

    "The Preacher's Confession"
    by Alberta Wilson Constant   117

EIGHT, Devices   136

    "Heaven Knows" by Ennen Reaves Hall   145

NINE, The Beginning   154

    "Comanche Son" by Fred Grove   163

TEN, The Middle   179

    "The Most Important Man in Town"
    by Ed Montgomery   193

ELEVEN, The End   208

    "Showdown at San Saba" by Al Dewlen   212

TWELVE, Ability Grows   228

    "Real Gone Guy" by William R. Scott   233

PART ONE

The Study of Source Material for Your Writing

CHAPTER ONE

BASIC NEEDS OF A WRITER

"Mr. Clemens," a new acquaintance stopped Mark Twain, "I have a bone to pick with you. I'd give twenty-five dollars if I'd never read your *Tom Sawyer.*"

"Why?" Mark Twain asked in surprise.

"It would be worth it," the man insisted, a sheepish grin covering his face, "just to have the privilege of reading it again for the *first* time."

Spontaneity and originality. How hard it is to get it into writing, and how wonderful it is when you find it!

There will always be a need and a demand for first-class writers. Although markets change and vary, demands rise and fall, styles and tastes reverse and alternate, the need remains for someone to depict our times as well as times past so that readers a hundred years from now can relive our experiences. A writer, if he masters his art well, can take his very limitations and reverse them into advantages.

Balzac did this. Irritated over the demands of his market that he write trivial short stories, first he fretted, then he deliberately depicted the individual small villages and revealed the way of French life. The result, according to his translator, was tremendous. "Balzac has given us a marvelous picture of French life and manners of the sixteenth century," he wrote. "The gallant knights and merry dames of that eventful period stand out in bold relief upon his canvas. After reading *Contes Drolatiques* one could almost find one's way about the towns and villages of Touraine unassisted by map or guide. Not only is the book a work of art from the historical information and topographical accuracy, but written in the nineteenth century in imitation of

3

the style of the sixteenth, it is a triumph of literary archaeology."

It was different, original, and done for the first time!

But how do you gain originality and that first-time feeling? What can you do to lift the reader into that he-was-there-seeing-it-happen sensation?

Today's writer's are swamped with advice and are still seeking the right answers. That is why you are reading this book: to find out what you need to know. You have heard practical people murmur, "Write what will sell"; crusaders ask you to exalt pet theories; some editors have limited the subject to interesting people, who include criminals, millionaires, and movie stars—at times, no others!

Victor Hugo insisted that there were no bad subjects, that writing is all a matter of skill and execution. Dante said that great literature must deal with *salus, venus, virtus*—war, love, and character. Dumas classified it similarly when he divided writing into action, emotion, and ideas. Horace said that if you wish your reader to weep, you must first shed tears yourself.

The late Walter S. Campbell used to tell his classes that whatever the writing problem was, it could be solved if the writer knew three things well. These were: (1) See that you know and love your subject. (2) Be sure you know and love your reader. (3) Develop the skill to take your reader into the heart and mind of your main character.

The better you know your material, the greater are your chances that you can write about it with enough interest and enthusiasm to make it glow in the heart of your reader. Real communication is the ability to plant the image that is within your own mind with the feeling which you, yourself, hold about it into the mind of the person with whom you wish to communicate.

In short, good writing builds a bridge into the mind and heart of your reader. This, in itself, is an art. It is also a skill. The simplest things are not always easy. Different words call up different ideas in individual minds.

A second-grade teacher put the sentence "Mary had a little

4

lamb" upon the blackboard and instructed the children to show which word indicated the girl, and which showed possession.

In the back an eight-year-old chewed her pencil. She had a cat named Mary, so that let the name out as being a girl; her cow had a calf that morning, but a cat couldn't have a lamb, so that let out possession; and she was stymied. So what seemed exceedingly simple became a hurdle.

Notice the difference between the following two answers to the question "What was the funniest thing you ever experienced?"

First answer: "Me on a camel."

Second answer: "At the age of thirteen, I was a Freshman in high school, barely five feet tall, and I still wore patent leather, flat-heeled shoes with a strap (Mary Jane shoes, I think they were called; anyway, they were fashionable only for girls aged one to ten!), my hair style was a 'Dutch bob,' and worst of all, I was straight up-and-down—flat-chested as any boy.

"It was mortifying when some dowager beamed toothily, patted me on the head and cooed, 'My, what a smart little girl you are—in high school already! How old are you, ten?'

"But I had the rest of the equipment other thirteen-year-old girls had. I wanted a boy friend. I wanted a strapless evening gown. And I wanted to be invited to the Junior Prom.

"As the date for the Prom approached, I realized I'd have to do something about my infantile appearance or nobody would ask me to go. After all, even Bob Stull, whom I'd known since Kindergarten and who wore sneakers and was knock-kneed, didn't want to rob the cradle. And with no mother to help—.

"So I bought the smallest bra I could find, a pair of silk stockings, a garter belt, and some curlers. With my nine-year-old sister Pat as an interested spectator, I rolled my hair in the curlers one night, about a week before the Prom.

" 'That won't help,' she prophesied darkly, 'your hair'll just stick out.'

"I ignored her and spent a sleepless night, trying to lie on my face and breathe at the same time.

"In the morning, Pat was on hand to view the aging process.

" 'I told 'ja your hair'd stick out,' she said.

"I refrained from answering. I also refrained from crying when I tried to comb my hair. My face always splotched when I cried.

" 'Every time you move, that toilet paper's gonna crackle in your brassiere.' Pat was entirely objective.

" 'Why don't you go in your own room and dress?' I snapped.

" 'I'd rather dress in here,' she said, 'so I can watch.'

"I put on the garter belt, struggling with the unfamiliar hooks in the back, then took the stockings from their tissue paper.

"Pat's eyes grew round. 'Gee, maybe they *will* help,' she said encouragingly. 'Your legs won't look so skinny.'

"At last I was dressed and went down to breakfast with my cheering section trotting happily behind me.

" 'Hey, Dad, lookit Honey!' Pat said as we sat down at the table. 'She's got a *bust!*'

"I hunched over my cereal, glaring at her.

" 'It's toilet paper,' she went on conversationally, 'but one side's bigger than the other.'

"Dad's opinion was terse and to the point. I retired to my room to remove the anatomical miracle and consider an appropriate method of torture for Pat.

"It was a beautiful spring day, and as I walked to school I scarcely noticed the weight of the books I carried. My hair could be worse; the stockings felt firm and luxurious. The garters were uncomfortable, but I'd get used to them.

" 'Hi.'

"I looked up at Bob Stull's grin. Maybe he *was* knock-kneed, but he was president of the Junior Class. I'd played "Tap-the-Icebox" with him since Kindergarten, but he looked different today. I hoped I looked different to him, too. . . .

"As we approached the school, my books grew heavy, and so did my heart. If he was going to ask me to the Prom, it would have to be in the next three minutes. I shifted my books to the other arm and felt something snap somewhere in the middle of my back.

6

" 'Say,' Bob said, 'You doing anything Saturday night?'

"Something terrible was happening. The pressure of the garter belt around my waist was gone. The no-longer-hooked belt was sliding past my hips. The stockings were sagging at knees and ankles.

" 'Uh—what?' I gasped, clutching the books against my stomach in a vain attempt to arrest the descent of the garter belt.

" 'Would you go to the Prom with me?' he sounded puzzled.

"I didn't dare look at him; besides, I was too busy trying to walk with my knees together.

"The catastrophe was complete when Pat came galloping up, waving my algebra book.

" 'You forgot your—.'

"That's as far as she got. She stared at me, open-mouthed. I slid my books down toward my knees to try to keep the whole apparatus—garter belt and stockings—from falling to my ankles. I'd heard of a girl who'd had the elastic in her panties break; she'd calmly walked out of them and gone on her way without even looking back. Well, some people had all the luck. I could see myself trying to walk out of a garter belt attached to my stockings.

" 'You sick 'er sump'n?' Pat inquired.

"Desperately, I looked at Bob. He was watching me strangely. 'I'll-be-happy-to-go-with-you,' I babbled, 'Thanks-for-asking-me-goodbye!'

"My dismissal was unmistakable and he turned to walk away, his expression indicating a definite doubt in his choice of a date for the Prom.

" 'Oh, *I* see!' Pat's voice carried beautifully. 'You're losing your *garter* belt! Gee aren't you glad that Dad made you take off that—.'

"Books, stockings, and garter belt hit the ground as I clapped my hand over Pat's mouth. Bob turned back, but didn't look at me. His face was crimson as he collected my scattered books and papers.

"Pat whisked that awful contraption off me so quickly that no-

7

body knew she was rescuing me from eternal disgrace. It took only a moment to roll the stockings into anklets.

"As Bob handed me my books (there wasn't anyone who could collect my scattered wits) he smiled warmly, his face still pink.

" 'I'll pick you up at nine Saturday,' he said.

" 'You taking 'er to the *Prom?*' Pat squealed. 'That's sump'n! Bet she won't wear stockings and a garter belt, though!'

"And she skipped down the street, one end of the garter belt dangling from her coat pocket."

   ❀ ❀ ❀

Now, do you see the difference?

Which student knew her subject, knew her reader, then took her reader into the mind and heart of her viewpoint character?

Before you can write with success you must have a sense of importance concerning that which you desire to share with your reader: something which you feel *needs to be said.* The things which come under this are experiences to be shared, truths to be demonstrated, and emotions to be experienced. Here is the clay with which the writer works.

And the writer must have the ability to make himself work. He has no taskmaster who stands over him demanding he finish the day's quota, no hours where an overseer watches his production. He may live where he pleases, work when he pleases, but if he is to succeed, work he must. Writing itself is work; good writing is hard work.

It is easy to bog down in dull routine. Technical studies which pay big dividends after they are mastered can be as dismal as dishwashing in the learning procedure. Not only must the writer train his brain to see and understand the writer's problems and know their solution, he must also teach, direct, and develop his own subconscious that it may co-operate with the mind in delivering the needed material and getting the working habits established.

How well can you take an incident of yesterday or last week and so visualize it, translate it, that pictures become words in a

8

way that tomorrow's reader may relive your experience? Words for such visualization are merely tools of the trade. So are sentences, paragraphs, patterns of various forms. As cloth can be cut into many kinds of garments to serve different needs, so various pattern forms can give the writer the skills he needs to produce his desired effect.

John Dryden put it this way: "The employment of a poet is like that of a curious gunsmith or watchmaker: the iron or silver is not his own; but they are the least part of that which gives value: the price lies wholly in the workmanship. The story is the least part; the problem of the real artist is the emotional pattern."

You, the writer, must learn to build these emotional patterns, to put them together in units as letters are put together to make words. As you do, you will find that you can play with life-material as a musician creates tunes upon the organ, making melodies sweep across the soul.

But you do not have to begin with the finished skill. Even an oak grows from a tiny acorn. If you have an intense desire to communicate, are anxious to share with others those things which you have discovered about life, and have the determination to make yourself work until your thoughts can stand up and march across the page into the heart of your reader, you will find that you have the basic seed of the writing skill. Begin and keep growing. You are on your way!

CHAPTER TWO

AIM FOR THE HEART

YOU'VE HEARD THE STORY that a person often has two reasons for doing something: first, the real reason; second, the reason that sounds good.

This is another way of saying that humanity travels in the direction of its desires and hides them by a covering of logic.

Every creative work starts with desire. This is true whether the work is painting a portrait, building a house, growing a garden, or writing a short story. Love for a thing starts the yearning (the desire) which stimulates thinking. Thinking produces ideas and ideas propel action.

It is your desire to write that prompts your reading this book.

Knowing this truth about individuals, you must learn how to aim first for the heart of your reader, then to go upward into his mind. So that we can understand what we are attempting, let us classify the mind as conscious-thinking and the heart as subconscious.

The conscious mind resides in the brain. It thinks rational thoughts; it reasons, weighs, and considers facts, ideas, and situations. It can establish habits that sink down to become part of the subconcious. Here resides the workaday part of the mind where thoughts flow and decisions are made. This, then, is the intellect, where reason is contrasted with feeling.

Feeling identifies itself with the heart. All your life you have been taught to suppress emotion and follow your head. From the first grade through the doctoral degree, you are commanded to let reason, judgment, and mental wisdom guide your activities.

More people think they are successful in doing this than are. Most individuals dream. They jump from subject to subject as

10

a grasshopper flits about a cornfield. There is no logical sequence
to their thought and little continuity. Ask somebody. Offer someone a penny for his thoughts. Chances are that he will glance up,
startled, and shrug, saying:

"Nothing, really, it's not important," or, "I don't remember."

Or they accept ideas secondhand, repeating glibly without
thought, or investigation, those things which their parents have
said or their teachers taught. Such thoughts are the hand-me-
down ideas of other minds.

If you feel that it is easy to control your thinking, try this exercise: Remember *in sequence* everything you did from the time
you awoke this morning. Do this very carefully, beginning with
first getting out of bed and following from there. Don't think,
"Oh, I went to the breakfast table; Oh, yes, before that I put on
my slippers." Be sure you put your slippers on first if that is what
you did, and deliberately refuse to get anything out of order.

Or take a night that you can't sleep. Deliberately move your
mind away from your mental problem that is chasing around like
a squirrel in a cage, and make your thoughts walk down the main
street of your town, seeing every store in its proper place, the
lights, the car meters, parked cars, etc. Cross the street and walk
back up, coming back to the place where you started again. See
if you can do this without having to do any backtracking.

The subconcious mind lies deep within; some call this the
heart. This is the part of man that feels. In this area there is no
logic, no ability to think. It can remember with distinct vividness, but it cannot reason, weigh, or calculate. Instead it follows
feeling.

Feeling cannot be conquered by reason. It must be mastered
and overcome by a stronger feeling. Spinoza pointed this out,
saying that one emotion can be mastered only by another more
powerful emotion, and by nothing else. Reason, will, feeling, duty,
faith conquer only by the force of emotional element contained
within. A soldier dying at his post does so because of his devotion
to honor or faithfulness. This sense of duty is more important to
him than other things. A man whose moral sense prompts him to

overcome his own passion does so because his love (emotion) for the moral is more powerful than all his other feelings.

Desires direct the mind's reasoning. Too long these have been considered fundamental differences, but the truth is, they are a matter of degrees.

If you doubt that emotion is the motor drive of people, try this little test with your acquaintances: Select an idea and present it to them using only the approach to the mind. Select forcible, bold, and logical reasons for its execution; accompany it by argument or proof; but keep all interest, excitement, or enthusiasm out of your voice and manner. Instead, keep a studied indifference, a shrugging-of-the-shoulders impersonal feeling about it, and watch the results.

Later, try it or another idea again; subtly insinuate in the nature of a hint your own feelings about the proposal, whether favorable or unfavorable. If you are eager, then glow with your own enthusiasm. Notice the result. Do you see any difference in the reaction?

Watch people. Include your family, friends, and persons on the street. What activates them? Are they moving toward the things they desire or things they need? A supermarket is a perfect place to study buyers. Are selections made according to the needs of the body or the tastes of the palate?

Observe a skillful lawyer—you see plenty of them on TV, if not in real life—and watch them use the power of imagination, as in, "You saw so and so, didn't you?" The statement of authority in itself can cause man to agree. It is easier to say "yes" than "no."

The advertising world is built upon this principle. Clerks will say: "This is a *beautiful* garment, isn't it? Don't you *like* this color?" making agreement easy.

Take a magazine, read it with the idea not of seeing the magazine's content but of seeing the man who buys the magazine, who finds entertainment or information behind its cover.

The editor has a vivid picture of this man, and he strives to give him, as best he can, what he wants. He does it with the reading matter, the advertising, and the entire layout. How well can you look into the mirror of the magazine and see the face of the reader it reflects? Go over a magazine with a pad and pencil, jotting down the things you would like that are left out; stimulate your own imagination actually to *see the reader.*

Take time to do this; then look at the following questions. How well have you covered these facts of the reader: sex, age, occupation, size of family, income, way in which leisure hours are spent, education, interests, hobbies, aims, desires, dreams, and ideals? What are the favorite sports, entertainments, and homes? What about health, appearance, and responsibilities?

Many things man understands because of his intellect, but there are other situations which he cannot possibly comprehend without his feelings. Mankind has always noted that "Birds of a feather flock together," "A full man does not understand a hungry one," and "One rogue recognizes another." Men have difficulty understanding each other because they live by different emotions.

So study people's emotions. Since you are a writer, you want to know how you can aid this subconcious mind of your reader to respond to the thoughts which you wish to share. And because you are a writer, you must do it with words.

Every word, written or printed, is the outward and physical expression of some inner state of being—resulting from the experience of the individual himself. Without his reaction toward it, words have no suggestive purpose. The total value of any word is limited to the meaning which leaps up within the mind of the person hearing it.

"Poltroonery" for instance, stirs no response from a person unfamiliar with the word. No matter how often you repeat it, even though you say it many times, there is no reaction—unless it is that of boredom. On the other hand, if you use the word "love," a direct physical and mental image is stimulated. Everybody has an idea of what "love" means.

Properly used, the feeling conveyed by the word itself can be produced. These feelings must have been experienced before, either directly or indirectly. Furthermore, the meaning of the term will depend largely upon the reader's personal experience. The word "love" will be responded to in different ways by different people. One person will imagine the love of sweethearts or of husband and wife. Another will see the mother-and-child relationship, while still someone else may snort that it is a low, animal passion. The same word may arouse pleasure in one and evoke rebellion in another.

How can you find out what words or arrangement of them will stir the response that you desire within your reader?

Begin with a study of yourself. You cannot write about an emotion which you have not felt, and you will discover, as you study your own reactions, that you have plenty for material. You need them all, the good and the bad. But begin with one. The particular emotion does not matter; the more you can remember, the better. Probe deep within yourself, recall the things that made you laugh with delight, burn with embarrassment, warm with amused affection—these are the things which you can best project to your reader in a way that he can share with you.

It is not the identical *experience* of the particular emotion but the use of the feeling in the material that you are projecting that you use.

One foggy night Ben Ames Williams rowed a boat out to a buoy and sat alone with the bell clanging beside him and smoked a pipe; a strong feeling swept over him, stirring his imagination. "The moment had meaning," he said telling about it later, "and at least a dozen, probably more, stories came out of that experience. Yet none of them used the sound of the clanging bell."

When Edgar Allen Poe was a child, he must have been punished by being put into a dark closet. Check his stories that tell of a frightful situation where someone was bricked up, enclosed in a box, buried alive, or thrust up a chimney. Some experience caused him to feel this horror, but whatever it was, he used it over and over as crisis material in a story.

Jack London wrote of his experiences in the North. Robert Louis Stevenson described the terror of his main character as he

14

heard the blind pirate tapping, tapping along the street with such vividness that you know he must have somewhere experienced this emotion. He repeated the incident in *The Black Arrow* with the bell.

Mark Twain recaptured his own boyhood days and its delights for his character Tom Sawyer. His love of the little town where he lived and his experiences with the Mississippi breathed life and excitement to his readers.

Study any author's works closely, mark the parallel passages, and you can spot their vivid personal experiences and strong feelings. These may be dressed up with different sets of facts and circumstances, but they are based upon an outstanding emotion experienced by the writer himself.

"Everything that happens to you," said Edna Ferber speaking to a group of writers, "is to your advantage, no matter whether it is bad or good. It can be stored away in your writing mind like keepsakes in an old attic trunk. You can go, in time of need, and pull out the experience which you require."

Think of items which you associate with certain emotions— a favorite song, picture, or a certain scene. Note how the unexpected hearing of the song or sight of the scene will arouse a distinct mood within you.

Now put your imagination to work. By this I do not mean the lazy daydreams and capricious imaginings of drifting thoughts. Imagination is not fancy; it is the image-making quality of your mind. Creative thought appears in pictures.

Use imagination in its positive sense. What lifts you with definite interest? What gives you a sense of excitement? What is excitement, anyway? Webster says it is stimulation, aroused activity. As you are animated by this reaction, you can see how you want to stir your reader.

The same things which lift you may not be the things which lift him, of course, for he will have his own set of memories in stories, songs, and places. But the feeling which lifts you is familiar, and by this feeling you can weave a pattern upon paper for him which helps him to respond.

A public speaker does this. Carefully he notes what things appeal by watching the response of his audience. As he communes with the group, he discovers that certain tones, manners, and ideas appeal; other gestures, tones, and opinions backfire. Quickly he discards those that backfire and develops those that stimulate the responses which he seeks, and so he develops his skill.

The playwright (who gets to see his plays) has a direct relationship with his audience, as well. He watches closely. If the group is swept away by the seeming reality of the situation he created, if there are laughter and tears, and the audience loses its sense of self-conciousness as it is caught up by the illusion, he has achieved his purpose.

You as a writer want to do the same in a more intimate, personal relationship. Guy de Maupassant put it this way: "The public is composed of numerous groups who cry to us, 'Console me, make me sad, make me sympathetic, make me dream, make me laugh, make me shudder, make me weep, make me think.'"

In Parc Monceau in Paris is a tribute to the great French writer's own skill in writing. There stands a marble memorial to De Maupassant where, underneath the bust of the author, sits a woman with an open book in her hand, a faraway look in her eyes, her entire body surrendered to the emotional effect of one of his master stories.

This is what you want to do to your reader. You want to make him thrill with adventure, glow with admiration and amazement for the hero, feel a romantic desire, emulate the brave deeds. You want your reader detached as if by some magic from his immediate surroundings, his body relaxed, while he is caught up with emotions, lost in delight, or terrified, uplifted, or inspired.

How can you, alone in your study, learn this? How are you going to know when you have crossed the threshold into this magic land? How can you tell when you accomplish this freshness and originality for which the world yearns?

It can be done. It has been done over and over.

Countless writers have learned the basic structure of accomplishment of this skill—and as their own skill developed, it became as simple as that of putting the right record on the phonograph.

It is said of Mary Coyle Chase that she was standing at a hotel window one day when she saw a woman below her who had just received the message that her two sons were killed in the war. As compassion filled Mrs. Chase, she wondered if there was anything she could write that would wipe the expression of grief off that woman's face and make her smile again. The desire to do this stayed with her, and out of the desire came the play *Harvey*.

When your desire to write is sufficiently strong, you begin to think and your mind sparks with ideas. Now how do you know which ideas create the reaction that you desire?

CHAPTER THREE

DEVELOP YOUR PERCEPTION

RETURNING TO HIS HOME one evening, an Indian discovered that his venison which he had hung up to dry had been stolen. His sharp Indian eyes studied the surroundings, and then he began tracking the robber through the forest. Crossing a road, he saw a man driving a wagon and motioned him to stop.

"Have you seen a little old white man, carrying a short gun, followed by a bobtail dog?"

"Yes, I passed him a mile or so north. He a friend of yours?"

"No," the Indian admitted. "I've never seen him. He stole my venison."

"Never seen him?" The driver lifted his eyebrows in amazement.

"But how could you describe him, if you've never seen the man?"

"Easy. I read the signs. He was a little man because he rolled up a stone to stand on to reach the venison. His short steps showed him to be old, and his toes turned out as a white man's do when walking. His gun left a mark on the tree where he stood it up. The dog's tracks were small and close together and when he sat on the ground, his bobtail marked the dust."

This is seeing with perception. You not only look at the thing itself, but you look at the signs that leave the telltale path behind. These are the things that you must learn to interpret.

Go to a café or a bus station and watch people. Don't listen to their words as much as you study their faces. Are they happy or unhappy? What little signs about the face, the way they stand, or the way they gesture reveals these things? Make a note of them. Watch your family; develop the habit of noting conscious-

18

ly the things that you have understood subconsciously so long. Junior is angry. How do you know it? What are his physical actions and his facial expressions that reveal it?

Increase your skill at taking in a full scene at a glance. Remember the experience which Kipling's Kim had in his contest of memory with the native boy of India:

Kim watched the store owner drop a handful of stones in a tray. The Indian took a look at them and handed the old man a newspaper, challenging Kim to look, handle, and study as much as he pleased, and then to beat him in a game of recall.

Kim looked and the man covered the tray with a newspaper. Proudly Kim named the number and color of stones—almost, but not quite, forgetting the last two. The native, however, stunned him.

He repeated the name, weight, and quality of stones, giving about twice the detail that Kim had been able to do. Disgusted, Kim requested the use of more familiar items. This was done.

Again the boy recalled the articles with far greater skill than Kim had ever seen. A third try proved to Kim that the young Indian was the unquestioned master. When Kim wanted to know the secret of the boy's skill, the answer was: repetition.

It must be repeated over and over, correcting mistakes, adding details, until the whole is done perfectly—that way, skill comes.

Emerson called Goethe Argus-eyed. "He seemed to see out of every pore of his skin and had a certain gravitation toward truth. . . . The Devil had played an important part in mythology in all times." Goethe considered him and murmured: "I have never heard of any crime which I might not have committed. So he flies at the throat of this imp. He shall be real; he shall be modern; he shall be European; he shall dress like a gentleman and accept the manners, and walk in the streets, and be well initiated in the life of Vienna, and of Heidelberg, in 1820—or he shall not exist. Accordingly, he stripped him of mythologic gear, of horns, cloven foot, harpoon tail, brimstone, and blue-fire, and, instead of looking at books and pictures, looked for him in his own mind, in every shade of coldness, selfishness, and unbelief, that, in crowds or in solitude, darkens over human thought—and found that the portrait gained reality and terror by every thing he added and took away. . . . and he flung into literature, in his Mephistopheles, the first organic figure that has been added for some ages, and which will remain as long as the Prometheus."[1]

Didn't Sinclair Lewis do the same thing with Elmer Gantry?

In addition to seeing others, Goethe looked within himself, and by studying himself he saw things that he could never have learned otherwise.

The word "idea" comes from the Greek and means "to see."

In your own study you examine the things which you have seen in others and in yourself.

Especially yourself! You must—as long as you write—live a double life: first, going about your daily affairs; second, as the spectator studying each action and reaction, the way you think, your habits, and above all your own emotions.

While you are experiencing strong feeling, try to capture it upon paper. Get it just as it is before it evaporates, showing just what this emotion made you, as an individual, experience.

If you are caught up high in its storm, you may discover that words flow more easily, that fresh forms and combinations suggest themselves to you. Or you may be operating at a lower level, where words and phases are trite. Nevertheless, catch them. You are not seeking the arrangement of words now, but the feeling itself. Obtaining it is like grasping elusive sunlight. Capture it in any kind of words, cement it on paper, and place it within your writer's file. Throughout your writing life it will prove invaluable to you.

If you will collect a variety of emotions, and put the pages in this file, later, in a time of need, you will find your own experience waiting. As you reread your words, the experienced moment will leap to life within your memory, giving you a true version of a needed emotional moment.

When days are on an even keel, practice. Constantly exercise the expression of your innermost visions, your ideas, and watch

[1] Ralph Waldo Emerson, *Representative Men* (David McKay Publishers, 1892).

your imagination grow. In your mind create various actions for your main characters; capture their actions in words as you watch them move about, acting, playing, living out their conflicts.

Do like the child and "play like." No one laughed when three blind men described the elephant, but how did it feel to be one of the blind men?

Stories in the Bible have pushed others over the hill to success, aiding, helping, and lifting with their messages of faith and courage when the individual reader had a problem that seemed too heavy for the next step. For instance, take the story of the Shulamite woman and the child's death (II Kings 4), and try to picture her deliberate refusal to accept dismay. The child died in her arms. She laid him on the prophet's bed, rushed to the field where her husband was working, and, without revealing her difficulty, announced that she was going to see Elisha.

"What for?" her husband said, in effect. "It isn't a holy day."

"It shall be well," she said, explaining nothing, and left. She smiled and greeted those she met along the way as though her world was calm. Only when she reached Elisha did she pour out her inward grief.

Such an act takes courage. Imagine yourself in that position, and behaving as this woman. Think on her courage and feel the emotion well up within you.

Practice other experiments with emotion. For instance, if you start feeling angry (even pretend to be) you will discover that your brows will furrow, your face will scowl, your jaws will clench together, and your hands will knot into fists.

Or without feeling anything, take the above physical attitude and keep it up for about ten minutes, and you will discover yourself actually growing angry.

In the middle of this experiment, deliberately think a pleasing thought. Some of the anger will fade, and your face will relax into more pleasant lines.

Think more on the pleasant thoughts and watch the bright, happy feelings fill you; watch also the way your physical features transform as the feeling floods your body.

When you are walking down the street, flash a smile at persons you don't know. Because you are unknown, they might not smile back, but they will smile at something near them. I've seen a mother's face lined with weariness from carrying her child on a shopping tour fill with a sudden rush of tenderness as she relayed my smile to her sleeping infant.

Watch the way emotions grow from a speck and spiral into an intensity and evaporate as something else attracts their attention and one emotion fades as another rises.

Take time to play with your work a bit. Be your main character and act him out—feel him in every fiber of your being, think what he thinks, see what he sees, feel what he feels, then sit down to write about him. Watch your work brighten up as you develop the capacity to do this. Writing is so much more than putting words on paper.

Watch your story as it happens in scenes. But don't sit and watch like a spectator; if you do, it will read that way and no one will enjoy it. You watch it much as one part of yourself watches you while you carry on your work or play, but giving yourself to the main part.

Be conscious of your reader the way an actor is of his unseen audience beyond the footlights; hear the laugh; feel the involuntary sob. It comes best when you feel it most keenly yourself.

Or better still, lose yourself until you *are* your character. Feel something of this student's experience:

"The first time I visited the pyramids of Mexico, we were with a guide. There were six of us together, but as we climbed the steps of the Pyramid of the Sun, I felt many people closing in about us—strange people with dark skin, dressed in ceremonial robes. They came between me and my family. Next, I was aware I had on robes, too, and a long, very heavy, elaborately embroidered and jeweled veil. It hung back of me and trailed down the steps. I felt obsessed by the one thought—I was giving myself to something glorious. I was a chosen one; I knew there would be pain. The back of my neck ached, but I kept on climbing, dragging the heavy veil. I didn't look back; I couldn't stop climbing.

I heard voices calling me to wait, but the voices and language seemed unfamiliar. I had a mission at the top of the Pyramid; I walked directly to what appeared like a small communion table. When I reached it I felt my body re-enact an ancient ritual."

Half the world is going about its business trying to present a face that is pleasant and carefree, hiding inner problems. This is only a façade, for human beings are wrapped up in problems, trying to overcome some disturbance, whether it is this week's bills or next week's difficulties. In your writing, present a strong problem; develop a good struggle that dramatizes its solution and ending with the light of truth which came to you in living it.

In private your readers can smile to themselves, and say with relief: "Well, I'm not the only one who makes stupid mistakes. And maybe there is a way out."

Think out these things; if necessary, act them out. The truth you have experienced in living may be a needed aid to your reader.

In the past, civilization has risen or dropped as truths were given or withheld. In his *General History of Freemasonry*, Robert Macoy said: "It appears that all the perfection of civilization, and all the advancement made in philosophy, science, and art among the ancients are due to those institutions which under the veil of mystery, sought to illustrate the sublimest truths of religion, morality, and virtue and impress them on the hearts of their disciples. Their chief object was to teach the doctrine of one God, the resurrection of man to eternal life, the dignity of the human soul, and to lead the people to see the shadow of the deity, in the beauty, magnificence, and splendor of the universe."

Sit at your typewriter and try to catch living truths. You have learned to bridge across to some reader who needs what you say. When you write it so sharply that he experiences it as though it had happened to himself and catches a glimmer of light, he can feel a lift in his soul, and rise to handle his own battle with high courage.

But after you know these things, how do you tie them together so you can demonstrate your truth or dramatize your theme?

PART TWO

Teaching Yourself Professional Habits

CHAPTER FOUR

YOUR CHARACTER TELLS THE STORY

SOMEONE HAS SAID that the most important words of the English Language are *within* and *now*. Certainly this is true for the writer.

Whatever you are writing about, whether it is fiction or non-fiction, it has two elements: (1) a problem; (2) an answer.

In fiction, biography, or personality sketches, the problem is that of a certain person. And, without conflict, your copy cannot be interesting.

With people, problems arise out of personality. Each person is a mixture of fine traits and weaker characteristics which war with each other. This is impossible for the reader to witness unless he is within the character having the problem.

Therefore, to create the magic carpet of the mind for your reader, you must slip him inside the character struggling with the conflict.

If you are dealing with facts, you naturally deal with the emotions and problems which correspond to those facts. If you are writing fiction, your task is to invent or create an outside problem which, when solved, brings the inside war into a state of peace with the conflict resolved. A boy, unwilling to fight for his own rights, must deal with a bully. A girl, timid and frightened at a party, must forget herself in making someone even more frightened than herself have a good time. And in the doing of these things, the problem, inside and outside, is solved.

To accomplish this, for the period of creation, you, the writer, must become the character and write as though you were that character—his weaknesses for the time being are your weaknesses; his strengths are your strengths.

If your main character is also your viewpoint (the point of view from which the entire story is seen) character, this then is your focus. You tell the story as though the main character were experiencing it for the first time, and from the point of view of this character's vision. If you are using a narrator, someone who sees and tells the story of the main character's problem, then your story must use the point of view of the narrator, telling what the narrator knows and what the narrator sees, and what the narrator interprets. In this case, the narrator is the viewpoint character instead of the main character.

But in most stories, and in the better ones as a whole, the main character and the viewpoint character are the same.

Actual people have many traits, many of them contradictory, some of them confused. As a writer, your story must be both credible and convincing, so it would be impossible for you to show all these traits. Therefore it is better for you to eliminate all but two for a short story—the dominant trait which English authors have called the "character core," which makes your character attractive, and the weak trait or flaw within him that is creating the problem and must be solved before the story is completed. You reveal these traits by your thoughts, feelings, and actions.

Readers must be able to see your character and see him in action.

Also, they must feel what he is feeling, as he feels it.

So you work with these three things: feelings, thoughts, actions. The reader forgets himself, his chair, and is inside the viewpoint character:

Thoughts: She tried to think of something that would console him. She couldn't speak of the pearls, that would only make him angry, but that would solve the problem for now.

Feelings: It was peaceful and quiet, but the fear in me grew. I hurried, afraid every second someone would—.

Action: Half-stumbling, I moved toward the river.

You weave these three points together as they naturally fall in life's pattern. These things in sharp focus help the reader to feel with the viewpoint character's feelings, cry his tears, or rage his anger.

A student said it this way: "If the writer transcends himself to become the self of the viewpoint character, then his words are charged with life. Words charged with life pulsate energy. As the reader reads the story, this energy is pulsated from the written word back to the reader. Because of this energy entering the reader, the reader is made to experience the emotion of the viewpoint character—actually passing through the emotional experience himself.

"It is through the viewpoint the reader gets into the story. If the viewpoint, the writing self, is genuine, the reader feels this is 'Me.' The reader has probably had, or would like to have, the strength of the viewpoint character; and admits, secretly, to the weakness of the viewpoint character."

Go through the following story and see if you can identify these important items. First, enclose in brackets every word that reveals the single viewpoint character. Second, underscore in blue pencil each word that reveals emotion coming from his strong character trait. Third, enclose in parentheses every word that reveals his critical feeling, or his emotion coming from his critical trait—i.e., his resentment of the Frenchman. Now, reread the story. Do you see how this helped you to identify with the main character and feel as if the story were happening to you?

Take some of your own copy and look at it. Have you achieved the same effect? If not, what can you do to improve it?

"Reconnaissance Patrol"

by Clifton Adams

A T division headquarters the general jabbed angrily at a place on the map. "Somewhere along this high ground the enemy has observation for artillery. Either here—or here—or here." He made three bloody circles with a red crayon, marking three small villages. "We don't know which one. Air reconnaissance hasn't been able to tell us anything. Our ground reconnaissance can't get through. The Germans have eighty-eights dug in and concealed along all roads and passages known to us." The general looked at the four men in front of him. At last he let his gaze settle on the French lieutenant. "Lieutenant Cortot, that is why I asked that you be released from your own French division and be attached to us."

The Frenchman said "Yes, sir," in precise, university-learned English.

"Do you know the situation, Lieutenant?"

"Part of it, sir."

The three other men knew nothing. Their tank had been taken from outpost a little more than an hour ago, and they had been told to report to division headquarters. They were combat men. In their reconnaissance company they seldom saw brass higher than a captain. They now stood rigid as they stared at the two silver stars on the general's shoulders.

There was Corporal Rodgers. He was a lean young man with old eyes. He had driven the tank all the way from the hedgerow country to this God-forgotten part of France.

And Bojinsky, the big Russian who had come from Detroit. He was the assistant driver on the tank. Nobody could tell Bojinsky anything about the art of killing with a thirty-caliber machine gun.

30

And, finally, there was Sergeant Ward. He had ridden point position on more reconnaissance patrols than he wanted to remember. He had seen St.-Lô, and Domfront, and Mortagne, and a lot of other places where men had died. But he had never been called into division headquarters before, and he didn't like it. And he didn't like the Frenchman. If it was a special mission they were in for, he wanted to select his own crew, and he wanted Americans.

The general went back to his map. He traced a line on the chart with a blue crayon."Here's where we are now. This whole armored division is massed in the woods along this river. We should have crossed yesterday, but every time our engineers try to put bridges across, enemy artillery blasts them out of the water." The general's face was worried and his eyes were tired. "G-2 tells us the Germans have reinforcements coming up to this point. If we don't cross before they get here—" The general spread his hands helplessly.

He didn't have to tell these men what it meant, taking tanks across a river with direct fire from the other side.

"We could make it," the general said. "We've made it before, but it costs us a lot of tanks. And a lot of men." The general consulted a piece of paper on his desk. "Corporal Rodgers, Bojinsky, Sergeant Ward. I asked for you men because you have the record of being the best reconnaissance crew in the division."

Bojinsky grinned. Rodgers looked serious. The sergeant wanted to spit. When a general took the trouble to pat an enlisted man on the back, there was a reason. And it wouldn't be good.

The general said, "This is your mission. One of these three towns is being used as a forward observation post by the enemy. We've got to know which one. There isn't time to make an attack with infantry before enemy reinforcements reach the river, so it's up to armored reconnaissance to get the information." The general paused for questions.

The sergeant said, "Are we to scout all three of the towns, sir?"

"No," the general said. "There will be two more crews like this one. Each one has the mission of observing a single town. You will

31

be in constant radio contact with Corps Artillery. If your town is the one with the enemy o.p., you will relay that information to them immediately."

Corps Artillery—that could mean only one thing, with the situation the way it was. A serenade. The song of hell, with every bellowing voice the entire corps could muster joining in on the chorus. It was something you heard a lot about in the army, but it was one of those things that you almost never saw. Every gun in the corps zeroed in on a single target, waiting only for a signal to blast it out of existence. In this case the target was a French town, and the sergeant would be the one to give the signal. If he lived that long.

But why the Frenchman? Why couldn't they take their own company commander or one of their lieutenants? The sergeant didn't like foreigners. He especially didn't like foreigners who had to have their wars fought for them.

Almost as if he had read the sergeant's mind, the general said, "Lieutenant Cortot knows this country well. It is his home. If there is a way of getting to your objective, he will find it."

Enlisted men don't argue with generals. The sergeant said nothing. He took an envelope containing call letters and frequency channels. The general said, "That is all. Until your mission is completed, you take your orders from Lieutenant Cortot."

He hesitated, as if there were other things he wanted to say, but only added, "Good luck."

A jeep took them to regimental headquarters. There a reconnaissance jeep picked them up and took them to their own company. A big blood-gorged sun moved sluggishly along the horizon. There was the sound of guns up ahead, and the air was heavy with the rotten smell of death. The company tanks and armored cars were coiled around a large field; big, shapeless beasts made more shapeless by the soggy camouflage nets pulled over them. The jeep pulled off the road and clawed its way into the field. It stopped beside the lead tank, where a man was waiting.

He was a gaunt man with tired eyes. And he was an angry man, angry at war, and killing, and fear. Angry because his men were killed and he could do nothing. Angry. To the sergeant, he was almost a god. He held a piece of K-ration cheese in one grimy hand and looked at his men.

"Well?"

The sergeant gave his company commander the envelope. The captain tried to shake the paper out with one hand. Finally he flung the cheese away in disgust, held the paper to the failing light, and read.

At last he said, "Who is Lieutenant Cortot?"

Sergeant Ward jerked his head at the Frenchman. Lieutenant Cortot got out of the jeep, clicked his heels, and saluted.

The captain stared. Then he cursed. "That's just fine," he spat. "What the hell do they mean, pushing a Frog into one of my tanks?"

If there was a change in the lieutenant's expression, it could not be seen in the gray light of dusk. He said, "It is the division commander's request that I accompany the captain's crew on this mission."

"So you speak English," the captain said dryly. There was no embarrassment in his voice. Only anger. It only went to prove that you couldn't trust foreigners. He unslung a map case from his shoulder, unsnapped it, and spread the chart on the ground. "I don't know what they told you at Division"—he glared at the lieutenant—"but I've had patrols out in this country and I know something about it. Here"—he drew a rough line across the face of the map—"are our outposts. From there on, you're in kraut country. All these roads and trails are covered by eighty-eights. A tank doesn't have a chance to get through. Why didn't they send infantry?"

"No time," the sergeant said. Briefly he told the captain about the German reinforcements coming up to the river.

The captain only said, "Oh." He too, knew what it meant to cross a river under direct fire. He wasn't angry now. He was afraid. But the fear was for his men, who he knew would die if they didn't make the crossing soon. The enemy observation point had to be found and destroyed. He stared at the map, as if he thought the answer would come to him if he stared hard enough. But no answer came.

Lieutenant Cortot dropped to his knees and put his finger on the map. "There is a way," he said. "Here."

The captain didn't believe it. Neither did the sergeant. On the map, the place was a scribbling of green, marking a woods. There was no road there. Not even a trail.

"When I was but a child I used to play there," the lieutenant said. "A tank can get through."

"When you were but a child," the captain said mockingly. "You're not a child now, lieutenant. That's kraut country, remember? They took it away from you, and now Americans are getting killed fighting your lousy war for you."

The lieutenant jerked to his feet as if he had been slapped. In that gray light the sergeant could see his face go white. "I think the crew had better prepare the tank," he said stiffly. "We will move out as soon as it is dark."

The sun had died. A chill seemed to seep out of the ground and cover this dead land. Up ahead, across the river, sudden flashes of guns flared.

"What are we waiting on?" That was Rodgers, down in the driver's seat of the tank. "I thought Frenchy said we were pulling out when it got dark."

"Maybe he changed his mind," Bojinsky said. "Maybe Frenchy figured it wasn't worth it, riskin' his hide just to save a few hundred Americans." He turned and peered up through the turret basket where the sergeant was squeezed in beside the breech of the small cannon. "How about that, Sarge? You think Frenchy will back out?"

"He'd look funny trying to explain it to the general," the sergeant said. "Now shut up, both of you." He squirmed around on the small turret seat and switched the radio on. After a moment, he pressed the button on the microphone and said, "Dog Mike Nan, this is King Fox George checking into the net. Over."

There was a power hum of a transmitter being turned on, back at Corps headquarters. "This is Dog Mike Nan. Roger. We're standing by."

The sergeant hung the microphone up and left the receiver on. Impatience began to gnaw at him. It had been dark for more than thirty minutes now and they hadn't even taken down the camouflage net. Then he saw two figures coming through the darkness. The sergeant stood up in the turret as the captain and the French lieutenant lifted the edge of the net and came under.

"Why the hell isn't this net down?" the captain said angrily.

The lieutenant said nothing. He seemed to be listening for something. Then they all heard it—the muted, pulsing hum of an airplane's motor. Bojinsky elevated his bucket seat, and his head came through the open hatch.

"Bed-check Charley," he said. "Maybe it was a good thing we left the net up."

The motor got louder. The plane seemed to be lazing somewhere in the blackness above them. Suddenly a miniature sun appeared in the darkness blazing with a furious blue light. Another sun spilled into the night. Soon there was a string of them floating gently down toward the river.

Rodgers had his head out of the hatch now. "Flares," he said. "Sauerkraut must be checking the river to make sure we haven't started another bridge. I'm glad we didn't get caught under that light. In fifteen minutes the news would have been all the way to Berlin that we were taking a tank toward their high ground." There was a respect in Rodgers' voice—respect for the French lieutenant who had kept them waiting.

But in the sergeant there was only anger. Trust a Frog to make a big show of it. There was no respect in the sergeant's voice when he said, "All right. Now do we take the net down and get started?"

The plane was gone. The flares floated to the ground and died, and the night was dark again.

The lieutenant said, "Yes. You may take it down."

The captain watched as they stretched the big net in the open field, folded it carefully, and lashed it on the back of the tank. He shook hands with the sergeant and said, "You're going to have to fight your way to that high ground. I'm glad I'm not going with you."

A break in his voice called him a liar. The sergeant was glad that it was dark and that he couldn't see the things in the captain's eyes. They would be old eyes, and incredibly tired. They would be the eyes of a man who was no longer sure of himself. He had made a mistake by wanting that net down, and it had been a Frenchman who had corrected him.

The captain turned suddenly and walked quickly into the darkness. The sergeant was helpless and angry. His god had fallen, and it was the Frenchman who had brought him down. He climbed stiffly up to the steel back of the tank and eased into his side of the turret. He jabbed his earphone into the jack and switched on the intraphone control.

"Can you hear me, Rodgers?"

"Okay."

"Then turn it over."

He had ignored the lieutenant on the other side of the turret and had taken over the tank himself. The Frenchman made no protest. He went quietly about his business of putting on his helmet and connecting his earphones as Rodgers started the motors.

"Take it out to the road and go right until we reach our roadblock," the sergeant said. "From there on, it is Frenchy's party."

He didn't know if the lieutenant had his earphones connected. He didn't care.

A pale moon lay behind a bank of clouds, occasionally letting shredded pieces of light crawl over the dark land. The roar inside the tank was a continuous thunder that worked on the mind until it was numb. It washed over you and tried to drown you, and every so often you had to shake your head or flex your arms in an effort to shake it off. Rodgers and Bojinsky were riding unbuttoned, with their heads sticking through the hatches in the front of the tank.

They came to the roadblock and the sergeant checked his watch: 2100. If they failed to contact a German patrol, they ought to make it to the observation point by midnight. If —.

They moved off the road and crawled slowly cross-country toward a dark mass that must be trees. Bojinsky's voice came through the sergeant's headset, "I hope the krauts didn't think to put antitank mines in this field."

The lieutenant's voice said, "Follow the edge of the wood up ahead until I tell you to turn in. There will be trees all the way up the slope. When we come out of them, we will be near Notre Dame de Catel."

The sergeant looked at the Frenchman for the first time. "Near what?" he asked.

"That is the name of the town. Notre Dame de Catal."

The sergeant watched an hour crawl by on the luminous dial of his watch. And he watched the woods and the trees until his eyes ached and jumped in his head. This was German country and there had to be Germans. He only hoped it would be infantry, something their light tank could kill. He felt himself getting tense as they crawled forward, stopped, listened, and crawled again. There had to be infantry. Krauts wouldn't set an eighty-eight here in this kind of country. But you can't tell about krauts. They do crazy things. The sergeant took his helmet off and mopped his face. He was getting jumpy, but he had been jumpy before.

He was almost relieved when he finally saw the half-track. It came out of the darkness of the woods and slid into a little clearing up ahead. Rodgers cut the motors before the lieutenant could touch the microphone to give the order. Bojinsky's head disappeared as if by magic, and his machine gun clicked as the bolt came back.

The lieutenant's voice came as a hoarse whisper, "Wait! Do not fire!"

The sergeant's head jerked up from the periscope where he had been getting the half-track in his sights. Then he saw that the lieutenant was right. The half-track hadn't seen them. It was going by, rattling and screeching off into the darkness of the woods.

The sergeant mopped his face again. One round from his thirty-seven millimeter could have knocked out the half-track. But the patrol would have been missed before long, and they would have had a dozen armored vehicles looking for them.

They waited and the night was as cold as death. The trees rattled their bones in a little breeze, and there was the sound of Bojinsky's heavy breathing.

At last the lieutenant said, "We can move on now."

They reached the edge of the woods, and the lieutenant said, "This is as far as we can go." He waved toward the flat darkness ahead of them. "It is open country between here and the town, about half a kilometer."

The sergeant said dryly, "And are we supposed to observe the town from here?"

"Yes," the lieutenant said. Then, as if with relief, he added, "But we must wait until morning."

Time dragged by. They had done what the sergeant had thought impossible—getting into position without making contact with the Germans. But it had been a long ride, and it was just as long going back. He didn't have to be told what the odds were on getting back from a mission like this. But the sergeant didn't resent being here. Any man in the company would have taken this job, because it was a chance to save a lot of lives. American lives. It was the Frenchman that the sergeant resented.

The lieutenant was now standing in the turret, leaning forward in the darkness with his head in his hands. The sergeant looked at him and saw for the first time what the man looked like. His face was thin, almost delicate. It seemed pale, but that could have been the moonlight. It wasn't an impressive face. It would get lost in the memory with a thousand others just like it.

"Lieutenant, you say you used to live around here?" That was Bojinsky. He had lifted himself up from the bucket seat and was sitting on the edge of the tank's hatch.

38

The lieutenant jerked upright, as if his mind had been far away and had suddenly snapped back to the present. He said, "Yes, my home is near here."

"I was just thinkin' about home," Bojinsky said. "Of course, I live in Detroit, and that's nothin' like these French towns, but just the same I'll be glad to get back. Do you ever get homesick, Lieutenant, bein' right here in your own country?"

The army hadn't been able to teach Bojinsky that there was a wide, impassable barrier that separated officers from enlisted men. The Frenchman didn't seem to mind. He said, "Homesick?" as if he were translating the word in his mind. "Yes, I get homesick."

"What kind of place is it?" Bojinsky insisted. "This home town of yours?"

The lieutenant thought. He looked out at the darkness and half-smiled as he remembered. "It is a little place," he said finally. "It sits on top of a small hill, and the valley around it is green. There is a white church with a steeple that seems to point at you like an accusing finger, and a stone wall on the north side to protect you from the winter winds."

"I mean the people," Bojinsky said. "What are they like?"

"The people? There are Cortots—my people have been there for two hundred years. They are much like the people in any town."

Rodgers climbed up to the hatch and took an interest in the conversation. Anyway, it was something to take his mind off the coming morning.

He said, "That sounds something like my home. I come from Oklahoma and there have been Rodgerses in that town ever since the run in eighty-nine."

The talk went on, but the sergeant didn't hear. He looked at the night and wondered if they would ever get out of here. He listened to a small wind and wondered if there was ever an end to war and killing. And at last, like the others, he thought of home. Most people wouldn't think it was much, his home. It wasn't a big place, and the people were just ordinary people. It was like Frenchy had said: they were much like the people in any town.

Guns sounded like faraway thunder. But it was quiet along the river, and in the woods, and in the dark distance that separated them from the town up ahead. The sergeant wondered what the town was like. Was this place the enemy observation post or was it one of the two other towns? There was only darkness there now, and only morning could give the answer.

No one—not even the general—had suggested a way to make the observation post show itself. No one had to; it was a scout's job to draw fire and make the enemy show himself. When it was light, the tank would move out of the woods and into the open. If nothing happened, then they had made a long ride for nothing, and there would be no escaping enemy patrols this time. But if their world suddenly burst into a roaring hell, then they would know they were a target for artillery, and that this town was the one.

" 'Way back in eighty-nine," Rodgers was saying, "my grand-dad made the Oklahoma run. I sure would like to see the place again."

And the sergeant wanted to see his home again. He wanted to see the town, and touch familiar things, and smell familiar smells. But he might never see or touch or smell another familiar thing, and he looked at the Frenchman and cursed him silently. He hated him because he was in his own country. Because the lieutenant hadn't been separated from his own people the way the sergeant and the others had. What did a Frenchman know about being homesick? What did a Frenchman care how Americans felt or how many of them died fighting his lousy war?

"I sure would like to go home again," Rodgers said for every American in France, and Africa, and England, and the South Pacific. "I sure would."

At last the sky in the east began to pale. The morning was cold and damp and sweet-smelling, putting a chill in the men's bones and a nervousness in their guts. The sergeant fastened his combat jacket up tightly at his throat, but the pressure there made him sick and he had to loosen it.

He sank stiffly down to the small seat in the turret and spoke into the microphone, "Dog Mike Nan, this is King Fox George."

A nasal voice came back, "This is Dog Mike Nan standing by." The voice was quarrelsome and full of sleep. The radio operator back at Corps headquarters didn't like being disturbed this early in the morning. The sergeant hung the microphone up. Anyway, they still had radio contact.

"It's beginning to get light," Bojinsky said. "You can see the town."

The sergeant reached down to his left and switched on the small auxiliary motor that powered the turret. He said, "You'd better check your gun, Bojinsky. If this town isn't the one we're looking for, we're going to have to fight our way out of here."

Bojinsky grunted and dropped down to his seat. The sergeant didn't have to tell them what would happen if it was the town.

The sergeant put his hands against the cold sides of the turret and pushed himself up. Off in the grayness the town was beginning to take shape; hazy at first and gradually fading sharply against the lightening sky. The sergeant guessed it was a quarter of a mile between them and the hill that the town sat on. The hill—that would be a good place for an observation point.

The sergeant got the tank binoculars, adjusted them to his eyes, and the town jumped into focus. It was a little place with winding cobblestone streets, and green pastures down in the valley that looked naked because there were no flocks of sheep to graze on them. To the north of the little town there was a stone wall to break the winter wind and to give protection to both animals and people. The town was quiet in the early morning, and inside the small houses there would be some people who would be too stubborn to seek the safety of the surrounding hills. The sergeant hoped for their own good there were no French people there. But he knew there would be.

He moved the glasses to the center of the town and saw a small white church with a steeple that pointed like an—. The sergeant

jerked the binoculars from his eyes. "Like an accusing finger"—
that was what the French lieutenant had said.

Suddenly everything made sense. This was the lieutenant's
town. His home. The sergeant's insides turned to ice, and then
melted with anger. He jabbed the binoculars at the Frenchman
and laughed quickly, without humor. "Here, Frenchy, take a
look at your home town before we blow it all to hell!"

It seemed to take the lieutenant a moment to hear the words.
He unfixed his gaze from the village and stared at the sergeant
with strange eyes.

"Go on!" the sergeant spat. He shoved the glasses into the lieutenant's bewildered hands. The heads of Rodgers and Bojinsky
came up through the hatches and stared at them.

"You had it figured real pretty, didn't you, French?" the sergeant said bitterly. "What would a few hundred American lives
mean to you? We'd cross that river whether or not we put an
end to this observation post. You heard the general say so. You
don't have anything to worry about. We'll win the war for you,
no matter how many men we lose."

"Sarge," Bojinsky said, "what the hell's eatin' you?"

The sergeant turned quickly in the turret. "I'll tell you what's
eating me. Somehow this Frenchman wormed his way into our
outfit. He convinced the general that he could lead us to one of
the towns that might be the observation post. Well, he did, all
right, but he never meant to give the order that would blast that
town off the map. Because it's his own home. His own people
live there."

Bojinsky's mouth fell open. Rodgers started to curse, but the
sergeant waved it away with an angry gesture. His hand went
to his shoulder holster and came out with a forty-five leveled at
the lieutenant's middle.

"Maybe I'll get court-martialed for this," he said, "if we live.
I'll worry about that later. Right now, Frenchy, we're rolling out
into the open, and you'd better not try to stop us. And if we draw
any fire from that hill, I'll radio Corps Artillery to blast it off the
face of the earth."

The lieutenant's face was white. He stared at the gun and at the sergeant, and his mouth worked. But no sound escaped him.

"All right, Rodgers!" the sergeant snapped. "Turn it over and button up!"

Rodgers and Bojinsky disappeared inside the tank. The motors whined, caught, then growled angrily. The hatches closed over the men's heads and locked. "We'll see what kind of guts a Frenchman's got when shells start falling."

The Frenchman slid down into the turret without saying a word. The sergeant settled on his side, with the breech of the thirty-seven-millimeter between them. He switched on the intraphone controls, then kicked up the periscope with the heel of his hand and had a quick look outside.

"Roll it out, Rodgers."

The tank lurched forward. They crawled out of the woods. The protection of the trees went away and left them with a feeling of nakedness.

"Keep it moving," the sergeant said into the microphone. "I don't think we'll get direct fire, but you can't tell." He pressed his face to the sponge-rubber padding of his periscope. The town was quiet. Nothing moved. Long minutes crawled by as the tank wandered aimlessly, inviting destruction. Cold sweat formed on the sergeant's forehead and soaked the rubber padding. More minutes went by and nothing happened. Maybe there was no observation post here. Maybe it was one of the other towns, and pretty soon they would hear shells screaming over to blast it to a heap of rubble.

Maybe. The sergeant glanced at the Frenchman on the other side of the turret. The lieutenant's eyes were wide and sick-looking as he glanced up from his own periscope.

The sergeant said, "Well, Frenchy, it looks like you won. There's no o.p. in that town or we'd be drawing fire by now." He felt empty inside. If they got out of here, the Frenchman would have a big laugh out of this. He could laugh the sergeant right to the front of the firing squad.

But there was something in the lieutenant's face that kept him from saying more. The Frenchman pushed his hatch open, stood up in the turret, and brought the binoculars to his eyes. For a long moment he searched the town with the glasses. At last he handed them to the sergeant and reached for the radio microphone. "Dog Mike Nan Six, this is King Fox George."

"What are you doing?" The sergeant jerked up in the turret.

The tank transmitter whined as the Frenchman pressed the microphone button. "Execute . . . Mission Red."

It took a wild moment for the sergeant to grasp what had been said. The lieutenant had asked for "Six"—that was the commander of artillery. And "Mission Red"—that was the firing mission for this town. The radio operator back at Corps headquarters made an excited sound. It ended abruptly as someone else snatched the microphone.

"This is Dog Mike Nan Six. Authenticate your message, King Fox George."

For just an instant the lieutenant pressed the button again. But there were no more words in him. He leaned against the turret and stared at the town. He didn't seem to notice when the sergeant snatched the microphone from him. He looked, and looked, as if he were trying to see enough to last him a life-time.

The sergeant shouted, "Stand by!" into the microphone and pressed the binoculars to his eyes. The village leaped up at him. Quickly he scanned the winding streets and the small houses. Finally he fixed the glasses on the church. And there he stopped.

First he shouted to the driver, "Rodgers, head for the woods! The serenade is on!" He fumbled for the coded authenticator wedged beneath the transmitter. His eyes raced over the maze of letters and numbers. At last he gave a challenge and received an authentic answer. After they had repeated the procedure in reverse, there was a loud sigh in the speaker from the commander of artillery. "Stand by to move out under smoke along co-ordinates Baker Able."

The sergeant said "Roger," and put the microphone away. He didn't have time to look up co-ordinates Baker and Able on the

44

map, but he hoped it was somewhere that would do some good.

The tank was back in the woods now. The sergeant tightened. He wanted to pound the steel side of the tank and pray for the gun crews to get smoke shells into these trees before the Germans hunted them down with armor. At last the shells screamed in. They thudded as they hit and spewed enormous mushrooms of white smoke. Heavy smoke that a tank could get lost in, thicker than any fog, better than any woods to hide in.

The sergeant felt good. He wanted to yell and laugh all at the same time. Then he became aware of the French lieutenant standing beside him.

"I . . . owe you an apology," the sergeant started. "A lot of them."

The lieutenant didn't hear. His gaze was lost in the smoke that swirled around them. His mind was lost in a little town that sat on a small hill overlooking a green valley.

"I was wrong about a lot of things," the sergeant said. "I was wrong about your people, maybe because I never got to know them. Until now."

The Frenchman said nothing.

"I didn't spot that opening in the church steeple where the kraut observer was. But you did. A lot of Americans are going to be around when this war is over because of what you just did."

But the town wouldn't be here. The place where Cortots had lived for two hundred years. The place where some of them might still be.

The lieutenant said finally, "Do you hear something, sergeant?"

The sergeant listened, and he heard the serenade begin. Shrill screams rent the air above them, and up ahead, on the other side of the smoke, harmless-looking puffs would start springing up in the little town. And buildings would crumble and fall. And there would be other screams—the kind that come with death. After a moment they heard the sound of the explosions, and even later, the sound of the guns reached them. It became a constant thunder, and no scream of one shell could be picked out of the hundreds above them. The sergeant couldn't look at the Frenchman. He didn't want to see what was in those eyes. He groped in his mind for something to say to the lieutenant. But there wasn't anything to say.

CHAPTER FIVE

TIME MOVES FORWARD

WRITING IN VIEWPOINT alone is not enough. Time must roll forward. The second important word is *now*, and the proper use of it helps the story unfold before the reader's eyes as though it were actually happening, as though the action were taking place now before the reader's eyes. You must write in such a way that your reader experiences a mental image of the story taking place as it happens.

For this, you forget words, grammar, formal style. You want your reader to forget himself, too, forget his sourroundings, the hard chair or soft couch, to lose all sense of time passing while he is caught up in the excitement, the drama happening before his mind's eye.

You cannot tell him about it as though you were talking about it long after it happened. If you write as though he were listening, much as you would write a letter to a friend, you help him to keep his own conscious awareness of himself in mind. Moreover, he is not likely to believe what you tell him about past facts. He will believe what he himself sees right now.

So you must master this sense of time's moving forward, letting it guide your stories. Your main rule is to let things happen *in their proper time sequence*. For example, do not write: "He said, 'Don't! You must not take that off in here!' "

Why? What is out of time sequence about that? You cannot hear something before the words have been spoken. Instead, write it this way: " 'Don't,' he said, 'you must not take that off in here!' " The change is minor, but the difference shows up in the aliveness of your copy. The sequence is correct; the "he said" comes after he has said something: "Don't!"

47

Write in the simple past tense. Today's readers have formed the habit of reading the past tense as though it were the present moving forward in time. If you change to the present tense, the reader has to struggle with the change before he can lose himself in the story. Not that writing in the present tense hasn't been done successfully; it has. Charles Lindbergh did it in his *The Spirit of St. Louis*.

At the same time *keep your verbs active*. Do not say: "He was angry." Change it to the active form: "Again he felt alien, surly." Or, "He clenched his fists trying to calm the rising tide of dislike."

Compare the differences in these two passages:

(1) The sound of the motor had grown loud. Somewhere in the blackness above them there seemed to be a plane lazing. A blue light became a sudden miniature sun. It was followed by another.

(2) The motor got louder. The plane seemed to be lazing above them. Suddenly a miniature sun appeared in the darkness blazing with a furious blue light. Another sun spilled into the night.

The second passage is from Clifton Adams' story. See how much better he wrote it, keeping the verbs active.

In the same manner, show the stimulus before the response to that stimulus. You see something before you react with an emotion toward it. It is backwards to say: "Mazie got the fright of her life, turning around, she saw—." Show the action that caused her to see the thing which stirred fear: "Turning around, Mazie got the fright of her life. Standing in front of her—."

Watch this throughout your copy. If your viewpoint character looks at something important to the story line, show what he sees at the time he sees it: "He glanced at her watch." "Odd how her tongue could prattle." "They came to the roadblock and the sergeant checked his watch." Let action take place in proper time-sequence.

After you have written your copy, fiction or non-fiction, check these points. This develops your seeing-eye. Your ability to spot your own flaws will grow. After you have practiced this for a time, a glance at your earlier efforts may shock you. Copy can always be improved.

In the story following, we have a confidential look inside for you. The fiction editor of *This Week* was not satisfied with the submitted version and wrote:

"We all thought that 'Violets from Portugal' by Helene Carpenter had a great deal of interest and charm, but from our point of view, two faults: It is one thousand words too long, and the method of writing, with frequent flashbacks, confuses the reader . . . it would be just right for us if Helene Carpenter would do some more work on it. I think she should, in cutting the story, omit some of the incidents and try, if possible, to eliminate some of the confusion."

To cut a manuscript is not easy. It is even harder to cut your own—but it is as important as cutting a garment; otherwise, no matter how beautiful the sewing, the dress will not fit or hang correctly.

The writer read the editor's letter and went to work. For your study, we are giving you both versions. Here you can see cutting and compression in the finished story and spot ways in which you may tighten your own work.

Now study it from the standpoint of the viewpoint character. Look at the character first objectively. Can you see her character traits? What is her problem? Why? What lack within the woman herself has caused her to be placed in this situation?

Can you feel with her as you read the story? Go back through the story carefully and study just what words the author used which called forth your feeling for the viewpoint character and caused you to sympathize with her problem. Does her mind agree with her heart?

Or look at it this way: Did her conscious thinking agree with her subconscious feeling? If not, what revealed the difference?

A good story is round like a wheel. The periphery and hub are related by spokes. The spokes are different views of the main character's problem. The hub represents the emotional conflict, and the periphery mirrors the character's problem in outside events or brings together a group of events where, if the main character solves the outside problem, he also solves his inner, emotional conflict.

Can you see this in the following story?

Now, how well do you have the sense of time moving forward in this story? Do you ever lose consciousness of the movement of the clock or the setting? In the flashbacks, do you have the sense of things having happened a long time ago, or do they, too, take place before your eyes?

How did the author manage this?

THE version of "Violets from Portugal" which follows is in the form in which it was originally submitted by Helene Carpenter to *This Week* magazine. When it was returned to her by the editor with suggestions for revisions, she immediately went to work on it, and in a period of twenty-four hours had made the alterations which you see here. The final, polished version of her story appears in this book on page 75 and following.

VIOLETS FROM PORTUGAL

by

Helene Carpenter

Blue smoke drifted in lazy sworls above the tables. The cocktail lounge was filled with ~~five o'clock~~ *late afternoon* customers crowding in from storm darkened streets.

A slender girl with gold hair curling softly under the edge of her mink turban stared into the tawny depths of her glass.

"I wish it were milk," she said.

Her companion, a square set young man with his heart in his eyes, said "I'll get you some," and turned to signal a ~~hurrying~~ waiter.

"Don't bother, ~~please~~ Edward." After all she was used to substitutes...for just about everything.

She raised her glass and the enormous topaz on her finger winked at the matching gems in her ears.

"Na Zdarovya!" she said.

~~Reaching across the table~~ He touched his glass to hers.

"Is that Russian for 'here's mud in your eye,' Susan?"

"Approximately. I learned ~~only~~ one other phrase, ~~that seemed adequate for all occasions.~~ Nitchevo. ~~It means,~~ what does it matter? Said with a shrug. Like this."

~~As she illustrated,~~ Her mink coat slipped from her shoulders, displaying a gold wool dress with an ornament of. barbaric beauty at its V neck. *Like the antique bracelet into which a modern watch had been set, it carried the stamp of the Zar.*

3 spaces

"This is stupid conversation," she thought ~~helplessly~~ as he adjusted the lustrous fur over the ~~back of her~~ chair, "for ~~two~~ people who ~~had~~ once meant so much to each other." But what do you say to the man you should have married -- and didn't? The man whose ring you returned to marry "Kelly" Westbrook; a scaramouche born with the gift of tongues and ~~of~~ laughter who swept you out of your small town orbit into a bewildering maze of military and diplomatic protocol. And now on to the ash heap of divorce.

It was good to see Edward again. ~~Unchanged after five years. He represented security in a world of insecurity.~~ She tried not to remember the hurt in his eyes the day he had looked at the small diamond glittering in the palm of his hand.

"I think you're ~~are~~ making a mistake," he had ~~told her~~ said.
"When you find it out, I'll be around and waiting."

Well she'd found it out. ~~And~~ He was waiting. Edward
who always ~~looked down at her feet and~~ broke his stride to
walk in step with her. With Kelly she had needed ~~wings.~~
~~S~~even league boots. And nature had failed to equip her.

She glanced at her watch. 5:15 Kelly should arrive ~~any minute.~~ in a few min
She must tell him cooly, briefly, she wanted a divorce. ~~Not~~ to lay
~~that he wouldn't be happy to be relieved of the fifth wheel~~
~~under the wagon for which there was never any need.~~

~~"Here I am boring you with details of my defence mission,"~~
~~Edward was saying, "and you haven't~~ Tell ~~told~~ me ~~a thing~~ about
your flight from Moscow, " Edward said, " Our mothers have been ~~discussing~~ your five
month ~~trip~~ trek over the garden fence, ~~every time you cabled. But~~
~~cables were too few and far between."~~

Odd how her tongue could prattle while
"There's ~~isn't~~ not ~~so~~ much to tell." Why she could sum up her dealt with g
whole married life in one command. "In the buggy, Suzie!"
That's what Kelly always said when he meant they were on the
move again. The words ~~became a~~ were prelude to nightmare.

Fly here. Motor there. Take a boat. Take a train.
Leave ~~Never mind~~ the trunks. Don't worry about the language, your
diplomatic visa will see you through. Boil the water. Don't
drink the milk. Goodby Sweet. Meet me ~~you~~ in Hong Kong, Manilla,
Moscow!

3 spaces

54

~~Only~~ This time ~~when~~ he said goodby at the Moscow airport. The Nazi's were marching on Russia, ~~and~~ Embassy wives were being sent to neutral countries on five hours notice, *although* Rumors had been flying thick and fast for months. Soldiers marching, ~~and~~ wheels rolling through the Red Square ~~by day and by night~~ *night and day* had formed a sinister counterpoint to daily living.

There was no laughter ~~quirk~~ at the corner of Kelly's mouth; no teasing gaiety in his ~~deep-set~~ eyes when he ~~kissed her.~~ *said:*

"You're going to Iran," ~~he said~~. "~~I'll cable you as soon as I know anything.~~" He kissed her hard, but ~~that last night~~ she had steeled herself against the feel of his arms about her, against the pressure of his mouth ~~on here~~. Her heart was a tightly wrapped cocoon. Her head was going to carry on from here.

"Okay," he said releasing her ~~and picking up her one suit case~~, "In the buggie, Suzie!"

She ~~didn't~~ *hadn't* look down when the plane circled the ~~flying~~ field swept with morning mist. She was trying to remember who it was that said, "Life is a comedy for those who think. A tragedy for those who feel."

3 spaces ~~5:30 the watch hand said.~~
Two career women settled themselves at a nearby table. Their inventory eyes ~~swiftly~~ dismissed Edward's neat pin stripe and rested on Susan ~~with microscopic interest~~.

"They're admiring the gold of your hair and the brown of your eyes, just as I am," he said.

"More likely the brown of my mink. It's about all I got home with." /~~3 spaces~~ Which wasn't quite true. She had the jewels Kelly was forever picking up at commission houses. Jewels and embassy intrigue! ~~When~~ All she wanted was a plain American home with a kitchen to hang her curtains. ~~Odd~~ How important *those* a few yards of red and white ~~checkered~~ gingham had become!

~~They'd only been married a short while; had taken a little~~ *Bought for their first* apartment ~~while~~ Kelly was on language detail at Columbia, *sewed every stitch by hand.* ~~She'd even bought lining for the gingham to give it body and had sewed every stitch by hand. A sewing machine had no place in their mobile scheme.~~

~~She was~~ Perched on top ~~of~~ a kitchen stool ~~just~~ about to hang ~~them~~ ~~first pair when~~ *had* Kelly burst in waving an official envelope.

"In the buggie, Suzie!" he cried swinging her off the stool, "~~We're on our way to~~ "California, *here we come!* "

"Oh Kelly," she wailed against his chest, ~~her feet dangling above the floor~~, "just when I had my ~~nice kitchen~~ curtains finished."

He kissed the tip of her nose ~~and put her down~~. "~~You know~~, I wouldn't be surprised if they had windows out there." He was ~~like a horse in a high state of collection~~, impatient to be off.

~~They had windows of course but they weren't the right~~
~~size and~~ By the time Susan ~~got around to~~ re-shap~~ing~~ed *the curtains* ~~them~~
they were ordered on foreign service.

"The day I get to <u>hang</u> these," she said fiercely, "I'll
know I've got a home at last."

"The nesting instinct dies hard, ~~doesn't it?~~" he teased.

"~~I remind me of the~~ *We had* sparrows in the ivy at home," she
~~told him.~~ *said* "Father was always pulling their nests down ~~with a~~
~~long pole.~~ The minute he went in the house they'~~would~~d pick
up the scraps ~~from the ground~~ and begin building ~~right~~ back.
I felt ~~so~~ sorry for them. Their nest grew ~~more and more~~ *so*
ragged."

He looked at her curiously ~~and when he spoke~~ His voice *was*
~~had a different quality.~~ *oddly soft* "Let's take them ~~with us.~~ *along for luck* People
carry old coins and ivory elephants. Why shouldn't we carry
spaces kitchen curtains ~~for good luck?~~"
5:40. Susan held her breath as a tall officer with majors leaves
"~~You're unhappy Susan,~~" ~~Edward said.~~ "~~Or am I mistaken --~~ *came in. No it wasn't Kelly -- she sighed.*
~~Is that sad expression for a husband who has no wife to look~~
~~after him?"~~

~~Susan's laugh was harsh in her throat.~~ "~~I can think of~~
~~nothing Kelly needs less than a wife to look after him."~~

"~~You've changed," he said slowly. "You're more beautiful~~
~~than even I remembered. But this lacquer you've acquired --~~
~~well I just can't seem to break through to the girl who helped~~

~~me draw house plans. To the Home Ec major who butchered~~
~~magazines for furniture illustrations and food recipes."~~
~~He leaned closer to her.~~

~~"I hope she's not lost. I cared --" he shifted his~~
~~tense deliberately, "care a great deal about her."~~

~~Now it was her move. But she couldn't say anything.~~
~~Not yet. Kelly had a right to know first.~~

~~A tall officer with major's leaves on his shoulder came~~
~~in and Susan held her breath. Why did she think every man~~
~~in uniform was Kelly?~~ *Edward looked up from the design*
he'd been making with matches.

"Your mother thought you might ~~be ready to~~ come home,"
~~Edward said. "Might travel West with me." He made a geometric~~
~~arrangement with matches on the table.~~ "I'm leaving on the
midnight."

Susan twirled the stem of her glass between her fingers
and the amber liquid swished up the side ~~dangerously close~~
to the rim. *"I must see Kelly first."*
~~"I should be able to conclude the necessary arrangements~~
~~with Kelly by that time," she said thoughtfully.~~

~~"With Kelly?"~~ ~~Edward looked surprised.~~

~~"I've had a cable from him.~~ *"*I left word at the desk to
meet us here." ←

~~Edward said nothing.~~

"He's flying from Lisbon," (she explained) ~~She wasn't sure~~
His cable read
~~of that really. He'd only said~~ 'Am bringing you violets from
Portugal.'

~~Still~~ Edward ~~didn't speak.~~ *seemed troubled*

"Didn't you <u>know</u> Kelly was recalled to Washington for conference?"

"Yes, ~~I knew,~~" he admitted, "but that was ~~a long~~ *some* time ago. When he didn't arrive with the ~~rest of the~~ *diplomatic* corps, I wondered --"

"Didn't arrive?" ~~Did~~ *Have* they... "What do you mean?"

~~Edward looked more puzzled than ever.~~ "Didn't you know?" Then ~~his~~ *Edward's* face cleared. "~~But~~ *Of* course not. You were ~~still~~ at sea."

"Tell me!" ~~A strange~~ urgency sharpened her voice.

"~~The papers said~~ *H*e wasn't on the plane when it left ~~from~~ Kuibyshev ~~with the diplomats and military attaches.~~ *The papers* ~~They~~ said he returned to Moscow. If Washington knew why, they weren't putting it out."

"But they were shelling Moscow ~~at that time~~!" she cried. "Why should ~~Kelly~~ *he* go back?" Kelly wounded? ... the cable didn't say. Just that nonsense about violets. Then she laughed inwardly for being a naive ~~sentimental~~ little fool.

"Kelly," she said dryly, "is indestructible." But she ~~quickly~~ drained her glass and slid it to the edge of the table ~~to be picked up for a refill.~~

Edward laid his hand ~~on hers~~ *over her watch* ~~covering the topaz.~~ "Susan," he said ~~earnestly,~~ "I know ~~an engineering professor~~ *construction engineer*

is pretty dull stuff. ~~But it isn't because I haven't wanted~~ I'd like
to be a plumed knight on a white charger."

Susan smiled ~~at him. "I wouldn't have you changed for~~ She couldn't say anything. Kelly had the
~~the world," she said.~~ right to know first.

— 5:45 — — — — — — — — — —

3 spaces

~~Besides~~ It was no white charger that had carried Kelly
into her life. It was a brown polo pony, ~~with sweaty, heaving~~ on a nearby army po
~~sides.~~ During the ~~Easter~~ holidays she'd gone ~~for a week end~~
~~at a nearby army post~~ with ~~a classmate,~~ home Dot Graham ~~whose~~
~~father was Colonel.~~ a classmate

Kelly had ridden up to their ~~parked~~ car ~~to be introduced~~
~~as the~~ Her blind date ~~Dot had made~~ for the post hop that night.
Susan remembered with painful vividness the quick charm of
his smile. Gray eyes in a lean brown face; ~~compelling,~~
~~dynamic, with~~ black triangular eyebrows that sharpened in
jest.

"Blondes should have blue eyes," he ~~told her reprovingly.~~ reproved her
"~~Now~~ I'll have to get you a yellow and brown orchid. ~~instead~~ I ordered a
~~of the~~ violet corsage."

"~~Oh but~~ I love violets," she assured him laughingly.
"I've just planted a whole border of them in my garden."

"You have a garden?" he asked incredulously as if she
said she had two noses.

"People **have** gardens," Dot said, "homes too!" She turned
to Susan. "Kelly doesn't believe that. He tucks his head
under his wing and goes to sleep like a duck on a pond."

60

That should have warned her. But it hadn't. ~~When~~ He rode back into the game ~~he carried~~ *Carrying* her heart with him.

The magic of that spring night! She wor~~e~~*'d* a white ~~organza~~ frock with ~~a square neck,~~ tiny puffed sleeves and a billowy skirt. The violets were perfect ~~for it~~. ~~When they came~~ ~~there was~~ *with* a cluster of ~~pinkish-gold rosebuds~~ *sweetheart roses* in the center. ~~Sweetheart roses.~~

~~After the dance he had parked his car~~ *B*y the lake ~~and~~ in a dawn filled moment, *he* kissed her.

"But I'm engaged," she protested ~~somewhat belatedly~~.

He lifted his dark head and she could see the laughter mounting behind his eyes. "I don't want to be engaged," he said. "I want to be married."

And they were. ~~Just like that.~~ Within the week she was the wife of Capt. William "Kelly" Westbrook, ~~of the~~ military intelligence. At that time G.2. was just a letter in the alphabet and a number from one to ten.

It was later. Three years later when Kelly was made military attache to Russia that the full force of her own inadequacy struck her. "Kelly darling," she ~~had said~~ *mourned*, "I can bake hot rolls ~~that will melt in your~~ mouth. But I'm stupid with languages."

"~~Just~~ *L*earn to say 'I don't know' and you'll get along."

"I can sew a fine seam. But I'm dumb about foreign affairs."

"Never speak unless you have absolutely nothing to say. That's a diplomatic axiom."

~~Kelly had the answer for everything.~~

Then she made ~~her~~ _a_ mistake. She tried to get him to resign from the army. "It isn't as if you didn't have a private income. Aren't we ever going to put down roots? ~~Have a home of our own.~~ ~~Lead a normal life?~~ Are we to be wanderers on the face of the earth always?"

She had wept but he didn't take her in his arms. ~~Didn't try to soothe her.~~ "Get this straight, Susan" his voice was rough ~~with anger~~. "I don't walk around draped in the American flag. But when I go out of the United States army it will be with taps playing."

~~Love used no judgment when it struck two such opposites.~~ ~~Incompatibility would be the grounds --~~

3 spaces

Edward's face swam into focus and she realized ~~he had~~ _she was talking quite coherently_. ~~asked her twice about the trip.~~

"~~It was ghastly.~~ We left the ~~Moscow~~ plane at Baku and crossed the Caspian by boat ..."

"We?"

"Zelda Higgins, and her little boy. ~~She is the wife of a foreign correspondent.~~ We stayed in Tehran until the news grew worse and the consul advised us to start working our

3 spaces way south."

It was in Persia that Zelda ~~had begun chattering~~ *talked* about
how her Jimmie was going to buy a small town newspaper as soon
as this fracas was over. "We don't want little Jimmie to
spend his life being dragged from pillar to post. It puts
a mark on them, don't you think?"

Susan didn't think. She knew. Kelly bore that mark.
~~He was born in Hong Kong where his father was military~~
~~attache. His wealthy mother had divorced him and remarried~~
~~into the diplomatic service. His boyhood had been spent~~
~~shuttling back and forth between them, which accounted for~~
~~his uncanny knack with languages.~~

~~"We crossed the desert to Basra," she told Edward, "and~~
~~caught a boat sailing for Bombay."~~

The long voyage home was taking on the quality of an
uneasy dream where everything is seen upside down like images
in a mirage. Even now. December in New York, and she could
still feel the blazing heat of the Arabian sea where a deep
breath seared the lungs ~~and produced nausea~~. Little Jimmie
who had ~~only managed to~~ *barely* survived the sunless killing cold of
a Russian winter had a sun stroke. ~~One day~~ Looking at the
child's bones thrusting through his skin, she had asked Zelda.

"Suppose big Jimmie wouldn't buy that small town paper.
Suppose he insisted on roaming the world ~~as a foreign~~
~~correspondent~~. What would you do?"

Zelda had gazed ~~out~~ over the rail where a pitiless sun danced on the copper sea and spoke simply. "Then I should say, like Ruth in the Bible, 'whither thou goest, I will go.'"

Susan couldn't afford to think about things like that ~~and was glad when Edward asked about Bombay.~~

~~"You stayed there so long we were terribly worried."~~
or her bout of fever in Bombay when
~~"I had a bout of fever," she said.~~

~~If it had only been a little worse it would have solved her problem. When she felt the sickness within her she had insisted on Zelda leaving without her. "You have little Jimmy to think of."~~

~~Ten minutes after bidding them goodby she fainted in the lobby of the Taj Mahal hotel.~~ In lucid intervals, ~~when she was~~ aware of dark faces and strange tongues, she wondered what was to become of her.

~~"We had a few days in Capetown," she went on. "Then Trinidad and home. Do I sound like a travel bureau?"~~

~~"I worried about subs," Edward said.~~
or the sub off Capetown
~~"Only once did we see one. And~~ that turned out to be
not before
English. ~~They had misunderstood our signals.~~ But₁a Polish
her
refugee ~~who had been~~ standing beside ~~me~~ went suddenly mad and threw herself in the sea."

~~Edward brushed his matchsticks into a careful little heap. "In a way," he said slowly, "I'm glad you had to~~

~~leave everything behind you. It may help you to forget what you've been through.~~"

~~An unsummoned agony washed over her remembering how~~ *Least of all could she afford to remember* ~~much she'd left behind; remembering~~ the bitterness of that night before she left *Russia*.

It had ~~really~~ started in the afternoon with a cocktail party. Elena, the wife of an important foreign minister was giving it. Whe was a red Persian cat of a woman ~~whose claws were in constant need of clipping~~. That she was half in love with Kelly was an open and amusing secret to everyone except Susan.

The Ambassador's wife ~~had~~ let it be known that she was going to call on Susan and together they would go on to Elena's party.

Susan was dressing when Zelda Higgins phoned, frantic, ~~and~~ distraut. Little Jimmie was ~~taken suddenly~~ ill. Looked like an emergency appendix and she couldn't locate a doctor. Would Susan come over and stay with the child while *she* ~~Zelda went out and~~ tracked one down?

Susan could and did; forgetting ~~about~~ the ambassador's wife; forgetting ~~about~~ Elena's party until Zelda, ~~hysterical from her long search, finally~~ arrived with a doctor in tow. *Then* ~~By that time~~ it was too late.

The Ambassador's wife was sweet and patient about it, like one is sweet and patient with a backward child. ~~But Elena refused to come to the phone when she called to explain.~~ *But*There was an Embassy dinner that night and Susan wondered in what sly way Elena would manage to humiliate her. Kelly had impressed upon her the importance of keeping things smooth between the legations. ~~Affairs were at a ticklish pass.~~ Nerves were on edge waiting for the inevitable blow, not knowing from which direction it would strike. Her fingers trembled as she fastened an emerald necklace set in heavy Finnish gold about her throat.

Kelly came in her room handsome in full dress. ~~A concentrated frown drew his brows together in a level black line.~~ She was wearing a new gown of honey beige satin, ~~simple in its sophisticated severity and~~ a perfect setting for the glowing emeralds. ~~But~~ *If* he noticed it he gave no sign.

"I'm sorry," she said ~~uneasily~~, "about this afternoon."

He ran an impatient hand over his thick, black hair springing up at the ends as it dried. "You're so damned impulsive, *Suzie* ~~Susan~~. Won't you ever grow up?" ~~He never called her Susan.~~ "Couldn't you have taken time out to send a message?"

"I didn't think," she defended herself. *Jimmy's* "~~His~~ fever was 104. I rushed right over." ~~She went to her vanity dresser and sat down.~~ "You see," she said hopelessly, "I'll never

66

learn that an artificial code comes before human sympathy."

He strode to the window. Through her mirror she could see him staring down at the rumbling cavalcade below. Finally, ~~he straightened his broad shoulders,~~ gave a short sigh and turned back to her. "Stop fretting, Sweet ~~girl~~." He dropped a ~~light~~ kiss on the top of her head. "Kelly can fix."

Sure Kelly could fix. ~~All~~ the stupid blunders his wife made. Bitterly she watched him doing it ~~at dinner and after-ward. Imparting his own special brand of charm~~ *with*; his adroit mixture of wit and impudence ~~that never failed him.~~ *after dinner,* The huge Soviet general with whom Susan was dancing gave an abrupt turn and she saw through the archway ~~a couple dancing in a deserted anteroom.~~ Red hair against black. Elena, tall and beautiful with ~~her~~ slavic cheek bones, over ripe lips and *a* thick creamy skin, was pressing her cheek against Kelly's as they executed slow turns to waltz time. Her slumbrous green eyes were half closed~~ and~~ Susan could almost hear her purr.

Kelly's lips moved, Elena smiled, and ~~indignation laced with~~ jealousy drove through Susan. "Why do I go on?" she asked herself. "It's going to be like this all my life. Only I'll be getting older ~~and less attractive~~ and there will always be an Elena."

~~"I'd like some champagne," she said unsteadily to the General.~~

Back in their apartment living room ~~neither made any motions toward getting ready for bed.~~ Silence hung like a heavy black curtain between them. In her ear drums the ever marching boots made hammers of sound; through the open windows drifted odors compounded of earth ~~smells~~ and body smells and the peculiarly strident perfume that all of Moscow ~~seemed to~~ affect*ed*.

In sudden revolt she rushed to the window and slammed it down. Kelly took a long drag on his cigarette and lifted *a questioning* ~~one~~ eyebrow ~~in questioning triangle. She didn't trust herself to speak.~~ Nervously she began to strip off her bracelets, and earrings, ~~and~~ necklace.

"I'm sorry I didn't buy you that ruby pendant we *w*~~saw~~ in Kiev," he said. "Too late now, ~~I'm afraid.~~"

~~Without warning the dam bro~~ke. "I don't want rubies," she cried. "I want an American gas stove and ~~an electric~~ refrigerator that works. I want to ~~stay put and~~ belong to garden clubs and the P.T.A. I want to bake pumpkin pies for Thanksgiving and trim trees at Christmas."

He uncrossed his long legs and watched her pace the rug. "~~You can say that?~~ *you're* Living ~~as you are~~ in the middle of history/"

"I want to live in the middle of America." The words tumbled from her lips ~~incoherently~~. "I'm sick of watching shore lines drop behind my ship, of earth falling away from

68

my plane, of landscapes flying by so fast I can't see the
homes or the people who live in them. I hate being cooped
up in an embassy -- Dining every night with foreign cats. ~~I
hate it with a passion.~~"

He was on his feet shaking her. "Make sense," he said
harshly. "You've got a ringside seat to the greatest show
on earth."

"You can have it," she flung at him. "I'll settle for
a little house with lilacs in the back yard and tricycles
in the driveway and --" her voice broke ~~into little dry sobs~~
-- "and a kitchen to hang -- my curtains -- in."

He let go abruptly ~~and~~ she almost fell. "So that's how
it is I thought you married me. What I sum up to as a man.
Not as a way of life." He shot her a hard level look. "The
next time you marry, remember that!"

His words killed the sobs in her throat. The next time
you marry. He was telling her what she'd begun to suspect,
that he was tired of carrying supercargo, ~~of racing with a
handicap?~~

They stood in the middle of the floor facing each other
across the gulf of words. The telephone ringing was like a
flash of lightning through a storm cloud. She stood rooted
to the spot while he answered it, listening without comprehension to his monosyllables.

~~He hung up and~~ W̲ithout explanation ^he banged out of the apartment. Dazedly, she went into her bedroom and set about undressing.

When he returned his face was a polite mask. ~~His mind was evidently no longer on personal problems.~~ "It's come," he said. "Hell's about to pop. You're leaving Moscow ~~in five hours.~~ Wives are being sent to neutral countries -- ~~or home as they prefer.~~"

"What will _you_ do?" Her voice sounded tinny and far off.

"Move with headquarters to Kuibyshev. Hurry!"

She began throwing things into a bag ~~helter skelter and~~ without recognition, until on opening a big carved chest, she saw neat folds of red and white gingham. Kelly coming ~~in~~ from the bath room with her ~~toothpaste and~~ toilet articles _saw them too_ ~~stopped on the threshold.~~ Their eyes met and held an instant. She let the lid fall. Even the sparrows in her father's ivy

3 spaces were eventually discouraged. — — — — —

_5:45_

Edward was holding a match toward Susan's cigarette when she saw Kelly. Heads turned to look at the tall man in uniform. _striding toward her._ Maybe others could hear the roar of planes, wheels on rails, ships turbines, just as she could. Her hand trembled. She put down her ~~unlighted~~ cigarette _unlighted._

~~He towered above her, and~~ S̲he was shocked by the haggard leaness of his face. ~~There was a flick of~~ _She_ gray at his temples, ~~and a~~ _the_ thin red scar on his forehead that had not been there five months ago.

"You know Edward," she said mechanically.

The men shook hands. "Quite a surprise," said Edward, ~~observing the social amenities.~~ "I was telling Susan what a stir it caused in Washington when you didn't arrive on schedule."

There was an awkward pause.

"Oh," ~~said~~ *spoke* Susan with a desperate *gaiety* ~~effort to fill in,~~ "Kelly's apt to show up any where, any time. He was born with a roving foot."

"But not a roving heart," Kelly said. His eyes held hers steadily. There was no laughter in *them* ~~their agate depths~~.

Edward stood up, embarrassed. "I'm taking the midnight west," he explained, "but I'd like to take you both to dinner if -- "

"~~Sorry,~~" Kelly cut in, "I'm hopping a plane for Washington ~~in half an hour~~."

Susan was hardly aware of Edward's going, so intent was she on Kelly's gaunt face. She thought wildly, "That scar! He <u>can</u> be hurt. He isn't indestructible." The bands about her heart threatened to slip. "Remember Elena," she told herself ~~sternly~~, "remember the forty-below cold of a Russian winter, the heat of the Arabian Sea, fever in Bombay."

"Scotch and soda," Kelly spoke to the hovering waiter. He laid his brief case on the empty chair and placed a small white box in front of Susan.

The name of a Lisbon florist was on the lid. With stiff
fingers she untied the purple ribbon and opened it. Nestling
in its bed of oiled green paper was a corsage of violets, in
the center a cluster of ~~pinkish-gold~~ rosebuds. Blindly she
looked at them, afraid to move her eyes lest tears fall. The
flowers were still fresh. Lovely rootless things, ~~to be worn
a few hours and thrown away~~.

"It was nice of you to remember," she said; and to herself: "But you can't go back to ~~the~~ beginnings-- ever."
She did not remove them from the box.

"I'm to be at the Russian desk in the War Office," he
said.

"You're not going back to Russia?"

"I may later." A wry smile twisted his fatigue-lined
face. "If that's what it takes to make the world safe for
Christmas tree trimmers."

"You will never change, will you, Kelly? Even after the
world quiets down?"

"I wish to hell I could say yes. But it wouldn't be
true." Even as he spoke she knew she wouldn't want him to.
~~It was because of men like Kelly that the American way of
life would be preserved.~~

"Are you coming to Washington with me?"

~~She wasn't prepared for that question, even if it were
only perfunctory.~~ She ~~had to~~ beat down the emotion that
bubbled to the surface, ~~and make her voice brittle~~.

"I want to die in bed with grandchildren about me. Not in a crash landing rushing half way across the world to meet you."

"Don't say things like that," he said quietly. "Don't ever say things like that."

The dispatch case slid off the chair. He picked it up and put it on the table. It reminded her of something.

"Why did you go back to Moscow? Or shouldn't I ask?"

A light flamed briefly in his eyes and died. "It wasn't official. Call it a sentimental journey. I see now it was a cockeyed idea."

But Susan saw a bit of goods sticking out from under the flap. She pulled at it, unbelievingly.

"Kelly!" she whispered. "You didn't go back -- didn't risk your life for kitchen curtains."

His grim mouth slipped sideways in a ghost of a smile.

"You used to say home was where my hat was. It isn't. It's where my heart is. You're my heart, Sue. A man's no good without his heart. The curtains were only part of the pattern. I thought they might prove something to you."

Hunger in his voice was unmistakable.

Tears pressed against her lids. The bands snapped and her heart seemed to break loose from its moorings. He did need her! Knowing that a woman could

do anything. Through mist filled eyes she saw men in uniform.
One day they'd be back in business suits on Main Street
because of men like Kelly; and wives like she was going to
be. The thought humbled her yet made her proud.

Silently she lifted the violets from their box and
pinned them to her shoulders.

A sudden joyous tear slipped down her cheek. Her lips
moved soundlessly to finish a quotation begun by another woman
on a sun-fired sea. "Where thou diest, will I die, and there
will I be buried."

"What are you saying?" His glance built a pedestal for
her feet.

"I'm saying -- What are we waiting for?"

Instantly he was on his feet, the old familiar laughter
mounting behind his eyes. His words fell like softest music
on her ears.

"In the buggie, Suzie," he said and pulled back her chair.

74

"Violets from Portugal"

by Helene Carpenter

Blue smoke drifted in lazy swirls above the tables. The cock-tail lounge was filled with late afternoon customers crowding in from storm-darkened streets.

A slender girl with gold hair curling softly under the edge of her fur turban stared into the tawny depths of her glass.

"I wish it were milk," she said.

Her companion, a square-set young man with his heart in his eyes, said, "I'll get you some," and turned to signal a waiter.

"Don't bother, Edward." After all, she was used to substitutes for just about everything. She raised her glass, and the enormous topaz on her finger winked at the matching gems in her ears. "*Na Zdarovya!*" she said.

He touched his glass to hers. "Is that Russian for 'Here's mud in your eye,' Susan?"

"Approximately. I learned one other phrase. *Nitchevo*—'what does it matter?' Said with a shrug. Like this." Her fur coat slipped from her shoulders, displaying a green wool dress with an orna-ment of barbaric beauty at its neck. Like the antique bracelet into which a modern watch had been set, it carried the stamp of the Tzar.

This is stupid conversation, she thought, as he adjusted the lustrous fur over the chair, for people who once meant so much to each other. But what *do* you say to the man you should have married—and didn't? The man whose ring you returned to marry Kelly Westbrook, a scaramouche born with the gift of tongues and laughter, who swept you out of your small-town orbit into a bewildering maze of military and diplomatic protocol. But now headed for the ash heap of divorce.

75

It was good to see Edward again. She tried not to remember the hurt in his eyes on the day he had looked at the small diamond glittering in the palm of his hand. "I think you're making a mistake," he had said. "When you find it out, I'll be around and waiting."

Well, she'd found it out. And Edward was still waiting. Edward, who always broke his stride to walk in step with her. With Kelly, she needed seven-league boots—with which Nature failed to equip her.

She glanced at her watch: 5:15. Kelly should arrive in a few minutes. A few minutes to lay the ghost of five years. She must tell him coolly, briefly, that she wanted a divorce.

"Tell me about your flight from Moscow," Edward said. "Our mothers have been discussing your five-month trek over the garden fence."

"There isn't much to tell."

Odd how her tongue could prattle while she dealt with ghosts. She could sum up her whole married life in one command: "In the buggy, Susie!" That's what Kelly always said when he meant they were on the move again. The words were prelude to nightmare.

Fly here. Motor there. Take a boat. Take a train. Leave the trunks. Don't worry about the language; your diplomatic visa will see you through. Boil the water. Don't drink the milk. Goodby, Sweet. Meet me in Hong Kong, Manila, Moscow!

This last time, Kelly had said goodby at the Moscow airport. The Nazis were marching on Russia. Embassy wives were being sent to neutral countries on five hours' notice, although rumors had been flying thickly for months—soldiers marching, wheels rolling through Red Square night and day.

✿　　✿　　✿

There'd been no laughter at the corner of Kelly's mouth, no teasing gaiety in his eyes when he'd said, "You're going to Iran." He kissed her hard, but she had steeled herself against the feel of his arms about her, against the pressure of his mouth. Her heart

76

had become a tightly wrapped cocoon. It was, she realized, her head that was going to carry on from here.

"Okay," he'd said, releasing her. "In the buggy, Susie!"

She hadn't looked down when the plane circled the field, swept with morning mist. She was trying to remember who it was that had said, "Life is a comedy for those who think, a tragedy for those who feel." . . .

She jerked her mind back to the present, glanced at her watch: 5:30.

Two career women settled themselves at a near-by table. Their eyes dismissed Edward's neat pin stripe, rested on Susan.

"They're admiring the gold of your hair and the brown of your eyes, just as I am," Edward said.

"More likely the brown of my mink. It's about all I got home with." Which wasn't quite true. She still had the jewels that Kelly was forever picking up at commission houses. . . .

Jewels and embassy intrigue! When all she'd ever wanted, from the very beginning, was a plain American home with a kitchen in which to hang her red curtains. How important those few yards of red and white gingham had become to her! She had bought them for their first apartment, when Kelly was on language detail at Columbia University. She'd sewed every stitch of those curtains by hand, and was perched on top of a kitchen stool about to hang them when Kelly burst in, waving an official envelope. "In the buggy, Susie!" he cried, swinging her off the stool, "California, here we come!"

"Oh, Kelly," she wailed against his chest, "just when I had my curtains finished!"

He'd kissed the tip of her nose. "I wouldn't be surprised if they had windows in California." He was impatient to be off.

By the time Susan had re-shaped the curtains, Kelly had been ordered on foreign service.

"The day I get to *hang* these," she said fiercely, "I'll know I've got a home at long last."

"The nesting instinct dies hard," he teased.

"We had sparrows in the ivy at home," she said. Father was always pulling their nests down. The minute he went in the house, they'd pick up the scraps and begin building back. I felt sorry for them. Their nests grew so ragged."

He looked at her, his voice oddly soft. "Let's take them along for luck. People carry old coins and ivory elephants. Why shouldn't we carry kitchen curtains?"

❖   ❖   ❖

Susan glanced at her watch again: 5:40. She held her breath as a tall officer with major's leaves came into the cocktail lounge— but no, it wasn't Kelly.

Edward looked up from the design he'd been making on the table with matches. "Your mother thought you might come home now," he said. "I'm leaving on the midnight."

Susan twirled the stem of her glass between her fingers. "I must see Kelly first," she said.

"Kelly?"

"I left word at the desk for him to meet us here," she explained. "He's flying from Lisbon." (His cable had read, AM BRINGING YOU VIOLETS FROM PORTUGAL.)

Edward seemed troubled.

"Didn't you know Kelly had been recalled to Washington for conference?" she asked.

"Yes," he admitted, "but that was some time ago. When he didn't arrive with the diplomatic corps, I wondered —."

"Didn't arrive? What do you mean?" Her heart skipped a beat.

"Didn't you know?" said Edward. Then his face cleared. "Of course not. You were at sea."

"Tell me." Urgency sharpened her voice.

"He wasn't on the plane with the others when it left Kuibyshev. The newspapers said he'd returned to Moscow. If Washington knew why, they weren't putting it out."

"But the Germans were shelling Moscow then!" she cried. "Why should he go back?" Had Kelly been wounded? His cable hadn't said. Just that nonsense about violets.

Then she laughed at herself, for being a naïve little fool.

"Kelly," she said dryly, "is indestructible." But she drained her glass and slid it to the edge of the table.

Edward laid his hand over her watch. "Susan," he said, "I know a construction engineer is pretty dull stuff. But I'd like to be a plumed knight on a white charger."

Susan smiled. She couldn't answer. She couldn't tell him now what she had decided to do. Kelly had the right to know first . . . .

It had been no white charger that had carried Kelly into her life. It had been a brown polo pony at a near-by Army post. During the holidays she'd gone home with Dot Graham, a classmate.

Kelly had ridden up to their car. He'd been her blind date for the post hop that night. Susan remembered with painful vividness the quick charm of his smile. Gray eyes in a lean brown face; black triangular eyebrows that sharpened in jest.

"Blondes should have blue eyes," he reproved her. "I'll have to get you a yellow and brown orchid. I ordered a violet corsage."

"I love violets," she assured him laughingly. "I've just planted a whole border of them in my garden."

"You have a garden?" he asked incredulously, as if she'd said she had two noses.

"People *have* gardens," Dot said. "Homes, too!" She turned to Susan. "Kelly doesn't believe that. He tucks his head under his wing and goes to sleep like a duck on a pond."

That should have warned her. But it hadn't. He rode back into the game carrying her heart with him.

The magic of that spring night! She'd worn a white frock with tiny puffed sleeves and a billowy skirt. The violets were perfect, with a cluster of sweetheart roses in the center.

By the lake, in a dawn-filled moment, he'd kissed her.

"But I'm engaged," she protested.

He lifted his dark head, and she could see the laughter mounting behind his eyes. "I don't want to be engaged," he said. "I want to be married."

And they were. Within the week she was the wife of Captain William Kelly Westbrook, Military Intelligence. At that time G 2 was just a letter in the alphabet and a number from one to ten.

It was later that the full force of her own inadequacy struck her—three years later, when Kelly was made military attaché to Russia. "Kelly, darling," she mourned, "I can bake hot rolls, but I'm stupid with languages."

"Learn to say, 'I don't know,' and you'll get along."

"I can sew a fine seam, but I'm dumb about foreign affairs."

"Never speak unless you have absolutely nothing to say. That's a diplomatic axiom."

Then she'd made a mistake. She tried to get him to resign from the army. "It isn't as if you didn't have a private income. Aren't we ever going to put down roots? Are we always to be wanderers on the face of the earth?"

She had wept, but he didn't take her in his arms. "Get this straight, Susan"—his voice was rough—"I don't walk around draped in the American flag. But when I go out of the United States Army, it will be with taps playing."

❀   ❀   ❀

So many things had happened since then—so many things. Again she pulled her mind back to this day, this hour. Edward's face swam into focus, and she realized she was talking quite coherently. "We left the plane at Baku and crossed the Caspian by boat —."

"We?"

"Zelda Higgins, wife of a foreign correspondent at Moscow, and her little boy. The three of us stayed in Teheran until the news grew worse and the American consul advised us to start working our way south."

It was in Persia that Zelda had talked about how her Jimmie was going to buy a small-town newspaper as soon as this fracas was over. "We don't want little Jimmie to spend his life dragging from pillar to post. It puts a mark on them, don't you think?"

Susan didn't think. She *knew*. Kelly bore that mark.

The long voyage home took on the quality of an uneasy dream, where everything is seen upside down, like images in a mirage. She could still feel the blazing heat of the Arabian Sea, where

every deep breath seared the lungs. Little Jimmie, who had barely survived the sunless killing cold of a Russian winter, had a
sunstroke. Looking at the child's small bones thrusting through
his skin, she had asked Zelda: "Suppose big Jimmie won't buy
that small-town paper? Suppose he insists on roaming the world?
What will you do?"

Zelda had gazed over the rail, where a pitiless sun danced on
a copper sea, and spoken simply: "Then I should say, like Ruth
in the Bible, 'Whither thou goest, I will go.' "

Sitting here in the New York cocktail lounge with Edward,
Susan put that answer resolutely out of her mind. What she
couldn't put out of her mind was the bout of fever she'd had in
Bombay. Aware, in lucid intervals, of dark faces and strange
tongues, she had wondered what was to become of her.

Nor could she forget the sub off Capetown that finally turned
out to be English—but not before a Polish refugee standing beside her had gone suddenly mad and thrown herself into the sea.
Least of all could she afford to remember the bitterness of that
night before she left Russia.

It had started in the afternoon with a cocktail party. Elena,
the wife of an important foreign minister, was giving it. She was
a red Persian cat of a woman. That she was half in love with Kelly
was an open secret, amusing to everyone except Susan.

The Ambassador's wife let it be known that she was going to
call on Susan, and together they would go to Elena's party.

Susan was dressing when Zelda Higgins phoned—frantic, dis-
traught. Little Jimmie was ill. It looked like an emergency ap-
pendectomy, and she couldn't locate a doctor. Would Susan come
over and stay with the child while she tracked one down?

Susan could and did; forgetting the Ambassador's wife; forgetting Elena's party—until Zelda arrived finally with a doctor
in tow. Then it was too late.

The Ambassador's wife was sweet and patient about it, as one
is sweet and patient with a backward child. But there was an
Embassy dinner that night, and Susan wondered in what sly
way Elena would manage to humiliate her. Kelly had impressed

upon her the importance of keeping things smooth between the legations. Nerves were on edge waiting for the inevitable blow, not knowing from which direction it would strike.

Kelly came in her room, that evening, handsome in full dress. Her fingers trembled as she fastened an emerald necklace set in heavy Finnish gold about her throat. She was wearing a new gown of honey beige satin, a perfect setting for the glowing emeralds. If he noticed it he gave no sign.

"I'm sorry," she said, "about this afternoon."

He ran an impatient hand over his thick, dark hair. "You're so damned impulsive, Susan. Won't you ever grow up? Couldn't you have taken time out to send a message?"

"I didn't think," she defended herself. "Jimmie's fever was 104, I rushed right over. You see," she said hopelessly, "I'll never learn that an artificial code comes before human sympathy."

He strode to the window. Through her mirror she could see him staring down at the rumbling cavalcade below. Finally he gave a short sigh and turned back to her. "Stop fretting, Sweet." He dropped a kiss on the top of her head. "Kelly can fix."

Sure Kelly could fix the stupid blunders his wife made! Bitterly she watched him doing it, later, with his adroit mixture of wit and impudence.

After dinner the huge Soviet general with whom Susan was dancing gave an abrupt turn, and she saw, through the archway, red hair against black. Elena, tall and beautiful, with her Slavic cheekbones, over-ripe lips and thick creamy skin, was pressing her cheek against Kelly's as they executed slow turns to waltz time. Her slumbrous green eyes were half closed. Susan could almost hear her purr.

Kelly's lips moved and Elena smiled. Jealousy drove through Susan. "Why do I go on?" she asked herself. "It's going to be like this all my life. Only I'll be getting older, and there will always be an Elena."

Back in their apartment living room, silence had hung like a heavy black curtain between them. In her eardrums the ever marching boots outside made hammers of sound; through the open windows drifted odors compounded of earth, body smells, and the strident perfume that all Moscow affected.

In sudden revolt she rushed to the window and slammed it down. Kelly took a long drag on his cigarette and lifted a questioning eyebrow. Nervously she began to strip off her bracelets, earrings, necklace.

"I'm sorry I didn't buy you that ruby pendant we saw in Kiev," he said. "Too late now."

"I don't want rubies," she cried. "I want an American gas stove, and a refrigerator that works. I want to belong to garden clubs. I want to bake pumpkin pies for Thanksgiving, and trim trees at Christmas."

He uncrossed his long legs and watched her pace the rug. "You're living in the middle of history."

"I want to live in the middle of America." The words tumbled from her lips. "I'm sick of watching shore lines drop behind my ship, of earth falling away from my plane, of landscapes flying by so fast I can't see the homes or the people who live in them. I hate being cooped up in an embassy—dining every night with foreign cats."

He was on his feet shaking her. "Make sense," he said harshly. "You've got a ringside seat to the greatest show on earth."

"You can have it," she flung at him. "I'll settle for a little house with lilacs in the back yard and tricycles in the driveway and—" her voice broke—"and a kitchen to hang—my curtains—in."

"So that's how it is!" He let her go so abruptly that she almost fell. "I thought you married *me*. What I sum up to as a *man*. Not as a way of life." He shot her a hard level look. "The next time you marry, remember that!" His words killed the sobs in her throat. *The next time you marry.* He was telling her what she'd begun to suspect that he was tired of carrying supercargo.

They stood in the middle of the floor, facing each other across the gulf of words. The telephone's sudden ringing was like a flash of lightning through a storm cloud. She stood rooted to the spot while he answered it, listening without comprehension to his monosyllables.

83

*   *   *

Without explanation he banged out of the apartment. Dazedly she went into her bedroom and set about undressing.

When he returned, his face was a polite mask. "It's come," he said. "Hell's about to pop. You're leaving Moscow. Wives are being sent to neutral countries."

"What will *you* do?" Her voice sounded tinny and far off.

"Move with headquarter to Kuibyshev. Hurry!"

She began throwing things into a bag without recognition, until on opening a big carved chest, she saw neat folds of red and white gingham. Kelly, coming from the bathroom with her toilet articles, saw them too. Their eyes met and held an instant. She let the lid fall.

Even the sparrows in her father's ivy were eventually discouraged! . . .

5:45. Edward was holding a match toward Susan's cigarette when she saw Kelly enter the lounge. Her hand trembled. She put down her cigarette—unlighted. Heads turned to look at the tall man in uniform striding toward her.

Maybe others could hear the roar of planes, wheels on rails, ship's turbines, just as she could.

She was shocked by the haggard leanness of his face, the gray at his temples, the thin red scar on his forehead that had not been there five months ago.

"You know Edward," she said mechanically.

The men shook hands. "Quite a surprise," said Edward. "I was telling Susan what a stir it caused in Washington when you didn't arrive on schedule."

There was an awkward pause.

Susan then spoke with a desperate gaiety:

"Kelly's apt to show up anywhere, any time. He was born with a roving foot."

"But not a roving heart," Kelly said. His eyes held hers steadily. There was no laughter in them.

Edward stood up, embarrassed. "I'm taking the midnight

84

west," he explained "but I'd like to take you both to dinner if—."

Kelly cut in: "I'm hopping a plane for Washington."

Susan was hardly aware of Edward's going, so intent was she on Kelly's gaunt face. She thought wildly, "That scar! He *can* be hurt. He isn't indestructible." The bands about her heart threatened to slip. "Remember Elena," she told herself. "Remember the forty-below-zero cold of a Russian winter, the heat of the Arabian Sea, fever in Bombay—."

"Scotch and soda," Kelly spoke to the hovering waiter. He laid his brief case on the empty chair and placed a small white box in front of Susan.

The name of a Lisbon florist was on the lid. With stiff fingers she untied the purple ribbon and opened it. Nestling in its bed of oiled green paper was a corsage of violets, in the center a cluster of rosebuds. Blindly she looked at them, afraid to move her eyes lest tears fall. The flowers were still fresh. Lovely rootless things.

"It was nice of you to remember," she said; to herself she thought: "But you can't go back to beginnings—ever." She did not remove the flowers from the box.

"I'm to be at the Russian desk in the War Office," he said.

"You're not going back to Russia?"

"I may later." A wry smile twisted his fatigue-lined face. "If that's what it takes to make this world of ours safe for Christmas-tree trimmers."

"You will never change, will you, Kelly? Even after the world quiets down?"

"I wish to hell I could say yes. But it wouldn't be true." Even as he spoke, she knew she wouldn't want him to.

"Are you coming to Washington with me?"

She had to beat down the emotion that bubbled to the surface.

"I want to die in bed with grandchildren about me. Not in a crash landing rushing half way across the world to meet you."

"Don't say things like that," he said quietly. "Don't ever say things like that."

The dispatch case slid off the chair onto the floor. He picked it up and put it on the table.

It reminded her of something. "Why did you go back to Moscow? Or shouldn't I ask?"

A light flamed in his eyes, then died. "It wasn't official. Call it a sentimental journey. I see now it was a cockeyed idea."

But Susan saw a bit of goods sticking out from under the flap. She pulled at it.

"Kelly!" she whispered unbelievingly. "You didn't go back— didn't risk your life for kitchen curtains!"

His grim mouth slipped sideways in a ghost of a smile. "You used to say home, for me, was where my hat was. It isn't. It's where my heart is. *You're* my heart, Sue. A man's no good without his heart. The curtains were only part of the pattern. I thought they might prove something to you." The hunger in his voice was unmistakable.

Tears pressed against her lids. The bands snapped, and her heart seemed to break loose from its moorings. He *did* need her! Knowing *that*, a woman could do anything. Through mist-filled eyes she saw men in uniform. One day they'd be back in business suits on Main Street because of men like Kelly; because of wives such as she was going to be. The thought made her humble, yet proud.

She lifted the violets from their box, pinned them to her shoulder. A tear slipped down her cheek. Her lips moved soundlessly to finish a quotation begun by another woman on a sun-fired sea. " 'Where thou diest, will I die, and there will I be buried.' "

"What are you saying?" His glance built a pedestal for her feet.

"I'm saying—what are we waiting for?"

Instantly he was on his feet, the old familiar laughter mounting behind his eyes.

"In the buggy, Susie," he said, and pulled back her chair.

86

CHAPTER SIX

ESTABLISH YOUR WRITING HABITS

Now THAT YOU HAVE PEEPED behind the scenes at the writing problems and have begun to perceive what a story is, the next step for you is prompt action. Make your writing habits professional.

The first sign of a fledging writer's future success is his shift into professional actions. Some of these are:

1. *Write daily.*

Good writing is not as easy as it reads. Like water in pipes, to be first-class, writing must flow crystal clear. When creative thoughts do not pour on paper, like water, they can rust the pipes, or thicken like sticky syrup, or solidify as honey turns to sugar. Almost all of us have other jobs. If you only have twenty minutes in which to write, there is not too much you can accomplish. But if you do use these twenty or thirty minutes in rapid writing, you will discover that your ease of expression is not so likely to freeze, but stays sharp, clear, and on tap when you call for it.

2. *Write rapidly.*

A warm-up period of *writing just as fast as you can* helps. You catch thoughts as they flow in your mind. This stimulates your creative thinking. Especially on those days when you are too busy for the writing work at hand, if you will write four pages just as fast as you can write, you will discover that you have kept the creative flow going and have brought out your thinking on your today's problems in an objective form where you can take a look at them. You will also be delighted at the story ideas that pop out. Another important thing: these ideas are on paper, easy to check on those dry days when you can't think of a story or article that you want to develop.

Before they go on stage, actors exercise for a warm-up. Fast writing helps you warm up before you start the work you have on hand to do. Your regular copy is more smooth, more alive.

3. *Finish what you start.*

You can't sell a half-written story or book. The practice of starting something without finishing it risks becoming a habit. It would appear that to start it—get it almost through—would make it easy to pick up later, but this is not always the case.

There is a sort of no-man's-land between beginning and getting into the story or the article. This crossover must be made each time you go to work. Many writers who have had outstanding success with short stories have found those stories were best which were written in one or two sittings. This has prevented that delving in and out where the transition is often marked by "wooden" writing.

One way to help yourself finish what you start is to make a list of the day's work. A list is objective and looks up at you with reproachful eyes. A list without a completion line drawn through it can reproach you like a baby without its bottle. Also, each time you are able to scratch a piece of work off the list, you will feel an upsurge of triumphant joy.

4. *Revise.*

We are so conscious of "slicks" meaning the smooth-paper magazines that sometimes we forget the origin of the term. It meant that the work itself had been polished, cleaned up, and made smooth—that is why it is "slick"! When you finish a story and it is neatly typed for the magazine to which you hope to send it, sometimes an idea will pop into your mind revealing a way to improve it. Or you show it to a critic who helps you see how to improve it. Don't go at it blind; that doesn't help; but when you do see a flaw, instead of feeling "Oh, that's too much work," tear into it and get it corrected. This squaring of the shoulders and settling back to redo a story into a more acceptable

88

form not only helps the conscious mind of the writer to get his vision on paper; it also helps free the subconscious mind so that his native, inborn but locked-up skill can break into the open. Here lies the difference between the good and the best.

5. *Use your subconscious.*

As you know, there are two steps in gaining knowledge. The first is the understanding of the theory, and the second is putting the theory into practice. A writer must work until he is skillful in the latter, which is, in effect, the joining of the conscious and subconscious mind.

Learning to use the subconscious is one of the writer's most powerful tools. How often that baffling problem straightens out when you "sleep on it." One writer I knew discovered how to plot this way: She worked hard on her story just before going to bed; then on arising, she caught the new ideas on paper before she rushed to class. Before long her plots were taking shape the way she wanted them.

In *I Will Lift Up Mine Eyes*, Glenn Clark wrote the entire book on the power of the conscious and subconscious mind tracking together.

6. *Write before you sharpen your pencils!*

Anything that keeps you from settling down to writing is "pencil-sharpening." It is in reality any kind of dodge that keeps your body busy and gives your mind excuses for not writing. In addition to the needed talent, the most important requirement for success, the late Walter Campbell insisted, is the ability to make yourself work.

A writer has to take himself by the scruff of his neck and force himself into a chair and begin pounding the typewriter. This is the one time that washing dirty dishes or mowing the lawn appears inviting.

Or you remember something else that needs doing—a letter to write, an imperative phone call, or a bit of research. Watch it; this is pencil-sharpening! All jobs will wait, unfortunately; and the doing of them after daily writing is finished gives you a lift.

7. Meet your deadlines.

If you are going to be of value to an editor, you must remember his problems. Unless you help him solve his, he cannot help you with yours. Editors have deadlines; if you are dependable, you will make your own and keep them, too. The writer who can do this often finds extra money in his pocket.

When a call came to a colleague of mine asking for his recommendation of a well-trained writer who could meet deadlines, he paused. He had many who were well trained, but their habits of turning in assigned copy late made him hesitate.

"This alone," he told his class later, "did the eliminating."

Because it is so easy to put writing off until "tomorrow," we may have to trick ourselves into forming the habit. One person I know has a high-school girl come in twice a week to type. This makes her keep her copy ready. Another sets a specific production goal. A third writer has a definite day to begin a story and will not mix with friends until he finishes his story. (He doesn't have a family.) Find out what works best with you and do whatever you must to get your copy done on time.

8. Keep growing.

In writing it is as easy to get in a rut as in any other field, and it is suicide to a writer. You are competing with the best minds in the land. Moreover, you work where the saturation point is reached very quickly.

Keep on your writing toes by developing yourself in three directions. First, delve deeply into the things that give you personal enthusiasm. This helps you to become an expert in your special field. Second, spread out in your writing areas. Keep a certain experimental growth going. If you do juveniles, try men's magazines, personality stories, or start a book. Third, develop your professional technique. Make studies of actions and reactions. Do character studies on the type of characters you have not written about. Seek new expressions for the standard movements. Tighten your writing. Finger exercises like these stretch the mind's writing horizons.

9. *Warm yourself by a fire!*

Writing is a lonely business. Sometimes, too lonely. Writers' magazines help you here. So do writers' conferences. You go, see what others are doing, and return home challenged and inspired. You can create, too, your own little group—not one where you talk instead of write, but one where you are challenged. Bring in a professional writer or teacher and conduct your own workshop. There is a charge of electric inspiration generated in such meetings which fills you with new enthusiasm. If you are already selling, the added spurt of production will more than pay the cost. If you choose your teachers wisely, you will build your skill as well.

Many a good, highly talented writer has fallen by the wayside because the flame burned low, when a little recharging would have caused the fire to blaze high enough to lift him over the hump.

10. *Tell the truth as you see it.*

Truth is vital—as much in fiction as in nonfiction. Before we study we have the vague idea that nonfiction articles are more lifelike. Possibly they state more facts, but they cannot demonstrate the inner principles of life as fiction does. And if fiction does not depict emotions honestly and reactions accurately, the reader tosses aside your work. He wants a world where he loses himself in other people's adventures. It is your business to create it for him.

When Mary Agnes Thompson first began to study professional writing, she revealed little conflict. She joined a private group where the members read their stories aloud to each other before handing them in to the teachers.

"You wouldn't believe it," one of the members later confided to me, "but hers were really among the worst in the class. None of us liked them."

That didn't stop Mary Agnes. She plodded on, working hard, writing children's stories, Sunday-school stories, confession stories, and finally she began selling to *The Saturday Evening*

Post. Had death not cut short her career, she would be among America's best sellers today.

But she first established her writing habits. When she saw what a story was, she promptly practiced it, persisted with her efforts, and later her habits established her.

The following story was written in two afternoons. She did not have to revise a single word. It sold to *The Saturday Evening Post*, who named it "Stubborn Bride."

"Stubborn Bride"

by Mary Agnes Thompson

LIEUTENANT FRANK PALCOUCEK slowed the car a little as New Czechy's white grain elevators appeared, slashing the purple-blue of the evening horizon. The vague uneasiness he had felt when he had suggested visiting his folks rolled over him now with a desperation close to panic. He felt like a little boy again. It was not that he was ashamed of the folks, he told himself over and over to lull the nagging uneasiness, but how could you say to reserved Linda Raeburn, one of Biloxi's elite, "Look, my old man is still pretty much old-country. He talks funny and loud, and sometimes he forgets and runs a bunch of Czech into it, and sometimes when I'm not watching I catch myself talking almost like him. And mamma —."

He gripped the steering wheel angrily. Well, mamma was something special that happened to a guy once in a lifetime. Old-fashioned, maybe. But mamma had been the buffer that had quietly eased itself between her youngest son and his tempestuous old man when the quarrels threatened violence. Nobody was going to hurt mamma!

"What's the matter, Frank?" Linda asked anxiously, her easy drawl carrying a nervous note. "You're awfully quiet. . . . It's pretty country. All wheat."

She waited, her dark head still at that expectant angle.

Frank glanced at the countryside. The wheat was turning, waving gently in the evening wind, icy-green and shimmering. He could tell the approximate yield of every field in passing. Old Bohomil Palcoucek had taught even his rebel son the fine art of wheat raising. Frank grinned wryly, but the thought of old

Bohomil was not amusing. He could see him, inspecting Linda carefully, then making his blunt pronouncements.

"It's all right, if you like wheat," Frank said with a brief shrug, his mind still on his father. "I never liked it. So the old man let me go, after a couple of rounds." He had an odd sense of loneliness akin to guilt now, coming home in June when the wheat was turning away from greenness. His Air Force uniform would be a sharp contrast to the overalls and blue shirts of the community Czechs.

"I'm the youngest son. I was supposed to farm next to the old man. He didn't want to let me go, so don't expect him to roll out the red carpet, honey." His mind flickered an image of old Bohomil coming in from the field, his huge body surging with the vigor of a man who has lived much outdoors and who rode his seventy-odd years triumphantly. His clothes would be wet with perspiration.

In the small mirror Frank could glimpse Linda, cool and serene in a pastel suit. Only a wisp of her dark hair showed from the scarf she wore around her head. She looked almost fragile. She was staring straight ahead, her lips parted slightly as though ready to speak, yet she hesitated.

"Scared?" Frank asked, trying to appear at ease himself to allay her fears.

"Your folks won't like me," she predicted moodily, her voice so faraway it seemed cold to Frank. "You know they won't. Is that what's worrying you?"

He drove the car to the side of the highway and slammed on the brakes. The vague irritation mounted in him. He stared straight ahead, as she was doing. She was getting into one of her brooding spells now when they were almost home. He'd hoped it wouldn't happen, but here it was. Funny that a girl like Linda would ever have to be plagued with the same doubts he'd known. But he'd had reasons. She hadn't. Yet she was afraid of strangers.

"Now, listen," he said doggedly. "Whether they like you or not doesn't make any difference. I'm the one who's marrying

94

you. I'll admit you're not like any of the Czech girls the folks thought I might marry. So you can't work like Czech women can. But my folks aren't like your folks, either. Well, maybe they won't like you. You probably won't like them either."

Her hands were in her lap, nervously clenched. "What're they like?" Her voice sounded childish, almost excited now. "Ever since I was a little girl, it's fascinated me where people come from and who their parents were and if they had grandfathers. Things like that.

"They came from the old country," Frank said shortly.

"You—you never talked about your folks before, Frank. Why?"

"There wasn't anything to say." He struggled uneasily and looked away over the icy-green wheat. "I didn't third-degree you about your folks, did I?"

"No," Linda said slowly in her soft voice. "You never asked me about my folks. Or where they came from. . . . I'm sorry, Frank."

Neither spoke any more. There were only the sounds of an occasional bird and the thrumming of wheat starting to ripen. Something about the sound brought the aching to Frank again. He had never known that feeling when he was still home. But now he had been gone and had come back, an alien, and the rustling of wheat in the wind hurt him.

He wanted to tell Linda how it was with Bohomil and Anna Palcoucek—big Bohomil who gave orders around New Czechy, and Anna who had loved him all through the rugged years with him. He wished he could explain how it was with Czechs, that no matter how long they were gone from the old country they never quite forgot how the Moldau ran its course or the sounds and smells of Prague—Praha they steadfastly called it. But he could not find the words without seeming to apologize for his parents. A boyish stubbornness kept him from either apologizing or explaining.

"I'm going to stop for a beer before I go out to the farm," he said instead as they drove into New Czechy. "I need one, that's for sure. Want to go in with me?"

Linda glanced around at the small town spreading about tall

elevators, like fingers leading to a strong palm. "The hand that feeds America!" Bohomil Palcoucek always called New Czechy. He was great on that American stuff.

Frank opened the door for Linda and she got out and looked around again. "I was afraid New Czechy would be bigger," she said.

They went inside and slid into a booth. After a while a dark-haired girl sauntered over. She stared at Frank, then tilted her head back and laughed. "Frankie Palcoucek!" She slapped him on the shoulder with familiar hilarity. "Look at the looie bars! I figured you'd get kicked out and have to come home!"

Frank wished she'd drop that Frankie stuff. He could feel a tinge of color working up over his neck. When he'd been a kid the other boys always made fun of him because he reddened when he got angry. "Hello, Suzy." He made his voice easy and finally flashed a smile at her. "Nope, I'm not kicked out. I see you're still around driving the fellows crazy."

"Oh, just dancing my head off, sure." Suzy watched him boldly. "I'll bet this is What's-Her-Name. Your old man said you were bringing her home."

"This is Linda Raeburn. Linda, this is Suzy Hrubeck, an old friend of mine."

"Friend is right." Suzy raised her eyebrows coyly. "Say, you got here just in time for the kolach festival. It's tomorrow, re-member?"

"Kolach festival!" Frank groaned and rubbed his hand across his forehead. "Well, you'll be up to your ears in Czechs, Linda, that's for sure."

They drank the beers, and Suzy followed them to the door. Linda got into the car. She was nervous to the point of silence. It was at times like this that she retreated so far within herself that Frank hardly knew what to say to her.

"Your old man said she was an outsider," Suzy whispered mali-ciously. "She's cold as an ice cube, Frankie."

"Shut up." He was already feeling the sullen irritation he had always known when he was home. He'd thought the Air Force had taken it out of him. Now it had returned. "Someone ought to put you in cold storage for a while."

"An old girl friend?" Linda asked when he got in. Her expression was remote. She applied make-up carefully.

"We used to hit the Bohemian dances together. That's about all."

"Are you sure it's all, Frankie?" There was a caustic tone in Linda's use of his childhood name.

"Oh, for Pete's sake!" he snapped, starting the car. "Let's cut the wrangling. It's bad enough we hit New Czechy in time for the kolach festival tomorrow. You'll need your nerves for that. So save 'em."

They drove down the old familiar road to the Palcoucek family home. The big two-story house looked clean and white, set in its mounting of clipped lawn. Bohomil always said you could tell the Czech farms easily. The houses were always painted. The lawns were always mowed. The barns were as well kept as the houses.

He parked the car under the tree in the back yard where he had always parked it when he wanted to have it ready for quick departure. Looking back, he realized that from the time he was little on he had always been ready to leave the farm. He had to take Linda through the back door, but it would not matter. Anna Palcoucek's kitchen was to her what Bohomil's barns and granaries were to him.

He opened the door and Linda stepped inside, but as he followed her, she turned and let him pass. His eyes moved quickly to the woman who was kneading dough at the kitchen table. Kolaches. Mamma was making kolaches, the sweet rolls the Czech women made by the hundreds for the festival. They were symbols, reminding the Czechs of the old country.

For a moment Frank hesitated in front of Linda. He should never have brought her home, he realized. How could he ever make her understand how it was about mamma and the kolaches, and Bohomil dancing the beseda on festival night, with hundreds of Czechs cheering him on? And following that, his thunderous speech about how Czechoslovakia would rise again from its chains and become another America, free to breathe again. Frank almost groaned.

Then Anna raised her head and the clear gray gaze moved slowly, fondly over him. He forgot all about Lieutenant Frank Palcoucek and the base at Biloxi, and the big Raeburn veranda where Mrs. Raeburn entertained the officers. He was Frankie once more, Anna Palcoucek's youngest son.

"Mamma!" he cried out, an agonizing joy making his voice boyishly raspy. "I'm home, see? I'm home, mamma!"

Except for the quick light that made her plain face beautiful, Anna Palcoucek might have been inspecting a casual acquaintance. She patted the kolach dough briskly. Then she rubbed the remaining dough from her hands carefully. But her eyes never left Frank. "So!" she said then, holding her arms to him. "So you come home, huh, Frankie?"

He took two quick steps and gathered her up in his arms, buried his face against her neck, and for a while they stood there, oblivious of the girl who was standing, alone and proudly erect, by the door. Frank could say nothing and Anna kept murmuring little pet phrases in Czech, over and over, her cheek nuzzling Frank's head, like a mare caressing her colt.

"I make kolaches, see? For the kolach festival tomorrow," Anna said when Frank dropped his arms and turned to Linda. "Poppy-seed. Apricot. Prune. You remember how you like the poppy-seed kolaches, huh, Frankie?"

"Sure, I remember, mamma," Frank said slowly. "I remember, all right." He forgot to introduce Linda. He looked past the two women, out the window and beyond, where in every direction the wheat rustled and crinkled in the sun. Again he felt alien, surly. "Where's the old man? Out tramping down half the wheat trying to figure out what the yield's going to be?"

The old bitterness against his father flecked him. He did not know why it should touch him now. But something about seeing mamma making kolaches had done it. They were so proud of being Czech, mamma and papa. He recalled the time at Biloxi when he had got into a brawl with one of the fellows who had lightly called him a bohunk. But he could not say whether it had been pride or humiliation that had made him fighting mad, and he wouldn't talk about it afterwards to Linda. No Czech wanted to be called a bohunk. He knew that. As Bohomil had once put it, "I call me a bohunk, but you don't!"

"Papa comes now," Anna said. "He comes, Frankie."

Bohomil stalked into the room, slamming the door behind him. There was the odor of wheat fields and barns and sweat about him. It surged through the kitchen in the wake of his steps. He tossed his straw hat onto a chair and ran one of his huge hands through his hair, only now graying a little. Then he slapped Frank on the shoulder.

"So you make it, huh?" he grunted. "This your girl, huh?"

"This is Linda," Frank nodded.

Linda held out her hand. It was only then that Frank remembered he had not introduced Linda to Anna. But once more Bohomil's immense vitality shoved Anna's personality to the background. He grasped one of Linda's small hands in his own and inspected her with the cautious suspicion with which he would investigate an animal before admitting it to his selected herd.

"So," Bohomil nodded only a little, his keen eyes running over Linda. "This goin' to be your woman, huh? Well, by golly, that Frankie can still pick 'em, huh, Anna?"

Anna nodded and smiled. Frank glanced quickly at Linda, remembering Suzy at the tavern. Everyone was determined to remind Linda that in his day he'd been quite a boy. Linda's eyes narrowed the way they always did when she felt somebody was disapproving of her. Couldn't she tell the old man was actually trying to be friendly?

"The old man likes his joke," he said in a low voice, touching her arm. "Well, you must be tired, honey. Mamma, can you show Linda where her room is?"

"You come in time for kolach festival." Bohomil was not yet through with Linda. "Then you see what kind of people you marryin' into, by golly. Tomorrow is all kinds of contests. Sokols do all kinds of crazy sport stuff and then at night is dancin' the beseda. Old-country dance. You dance, huh?"

"Yes." Linda was still staring at Bohomil, her eyes fixed on him as though hypnotized, her hand still imprisoned in his great one. "I dance." She hesitated, then the soft words came faster, almost tumbling over one another in her haste to assure him she could compete with the Czech girls. "I dance all kinds of popular dances."

"We see. I dance the beseda with you tomorrow night and we see if you enough woman to marry Czech man. That beseda, that some dance, huh, Frankie?"

"Yeh." Frank nodded nervously. "It sure is some dance. It winds you. Linda didn't bring the right kind of clothes to dance the beseda in, papa."

"Mamma she used to dance the beseda, huh, Anna?" Bohomil went on, ignoring Frank. "Back in old country, Anna and me we showed 'em how beseda oughta be danced." He was quiet a little. "The night of our weddin' dance we showed 'em, huh, Anna? Anna she went all the way to Praha to get her weddin' dress, and not many girls in our village ever got to go to Praha, let alone wear no dress from the city."

"All the way from Praha," Anna said softly, looking out the window.

Why couldn't they call it Prague, Frank thought irritably, the way everyone in America except Czechs called it? He moved toward the living room.

"Linda's tired, mamma," Frank said, frowning. "We drove all the way today from Tulsa. We stayed overnight with some friends of hers in Tulsa."

"By golly, I betcha they haven't danced the beseda in the old country since the soldiers come." Old Bohomil stood, slowly pounding his right fist into his left palm, almost like the ominous beating of a drum, fierce and warlike. "But someday they goin' to, believe me. Someday it's goin to be like here in America."

"Papa," Frank broke in.

"I tell 'em tomorrow night." Bohomil nodded savagely and shrugged as though to shake off his anger if only for a time. "After we dance the beseda and everybody all worked up, I tell 'em how it is with the old country. How it is here in America better."

"I show you to your room, Linda." Anna said softly, leading the way to the living room and toward the staircase leading upstairs from the hallway just next to it. "You tired, maybe so."

The old man was taking over as usual, Frank thought impatiently. He couldn't be in a room or a tavern or a meeting with any amount of people in it for one minute without overwhelming everyone, and if anyone objected, he just overwhelmed their objections too. It had always embarrassed Frank the way old Bohomil took over.

"I'm goin' to tell 'em . . ." Frank could still hear Bohomil, muttering to himself in the kitchen.

"He's right, Frankie," Anna sensed Frank's antagonism. "Papa's right."

"Sure," Frank muttered savagely, moving out the door to get the bags out of the car. "Sure. Papa will tell 'em, all right. Papa's right, you can bet on that."

✿   ✿   ✿

Anna put Linda in the bedroom that had been Frank's when he was home. It was an old-fashioned room in old-country style. It had once been the main bedroom. The cradle Bohomil and Anna had brought along when they had crossed over to America was sitting in one corner, well-used and weary now. Souvenirs of Frank's school days were still on the wall.

He glanced into the mirror on the old dresser and was startled by the expression on Linda's face. It was a mixture of sullen resentment and an emotion that was almost fear. Frank slipped both arms around her and held her close, shaking her in his aggravation. "Stop it," he whispered fiercely. "Stop being so

101

standoffish. All right. So my folks are old-country. We won't be living with them. But," he added with a sharp touch of viciousness, "we won't be living high-society style with your folks either."

"I never asked you to, Frank." Linda was angry now. She tried to break away from him.

"You don't have to go to the kolach festival tomorrow if you don't want to, and you don't have to dance the beseda with my old man, if that's what's put the chill on you." He tried to twist her face toward his, but she jerked away. "Do you think I want everyone saying I married an ice cube? We go back to Biloxi day after tomorrow. That's just one full day."

"One full day is right." Linda laughed scornfully. I should go to town and run the gauntlet of all these Czech people you grew up with. I should dance with your father while you dance with that—that —."

Frank narrowed his eyes and dropped his arms from around her. "That's it!" he muttered. "Well, I've known you when you were scared and when you seemed to hate the whole world, but I never thought I'd see the day when Linda Raeburn of Biloxi had to be jealous of someone like Suzy Hrubeck."

They were both silent then. They were ruining something that had been beautiful in spite of its shaky, uncertain moments, he knew. They had never quarreled like this.

They had been a popular couple, with Frank's blond good looks in sharp contrast to her brunet, almost elfin beauty. He had never felt certain of her, as he had felt with the Czech girls he had known. Sometimes her quicksilver changes made him feel afraid he was losing her. Frank, accustomed to the robust boisterousness of his Czech background, never quite knew how to analyze her brooding spells. But he had accepted and liked Linda's mode of life in Biloxi. Now she was openly resentful of his.

Linda sat down on the bed and ran her finger over the patchwork quilt, following its pattern. Frank recalled once more her house in Biloxi, modern with a touch of the old South to give it

an air of quality. But no hand-sewn quilt, with patches he recognized. The brown-and-white checked shirt that had been his
first ready-made garment. A patch from his older brother Anton's
vest lining. Everything about the Palcoucek house had threads
running back to ancient things that embroidered memories of
the old country, gentle as the flow of the Moldau at times and
then exploding violently into action.

He did not know what he expected her to say when she raised
her head. But he had not thought it would be, "Were you born in
this room, Frank?"

"Yes," he said, startled by the change in the conversation.
"Mamma has never been in a hospital." He heard his voice, de-
fensive to the point of defiance. He could not explain to Linda
about mamma's strange mixture of shyness and strength that
had kept her from going to the hospital for the birth of any of
her seven sons. "Some women don't want pampering," he added,
and knew immediately he should not have said it.

Linda rose and whirled on him. "The only reason I didn't take
a job was because we got engaged right after I finished college,"
she reminded him, her blue eyes flashing. The breach was growing wider with every word.

We shouldn't have come home, Frank thought again. *I don't
know Linda at all now. The folks don't even act as though she's
company. They don't realize what a long ways it is from the
Mississippi to the Moldau. She's not a Czech girl.*

"I know, Linda." He lowered his voice. "I just meant mamma is
—well, like I said, old-fashioned. You don't understand each
other. You're miles apart."

"I'm sorry, Frank," Linda said. "I told you. You can't say I
didn't tell you." She sat back down on the bed and her eyes were
cool again, her expression unfathomable.

Anna came back into the room then. She was carrying the
dress Bohomil had liked. "All the way to Praha I went for my
dress," she said softly, laying it out on the bed. "Bohomil wanted
I should have my wedding dress from Praha."

"It's—a pretty dress," Linda managed to say politely, not looking at Frank. She stared down at the dress, but she did not touch it as she had the quilt.

Anna touched it. She fondled the lace at the neck, pressed it out with fingers. She spread out the full skirt lovingly. The tiny waist could no longer contain her ample form, and a slight smile edged her mouth as her fingers caressed it. "Seven sons I had." She nodded. "When you have seven babies you can't wear your wedding dress, either, maybe so."

"Mamma," Frank broke in sharply.

"So small you are now," mamma sighed, shaking her head. Then she said proudly, "You wear it tomorrow night when you dance beseda with papa. Papa like that."

Linda stared past Frank and mamma, her eyes fastened on the full-skirted white dress lying on the bed. There was a touch of horror in her eyes and she rose quickly from the bed. "I—I couldn't wear the dress," she said quietly. "Thank you anyhow, Mrs. Palcoucek."

She walked past the two others and out of the room, walking almost stiffly.

Frank halted, uncertain and confused. He looked at Anna. She was still caressing the dress, her fingers touching the creamy-white old fabric, following the embroidered threads that wended their dreamlike way along the banks of the Moldau and through the villages of old Czechoslovakia. She had been a girl of sixteen when she married the stalwart Bohomil and had followed his dream to America, shy and almost speechless before his passionate fervor with all things. Of the two, it had been Anna who remained the most old-country. It had been the woman whose heart had wept for the Moldau and its rich land, its dancing and its music. How many times her heart must have made its pilgrimage back home!

"Mamma," Frank said gently, his voice hoarse. He touched her arm, "Don't, mamma!"

But Anna did not turn. She did not even blink her eyes. She stared at the dress which had come all the way from Praha so many years and so many sons ago. There was in her eyes terrible loneliness for the days gone, for the laughter of her girlhood in the old land she loved.

A furious anger swept over Frank, pushing back the boyish uncertainty, cutting through the confusion that had always marked his actions. He turned and walked out of the room, leaving Anna with her memories and her dress from Praha. He took the stairs two at a time and went out the front door, then stood for a few moments on the porch that stretched across the front of the house.

Linda was sitting in the lawn swing under the big elm tree. She was almost a carved portion of the swing, still and cold. She was staring straight ahead, her expression immobile as a chiseled mask. She did not even turn her head as Frank strode down the steps and across the neat, clipped lawn. He halted in front of her, his breath coming short and fast, like the sounds of an angry animal turned loose. He could feel his face coloring from the force of his emotions.

"This is how it's going to be," he said slowly, not even touching her. "You're going to wear the dress tomorrow night. You're going to wear it and you're going to dance the beseda with papa. Not to please papa, because a lot of things please and displease papa. To make mamma happy."

"And how about me?" Linda said without turning to him. "I've got to make myself unhappy to make your mother happy is that it?"

"Maybe so," Frank went on. "Maybe you don't understand how it is with mamma. So I'm telling you, Linda. And you listen." He heard his voice, heavy with Czech accent the way it always was when he talked with mamma. He noticed the dogged tone of his own words and remembered how he had always tried to hide it when he entered the Air Force. Now he caught the Czech determination and he did not try to stop its force. "With mamma it's different. You don't know how it was with her, coming over to America when she'd never been anywhere in her life except to Praha. She won't ever go to Praha again. That was a big thing in her life, and all she's got to remember it by is her wedding dress. And you're going to wear it tomorrow night to make her happy or there's not going to be any wedding for us. Because nobody, not even Linda Raeburn of Biloxi, is going to hurt mamma!"

Linda looked at him now, and there was, he saw, anger and amazement and quite a good deal of scorn in her eyes.

"Now, you can talk about your folks, can't you, Frank?" she said, her soft voice cutting in its contempt. "Now you can talk about mamma. All the while I knew you at Biloxi you never spoke about your parents except to say they were farmers. I waited and waited for you to say sometime 'Let's talk about our folks!' But you never did."

"I wasn't ashamed of them," he protested doggedly. Yet he wondered about the truth of it. "There just wasn't anything to say. And I knew your folks."

She got up. One hand was clasped behind her, and for a moment Frank thought she was going to run. The knuckles of her other hand were white from gripping the chain of the swing. "Then you know more than I do!"—her voice was hoarse, filled with an odd panic—"because the Raeburns aren't my parents. The police caught me when I was ten, looking for something to eat in the alleys of New Orleans. They found my mother in a bar, and the Raeburns, who are distant relatives, took me in because my mother didn't want me. They took care of me beautifully and gave me a good education because they are responsible people, but they didn't really want me." Her voice rose, shrill, almost hysterical. "Nobody ever really wanted me."

"I want you. Do you hear me, Linda?" He tried to shake her from her hysteria, but it was feverish in her and she had to burn it out, now that it was loosed. She jerked away from him and stood, shrinking back against the swing, one hand held out to ward him off.

"It was all over in the papers that nobody wanted me," she cried out, and the anguish in her voice cut through him. But he could not touch her. "Somebody always wanted you. You even

106

know exactly what room you were born in. I watched your mother when you came in. She wanted you, and I hated you then, Frank. I hated you because she wanted you and nobody ever wanted me. I don't even know who my father was or where my mother is now. Don't you see why I can't wear her dress?" Her voice held horror now. "Not her wedding dress! Not the dress she got when she went to Praha!"

   ❀ ❀ ❀

Her voice caught then on a high sound like a sob. But she did not cry. She pressed her hand against her mouth and turned to run as Frank stepped toward her again. But Anna had come sometime during the quarrel and was standing on the steps. She gazed at Linda with her quiet eyes, and the girl halted, glancing wildly about her.

"So?" Anna asked softly. "You cry because nobody want you?" She came down the steps in her slow manner and walked across the grass to the swing where Linda stood, terrified and uncertain.

"Nobody wants me . . . " The words were hysterical and automatic now, harsh sounds breaking uncontrollably from a heart that had nursed hidden wounds too long.

Anna held out her arms slightly and Linda fled past Frank and into them. The tears came then, and they beat cruelly against Frank's own heart. He felt a fierce protectiveness toward her he had not known before, a tenderness he had been unable to reveal. Yet there was nothing he could say. It was Anna who said it.

"Seven sons I have," she said slowly, "and not one little girl to dress. When Frankie come to me so long after the others, I think maybe now I have little girl. But, no, is another boy. Now he brings me little girl."

She rested her face against Linda's black hair, caressing it with her cheek. She crooned to her, soft little Czech pet words. She cradled her back and forth in her arms as a woman does her firstborn. "Tomorrow night I dress my little girl in my wedding dress, my dress I got when I went to Praha," she murmured, almost as though Frank were not there, and she and her child were alone. "And we go to kolach festival, and my little girl dance the beseda with papa, huh?"

"Yes, mamma," Linda whispered hesitantly, like a child who has rehearsed words hoping to use them sometime.

"And I show everybody Anna Palcoucek she got her a little girl finally. I show everybody my little girl, dancing with papa the beseda, huh?" She laughed softly.

"Yes, mamma." A small hint of laughter touched Linda's choked words.

"And afterwards"—the quiet eyes had erased their memories and Anna's gentle gaze moved across the girl's head to the barn down the slope where big Bohomil was milking the cows—"afterwards papa he tells everyone how here in America is better for the Czechs. We do that, huh?"

"Yes, mamma," Linda nodded quickly. She clung to Anna.

Frank looked out across the field where the wheat was waving icy-green in the wind, thrumming a soft song like the rippling sounds of the Moldau whispering of yesterday to its banks. From the kitchen came the sweet smell of prune and poppy-seed kolaches, and down at the barn the cows that were waiting their turn lowed impatiently.

Linda raised her face finally and looked at Frank. He smiled at her and laid his hand against her cheek. A feeling of contentment warmed him. There was a oneness between himself and the girl he loved now. It had never been there before. Strange, he thought, how simple things were when mamma took over.

"Better you go change your clothes now, Frankie, and help papa milk the cows, so?" Anna said, her cheek still resting on Linda's hair.

"So," Frank said, nodding, "I go help papa milk now."

PART THREE
The Study of Technique

CHAPTER SEVEN

SEE WITH SCENES

How do you make a story take place before the reader's eyes? How can you make him feel that he is watching it happen instead of hearing about it?

This is a skill needed in both fiction and nonfiction. The successful article, like a story, is created whole. With build-ups, tension, drama expressed in dialogue, and climaxes, it has a beginning, a middle, and an end.

The materials of the short story are invented or at least altered. The materials of nonfiction are taken as they were. The difference lies in the fact that the names, the places, and the incidents are real and unchanged in nonfiction, but are changed, sometimes tremendously, are added to or subtracted from in fiction.

But how do you make these fictionized things seem alive? As though they were actually happening? Real?

You do it with scenes.

The scene takes place in the reader's mind as clearly (if it is well written) as if he were seeing it performed upon a stage in front of him.

Your scene is the dramatic unit of your copy. It has no relation, of course, to the scenery or background, nor to what the viewpoint character sees. Nor is it a detailed picture of something taking place without purpose or story-conflict.

Old Sam sitting on the riverbank—no matter how beautifully you write it, it is still not a scene. Neither is Sam stepping outside his house, walking down the sidewalk, going for a casual walk a scene. Why?

It is not a scene because there is no conflict.

A scene has a minor or major crisis created by conflict. Your main character starts toward his goal. An opposing force rises to threaten him. He may succeed in spite of the force, or he may veer into a tangent, or even be turned into the opposite direction, making it harder than ever for him to reach his goal. As the scene ends, as the result of the conflict, the main character has a change of emotional reaction and meets a new set of circumstances. This we call the twist.

As you plan the outline of your story, jot down a list of scenes that best show the conflict within your story. Now, run through that list and underscore those scenes that are most important to your story's development. These are the scenes you work out in detail. Those that are of less importance may be summed up in a narrative form. However, if you handle your story so that it is filled with scenes and a little narrative, you multiply your skill.

Some writers expect dialogue to make a scene without giving any background. It reaches the reader with no more effectiveness than a TV set does with the sound turned on and the picture blank. So, early in your scene, give the background picture—where your characters are and why they are there. You may do this with the minimum of suggestion, drawing in broad outlines the needed surroundings.

The main character enters the scene with a definite purpose and plans to accomplish something (or his antagonist plans to do something with the main character). At least one, or perhaps both, of the characters have a goal.

As emotions rise within each character, sketch in greater detail, showing the conflict taking place. It may be a mere argument, or the action may grow to one of force, but the emotions are clashing. Show each step of the stimulus and response in the emotional reactions. The purpose may be accomplished, but for the main character things take an unexpected turn. This turn, or the twist, plunges the main character into a new set of circumstances and it also affects his feelings concerning these circumstances.

In your scene, build toward your scene purpose, then when

it is achieved, close it quickly, giving the main character's re-action; this adds the dramatic quality.

Study the examples of scenes which follow. Then go through "The Preacher's Confession" and divide it into scenes.

A Scene—Example I:

Edith walked carefully toward the child playing at the edge of the brook. He had his foot in the sand and was patting a mound of dirt over it. She stood silent, waiting.

Yes, this towheaded blond must be the child. He wore the tan sweater, the blue jeans about the right size. How relieved his mother would be to get him back. And how she could use the reward!

The boy began an easy vibration of his leg, moving it gently as if testing. Edith watched until he pulled his foot away from the mound, leaving an open-faced cave. He seemed totally absorbed.

Kneeling beside him, she pretended to admire it.

"That's nice," she spoke softly in order not to startle him. "Is it for elves?"

"Naw," he looked at her with disgust. "It's for trolls."

"Of course," she corrected herself quickly and motioned to her aunt's car under the big pine. "I'm going for a ride in that pretty car; want to go with me?"

"Why?" He looked up at her wide-eyed, his voice matter-of-fact.

"Your mother wants to see you."

"No, I'm busy." He turned back to his sand.

"Oh." She gauged his size, letting her eyes note the thinness of him. "I think you'd better. In fact, I'm taking you." Her arm shot out, catching him close; and in spite of his kicking and struggling, she managed to get him in the car. As she slipped under the steering wheel, she breathed a sigh of relief; thank goodness she'd had the foresight to lock all doors but hers.

He slumped pouting in the seat corner. She drove swiftly, checking the address in her purse only once. Her hands tightened upon the steering wheel as she tried to calm the pounding of her heart. She'd found him; all alone she'd found the little boy that everybody thought kidnapped. And the reward money would be hers, a whole beautiful thousand dollars of it!

As she turned the corner where the house was, she saw the woman who had been pictured over TV talking to someone in the yard. She pulled the car to the curb and caught the hand of the youngster beside her.

"Come on, sonny," she pulled, opening the door, "let's tell your mother you are all right."

The child sat up and glanced around.

"Where is she?"

"Right there," Edith waved her hand toward the woman.

"No!" The child pulled back. "She ain't my mommy."

"She isn't!" Edith gasped, alarm beginning to stir. Oh, heavens, what had she gotten herself into now?

A Scene—Example II:

But none of that was in Tom's mind now. All he was thinking about—all he'd thought about all day—was Sara Bell. He turned off the road and hitched the mare down by the turn of the creek that gave the place its name, and started through the woods toward the steppingstones.

The water was talking to itself, saucy and happy, and there was a spicy smell from the cedars. The sun left a pink trail as it went down, and the light that slanted through the trees had an unearthly glory to it. Would she be there? Would she?

Then he saw her, standing on the first steppingstone with a water bucket in her hand, but she carried it like it was a poor excuse.

"Sara Bell—Sara Bell!" he called, savoring the delight of her name.

"Tom! Oh, Tom! I thought you'd never come."

He crossed the creek like a buck deer in flight and reached the steppingstone where she stood, and all at once his arms were around her and he kissed her. Neither of them heard the splash of the bucket falling into the water.

"I love you, Sara Bell. I love you. Will you marry me?" He could have fallen into the creek himself to hear those words spoken, but once he heard them he knew they had been in his mind since early morning.

"I love you, Tom," and he smiled at her sweet honesty, for most girls would have kept him dangling, if only for the sport. "I love you, but I mustn't ever see you again. I only came down here to tell you—good-by."

"Then you've taken a poor way to do it," Tom said, "for I tell you, fair and square, I'll never let you go now." And he kissed her again.

"Oh—you mustn't—you mustn't," she said, between times. "Pa'll never let me marry a fiddler. Never in this world."

"If you're willin'," Tom said, "I'll bring your pa 'round."

"You don't know pa." Sara Bell wailed, and the recollection of Brother Calhoun's rocklike jaw jabbed Tom. "Nobody's ever changed his mind! Not since ma died!"

"Then there's other ways," Tom said, testing his words like a horse tests a shaky bridge. "My mare's hitched down by the road. She'll carry double and we can make it to Horn's Ferry before meeting's over. Elder Kincannon'll marry us and —." But he stopped, for he could tell by the feel of her that it was no use at all.

"I can't," she whispered into his shirt ruffles, "I just can't. I promised ma when she was dyin' that I'd always look after him, and I can't go back on her. Nor him, either, because"—and her voice dropped so low he could hardly hear it over the ripple of the water around the steppingstones—"because he loves me, too."

"And no blame to him for that," Tom said, hating himself for understanding, "but my love's a different thing, and stronger, and so it's got to win out." He took a deep breath and said out loud the thing he'd been shying away from all day, "Supposin'— I gave up—the fiddle?"

That last of the daylight caught in her widened eyes. "Oh, no! You mustn't ever do that! Why it'd be like I'd killed part of you! Oh, Tom, no!"

A tide of voices washed down from the meetinghouse, "There is a Fountain filled with Blood —."

"I'll be late! He'll miss me." And she was gone.

Tom sat down on the creek bank and pitched pebbles at the riffles that curled around the steppingstones as long as he could see. Dark settled around his shoulders and he still sat, slumped on the bank, his mind running in weary little circles. Sara Bell— Brother Calhoun—the fiddle.

"The Preacher's Confession"

by Alberta Wilson Constant

THOMAS DONEGHY NORMAN was the finest fiddler in Green-brier County. When he laid bow to string not a soul could stop dancing till he stopped fiddling. Add to this that he was hand-some, that he owned two hundred acres of prime Tennessee tobacco land that his gran'pap got from the Indians by trade and by musket, and it comes out a plain wonder that at twenty-four he was still unwed. It caused talk in the county.

Some said Tom was wedded to his fiddle. Some said he hadn't found the right girl—though not for want of trying, on both sides. To tell the truth, Tom himself got to wondering about it, now and again. It was on his mind this morning as he rode down the stretch between Pink Hill and Old Salt Lick, playing his fiddle as he rode.

It wasn't important playing like he'd do for a wedding or an infare, or like he'd done the time Andy Jackson asked him to The Hermitage. It was just fooling along, making music about the pretty girls at the dance last night, and the sun on the back of his shoulders with the neat sound of the mare's hoofbeats coming into the tune. He topped the rise by Robertson's place playing "Money Musk" a new way that'd come to him in the night, when he caught sight of a big black carryall pulled over at the side of the road with a roan pair cropping at the grass.

The carryall curtains were down tight, which was odd, for it was as fair a morning as you'd ever see in this vale of tears. It made Tom curious and he slowed the mare down with his knee and rode alongside, fiddling all the time, but keeping his eye on the rig. Just then a girl's head popped out of the curtains and he broke his trill and stared. He thought he'd seen all the pretty girls in these parts—and some at mighty close range—but he'd never seen one the like of this.

Her hair caught the sun and held it in tight curls. Her nose hesitated just on the right side of being tilted. Her big brown eyes were like a fawn's, they were that gentle and trusting. And her mouth—nothing to say about that mouth but that it was made to kiss. Tom would have kissed it, too, then and there, but for looking at the eyes first. Because of them, he took off his fine black felt hat and made a bow.

"Howdy, ma'am," he said, trying to put all he was feeling into two words.

"Howdy," she gave him back, and it delighted his fiddler's ear that her voice fitted her face. "Was that you I heard? Down the road a piece?"

"I reckon it must of been," Tom said. "I'm about the only one in these parts that plays the fiddle ahorseback." He grinned to show her he knew it was foolish, but he hoped she'd understand.

"A—fiddle?" she asked, and her voice dropped a note.

"Why, yes, ma'am, and a finer one you won't see in Middle Tennessee. Gran'pap brought it from Carolina and some say it came from France. There's foreign words inside."

He held it out to her, which was a special thing, for few had touched it since Tom grew up. When she jerked back inside the curtains he was that taken aback that he almost dropped the fiddle, and that was like dropping the arm off his shoulder.

"I didn't go to give offense, ma'am," he said to the black curtains.

Out popped her head like a mud turtle, if you can vision a pretty one. "Oh, you didn't give offense. I'm the one to ask pardon. It's just that—." And she stopped, dead stuck.

"I'd take it kindly if you'd tell me, ma'am," Tom said, puzzled but determined.

She parted the curtains and stepped down into the road. Tom wouldn't have been the man he was if he hadn't noticed she had a fine ankle.

118

"It's just that—I've never seen a fiddle—not real close." She looked at it as if it ought to sprout horns and a tail. "Pa doesn't hold with fiddles. He's here to preach at camp meeting at Crooked Elbow Meetinghouse, and he thinks the fiddle is an—an instrument of the—devil."

Tom leaned down toward her till the saddle creaked. "And what do you think, ma'am?"

"There's no need to keep callin' me 'ma'am,' " she said, chipper as a blackbird. "My name's Sara Bell Calhoun."

Tom got off the mare and bowed low and allowed it was an honor and gave her his name. But he came right back to the question, for all of a sudden it was almighty important to him. "And what do you think of the fiddle, Miss Sara Bell?"

"I've not rightly had time to think at all," she said, "but it did have a right happy sound to it."

"Well, if you think that was fiddlin'—." Tom laughed and swept the fiddle with the bow. He played "Hop Light Ladies," and "Chase the Kitten," and then he played something he'd made up and never put a name to, but he knew now he'd made it up for this minute. He played for pride of himself and his fiddle till he saw Sara Bell's red delaine skirt swinging, and he knew skirts didn't move of themselves. From then on, he played for her, and her feet answered the way he knew they would.

He hadn't a notion of how long it went on, but all at once everything stopped. The fiddle stopped, Sara Bell stopped, and the sun ducked behind a little white cloud. Astraddle of Robertson's rail fence, and big enough to keep both feet on the ground, too, was a man in a black broadcloth suit. He had a red face and a plume of white hair that lifted like a fighting cock's hackles. Tom braced himself, but the big man didn't appear to notice him. He just came striding up to Sara Bell and took her in his arms.

"My child," he said, "my poor motherless child! Can't I leave you for a minute but that the wiles of Satan tangle themselves around your feet?"

Tom's muscles were all ready to take a beating or give one, but talk like that made him uneasy. "I meant no harm," he said,

119

louder than he intended. "It was only a tune I hadn't put a name to."

The big man looked straight at him, and it gave Tom a fair start to see Sara Bell's brown eyes in his massive weather-beaten face. "It's not you I mean, young man, when I speak of the Evil One. It's that—thing you hold. That viper in your bosom."

"You mean my fiddle?" Tom asked, unbelieving. "But it's the finest one in these parts. I was just tellin' Miss Sara Bell that it came from —."

The big man held up his hand and seemed to ram the words back down Tom's gullet. "It came from the devil!"

"Pa," Sara Bell put in stoutly, "it didn't sound like a wicked thing."

"You can leave it to me, Sara Bell, what's wicked and what's not. I've kept you unspotted from the world these eighteen years and I aim to go on. Get back in the carryall where I left you and read five chapters of the Word. By that time I'll have this axle fixed." It wasn't in reason to hope she'd refuse to go, but it gave Tom's heart a tickle to have her smile over her shoulder as she mounted the step.

It was plain as daylight that Tom was supposed to get on the mare and light a shuck for other parts, but he couldn't give up that easy. Not with that smile in his pocket. "I hope you won't hold my fiddlin' too much against me to let me help you fix that axle," Tom said.

"Now, that's downright neighborly of you." The big man was as polite as a basket of chips, once Sara Bell was out of harm's way. "Brother Robertson and all his hands were in the field, so I asked the loan of some tools, but a helpin' hand's better'n a jackknife, any day."

Tom put his fiddle into the brand-new case that had just come from Philadelphia and hitched the mare to the rail fence.

The big man put out his hand. "If we're goin' to do a job together, we'd best swap names. Mine's Calhoun—Clayton Calhoun, from the state of Maryland, but a long time on the road."

Between shaking hands and saying, "I'm Tom Norman, from

this side of Old Salt Lick," and getting down to squint at the axle, Tom got in a sight of thinking. That name cleared things up like a lightning flash on a dark night. All over Tennessee, Kentucky, and even as far west as Missoury, Brother Calhoun was known as a powerful preacher. When he stood up in the pulpit the devil took to the tall timber. He could bring fire down from heaven and brimstone up from hell. Folks said nobody could stand against him. That anybody who listened to him three nights hand-running would never be the same again. He was death on whiskey-drinking, cockfighting, and gambling, besides all the regular sins, but the thing he preached against most was music and dancing. And of all music it was the fiddle that made him burn like a pillar of fire.

Lots of preachers felt that way. That was one reason Tom quit going to meeting after ma died. As long as she lived, he went with her and played hymn tunes for her at home in the evenings, but it hurt him the way the preachers talked, for the fiddle was just about religion to him. Whenever he heard one of 'em going on about how sinful fiddlin' was and how it brought out the Old Nick in folks, Tom called to mind what gran'pap had said the day he laid the fiddle in his hands.

"It takes an honest man to be a good fiddler, son. She won't answer true to a liar or a thief. She'll keep you straight if you've got the ear to listen." And it was the truth. Whenever he got out of line, the way a young buck will, he couldn't play for sour apples till he'd straighened things out. But you couldn't tell a preacher a thing like that. Tom sneaked a look at Brother Calhoun's jaw line. No, he'd never believe it.

Fixing an axle is a tricky job, but it's a good way to get acquainted. Before they were halfway through, Tom felt as if he knew why folks loved Brother Calhoun and came to hear him in spite of his harsh preaching. He was a bedrock sort of man. He was the kind you'd want on your side in a tight place.

They were just about done when Tom caught sight of something white fluttering around the corner of the carryall. He stood up as if to ease his back and stepped over, light and easy. Sure enough, there was a white handkerchief in Sara Bell's hand, held right between the curtains. Tom caught at the hand, but she pulled it back so that all he kept was the silky feel of it and the handkerchief, that smelled of lemon verbena. Then he heard a whisper, and he put his ear to the crack in the curtain.

"I like the fiddle," she whispered. "I don't think it's wicked."

"I'm comin' to camp meetin', Sara Bell," he whispered back. "Meet me down by the creek at the steppin'stones at sundown."

"No! Oh, no!" she gasped, but there was something in her "no" that made him think "yes" was riding double right behind it. He didn't get a chance for another word, because out of the corner of his eye he saw those black coattails come off the ground. When Brother Calhoun turned around to Tom, there wasn't a thing to be seen but a young fellow scanning the sky for weather signs like any honest planter would.

"Thank you kindly for your help." Brother Calhoun brushed the dust from his trousers. "I think that'll hold till we get to a blacksmith. It's a far piece to Crooked Elbow, so we'd best be on the road."

"Then good-by and good journey," Tom said, bold as brass, "but I'll see you at meetin', Brother Calhoun."

He bore down hard on the "Brother," and Clayton Calhoun turned red as a turkey gobbler and his mouth stiffened to a straight line. It seemed like half of him wanted to knock down this impudent fiddler for daring to smile at his daughter, but the other half, the preacher half, wouldn't let him do it. Finally the mouth loosened up a little and a half smile touched it, and Tom knew the "Brother" had got in its work. There's not a preacher living can resist the chance to snatch a brand from the burning.

"Come and welcome. I'd be a poor servant if I turned a man away from the Word. But I warn you, I preach against fiddlin', and I preach hard."

Watching after them, Tom felt the kind of chill ma said came when a goose walked across your grave. Only the sight of Sara Bell's hand waving out between the curtains made him feel warm again.

It takes hot weather for camp meeting. Folks open up their hearts easier when the sun cracks the earth and the corn grows all night. It was near to sundown, but the heat was still heavy when Tom came riding up to Crooked Elbow Meetinghouse. The camp ground was crowded. He saw rigs from as far away as Chauncey. The smoke of scattered campfires mingled with the kicked-up dust and made a blue haze over the valley.

Crooked Elbow hadn't always been a meeting house. Tom could remember tales gran'pap told about the days when it had been Crooked Elbow Fort and the settlers and their families— or what was left of them—hustled in for protection when Dragging Canoe took his braves on the warpath. The stockade that had been around it was long since gone, but there were still signs of those times, if you knew where to look. The little shuttered windows, high up in the wall, so they couldn't be forced by a war party. The open fireplace back of the pulpit where gran'-ma'am helped to mold bullets. And the big old door where the settlers could make a foray out, if need be. But it wasn't big any longer. Elder Pennington had it nailed up and a little door cut at the side. Little and in-opening, so that nobody could move one of those ungodly, newfangled organs into the meetinghouse.

But none of that was in Tom's mind now. All he was thinking about—all he'd thought about all day—was Sara Bell. He turned off the road and hitched the mare down by the turn of the creek that gave the place its name, and started through the woods toward the steppingstones.

The water was talking to itself, saucy and happy, and there was a spicy smell from the cedars. The sun left a pink trail as it went down, and the light that slanted through the trees had an unearthly glory to it. Would she be there? Would she?

Then he saw her, standing on the first steppingstone with a water bucket in her hand, but she carried it like it was a poor excuse.

"Sara Bell—Sara Bell!" he called, savoring the delight of her name.

"Tom! Oh, Tom! I thought you'd never come."

He crossed the creek like a buck deer in flight and reached

the steppingstone where she stood, and all at once his arms were around her and he kissed her. Neither of them heard the splash of the bucket falling into the water.

"I love you, Sara Bell. I love you. Will you marry me?" He could have fallen into the creek himself to hear those words spoken, but once he heard them he knew they had been in his mind since early morning.

"I love you, Tom," and he smiled at her sweet honesty, for most girls would have kept him dangling, if only for the sport. "I love you, but I mustn't ever see you again. I only came down here to tell you—good-by."

"Then you've taken a poor way to do it," Tom said, "for I tell you, fair and square, I'll never let you go now." And he kissed her again.

"Oh—you mustn't—you mustn't," she said, between times. "Pa'll never let me marry a fiddler. Never in this world."

"If you're willin'," Tom said, "I'll bring your pa 'round."

"You don't know pa." Sara Bell wailed, and the recollection of Brother Calhoun's rocklike jaw jabbed Tom. "Nobody's ever changed his mind! Not since ma died!"

"Then there's other ways," Tom said, testing his words like a horse tests a shaky bridge. "My mare's hitched down by the road. She'll carry double and we can make it to Horn's Ferry before meetin's over. Elder Kincannon'll marry us and —." But he stopped, for he could tell by the feel of her that it was no use at all.

"I can't," she whispered into his shirt ruffles, "I just can't. I promised ma when she was dyin' that I'd always look after him, and I can't go back on her. Nor him, either, because"—and her voice dropped so low he could hardly hear it over the ripple of the water around the steppingstones—"because he loves me too."

"And no blame to him for that," Tom said, hating himself for understanding, "but my love's a different thing, and stronger, and so it's got to win out." He took a deep breath and said out loud the thing he'd been shying away from all day, "Supposin'—I gave up—the fiddle?"

124

That last of the daylight caught in her widened eyes. "Oh, no! You mustn't! You mustn't ever do that! Why it'd be like I'd killed part of you! Oh, Tom, no!"

A tide of voices washed down from the meetinghouse, "There is a Fountain filled with Blood —."

"I'll be late! He'll miss me." And she was gone.

Tom sat down on the creek bank and pitched pebbles at the riffles that curled around the steppingstones as long as he could see. Dark settled around his shoulders and he still sat, slumped on the bank, his mind running in weary little circles. Sara Bell—Brother Calhoun—the fiddle.

Up at the meetinghouse shrill shouts told him some sinner had prayed through and found glory. He wished it was that easy for him. His head ached as if he'd been butting it against a stone wall. The water that sounded so saucy and happy as he came through the woods changed to snickering laughter. It had been a long day. *Falling in love is hard work*, Tom thought, and put his head back against the rocky bank and stared at the stars through the dark cedars. The little circles began again. *Sara Bell—Brother Calhoun—the fiddle.* Then he slept.

It was a dream that waked him. A dream of Brother Calhoun standing on a ledge over a great pit, thundering, "That's where you'll burn—burn—burn." A fiery light leaped up from the pit and Tom saw his fiddle in the preacher's hand. He jumped to save it and everything vanished away. He awakened with cold sweat on his forehead and in his palms. The fear that held him was so strong he hardly knew where he was. Then, piece by piece, things came back. Sara Bell came back. He knew suddenly what he must do.

He must go to Brother Calhoun and have it out, then and there. It was quiet at the meetinghouse and the way the stars looked Tom knew it was late night, but he had no stomach for waiting. This was the time.

He made his way up the path to the camp grounds. Tents and wagons and carriages were all about and pallets were spread in the open. Here and there he heard heavy snoring or the rain crying of a baby or the warning growl of a watchful dog, but for the most part a heavy quiet lay over Crooked Elbow. Folks worn out struggling with their sins slept hard.

Off by itself, as befitted a preacher's rig, he saw the bulk of the black carryall, and he went toward it, the flavor of what he was going to say hot in his mouth. He'd tell Brother Calhoun that he was narrow-minded and hardheaded, that fiddling was an honorable thing that went back to the kings of Rome, and further, and besides that—. Then he stopped dead in his tracks and anger fell from him like an old coat. You can't quarrel with a man you find on his knees.

Brother Calhoun prayed with his head thrown back and his eyes open. He could see him plain in the light from the campfire still burning. It came to Tom that he was like a man talking to a Friend. Without hearing a word, he knew the preacher was asking counsel about his motherless daughter who danced to the fiddle and smiled at the fiddler. It made him feel mean as a weasel that he'd tried to steal her away like a thief in the night.

Then he stumbled over a stone or a stick, and Brother Calhoun came up from his knees, and when he saw who it was, he came stalking over in a way that curdled Tom's soft feelings like cream in a thunderstorm.

"I take it you decided to heed my warning, Tom Norman," he gibed. "I didn't see you at meetin'. Or mayhap you've been out fiddlin' poor souls to their damnation. What brings you here at this hour?"

Tom's temper broke like a quarter horse, but he fought it to a standstill. When he spoke out, his voice was steady. "I've come to ask your daughter's hand. I know it's a sudden-sounding thing, but —."

Brother Calhoun pushed his words aside. "Are you of a mind to give up the fiddle?"

"I am not," Tom said, and knew he was speaking wrong, but couldn't help it. "A fiddle's a good thing."

"It's a sinful, worldly thing." It leads to dancing."

"David danced before the Lord."

126

"David did a lot of things I wouldn't countenance in my son-in-law."

Tom knew the preacher had him there, so he took another tack. "This life on the road's no life for a woman. My folks would make Sara Bell welcome. Our place is this side of Old Salt Lick. My share's two hundred acres, prime tobacco land, and besides that——."

The white plume shook impatiently. "I know who your folks are, Tom. I haven't ridden the roads of Kentucky and Tennessee all these years without hearing about the Normans. I made inquiry from the elders here today, and I'm bound to say they gave you a good name—saving your fiddle. There's nothing against you or your family, but you could be the king's own and have title to the land for a hundred miles down the Natchez Trace and if you were a fiddler I'd still say 'No.' "

He slung the word like a chunk of granite. Tom knew in another minute he wouldn't be able to stand there talking. He made himself remember Sara Bell's voice saying, "Because he loves me, too," and it unclenched his fists and let him walk off.

"Stop!" The word hit Tom between the shoulder blades and spun him around. "You think I'm a narrow-minded, pigheaded old fool, don't you?"

"Now that you mention it," Tom said, "that's right."

"What you think about me is no matter, but I won't have you looking down on the Word. As the Lord's servant I challenge you to come to meetin' three nights hand-running!" He leaned forward and power seemed to crackle around him. "Do you dare?"

"I dare," Tom said, "and what's more, I'll bring my fiddle with me."

"Bring it," snapped Brother Calhoun, "let the devil's instrument witness the power of the Word." And with that he walked off, leaving Tom staring after his shadow, big and black and proud in the light from the dying fire.

When Tom Norman took his seat at Crooked Elbow Meetinghouse the next night with his fiddle case under his arm, a rustle and a whisper ran over the congregation like a breeze through a cornfield. Men on the same bench gave him room aplenty, though there were many standing at the back of the house. Through the rows of turned heads on the women's side of the meetinghouse he could just catch a glimpse of Sara Bell. The sight of her twisted his heart the way it had when he kissed her, and he fixed himself so he could see her face plain. Then Brother Calhoun began to preach.

He preached of the terrible end that waits for evildoers. He dangled them over the coals. He told of fiddlers standing in banks of undying flames playing red-hot fiddles while dancers stumbled over the blazing floor of hell. Two women fainted and had to be dragged out. Ed Bledsoe went screaming to the altar where he hadn't been in forty years. But Tom sat solid and didn't give an inch. Damned he might be, but he wouldn't be scared into heaven. He saw the shine of tears on Sara Bell's cheeks and he longed to tell her that he feared the bleak years without her more than twice the punishment her pa preached about. Though he waited till the last mourner left the bench, Brother Calhoun kept her under his eye all the time.

The next night Brother Calhoun preached on the glories of the Promised Land. The puncheon floor seemed to glitter and the taste of milk and honey was sweet in Tom's mouth. He longed to see ma's face and to hear the angel choir. He thought how Sara Bell would look in a robe and a crown and how sweet the passing of eternity would be by her side. Still, he didn't join the folks who crowded forward at the invitation. If he wasn't going to be scared in, he wasn't going to be bribed in, either. He kept his eyes on Sara Bell and his hand on the fiddle case.

The third night there was the biggest crowd ever seen at Crooked Elbow Meetinghouse. The little old in-opening door was propped back with a hickory chunk long before sundown, and late-comers stood in ranks at the back. Even at that there was plenty of room made for Tom when he came in with his fiddle. He took a seat near the front, and the next man on the bench gave him space for his fiddle by moving clear to the back. Across the aisle and around the massive bulk of the Widow Barton, Tom saw Sara Bell. Her face was white and tired-looking, and the little smile she managed for him hurt worse than tears. The ache he felt to take her in his arms was the ache of swamp fever that works on a man's bone marrow.

Brother Calhoun stood up behind the pulpit and the tension came up the way the turn of a peg tightens a E string. He shook his white hair back like a banner and there was a pride and confidence in the way he gave out the hymns that made Tom uneasy. Palm leaf fans were waving all around and Tom took out his silk handkerchief to wipe the sweat from his forehead. Folded into it was Sara Bell's little white handkerchief. The smell of the lemon verbena made him feel better, but, still and all, he had a queer sensation in his middle as he used to before a wrestling match or a fiddler's contest.

All of a sudden there came a stir at the back of the room and everybody turned around to look. Through the little in-opening door marched four exhorters, each one carrying a load of firewood. They made their way through the crowded aisles and laid a fire on the bed of last winter's ashes that hadn't been cleaned out since Christmas exercises. They laid it from kindling to top log and then Brother Calhoun lighted it from his tinderbox. The congregation buzzed with questions, but Tom didn't ask a one. He was recollecting the dream he had down by the creek, and the sick feeling in his middle ran all up and down his body and he could have sworn the fiddle moaned in the case beside him.

"I've kindled an altar fire," Brother Calhoun shouted, "an altar fire where you can burn your sins away and start a new life! Are you strong enough to do it? You are if you have love! Love will make you strong! Love —."

And he preached on love. Love that fills a man's life and lets him do the impossible. Love that will not let a man go. As the flames mounted, his voice mounted till it rang like a bell and filled the meetinghouse with sound that matched the fire for intensity. Tom knew it was divine love Brother Calhoun meant, but to him love and Sara Bell were the same. Could he lay his fiddle in those searing, twisting flames for her? Could he?

The struggle in him was so strong he hardly noticed when Lije Johnson stumbled up the aisle and flung a demijohn into the fireplace. The jug cracked and the rank smell of green whiskey sizzling on the stones filled the room. Jamey Munger tossed in a deck of cards that whirled up the chimney in the strong updraft in one last gambler's fan. "Glory! Glory!" the exhorters chanted. Amaryllis Bedford, the vainest woman in Greenbrier County, threw in a red satin carriage cloak and screamed in ecstasy as it caught fire. Old Lady Parsons started jerking like she was pulled by strings. The line at the mourners' bench swayed back and forth. Brother Calhoun leaned across the pulpit and pleaded with Tom, sweat pouring down his face, "Give in—now! Do it now! Burn your sins away! Put them on the altar now—now—now!"

Tom didn't hear him. The chant "Glory, glory, glory!" beat up through the floor and through his body. Over it all, like another chant, he heard Sara Bell's voice saying, ". . . love—I love you, Tom—I love you."

Suddenly he was standing in the aisle. The fiddle weighed like an anvil in his hand. He wanted to hurry, but he moved like a man with his feet hobbled. Somehow he got to the fireplace. The fierce heat smote him and made him wince. Not for himself, but for the fiddle—the fiddle. For an agonized minute he opened the case and looked at the sweet curved brown body that had been his more than any woman would ever be his. Tears scalded his eyes. He snapped the case shut and laid it on the top log.

Brother Calhoun's arm was heavy on his shoulders. The meetinghouse rocked with shouting, "Glory, glory, hallelujah! Glory!" This was the moment when happiness should come to him in a great, rushing wave. Numb with the thing he had done, he waited. Nothing happened. All at once he wanted to run and hide. The smell of scorching leather sickened him. He looked for Sara Bell, but the bulk of the Widow Barton cut her off. Men wrung his hands, women hugged him, Brother Calhoun pounded his shoulders joyfully, but he had never felt so alone in his life. The fiddle—Sara Bell—the fiddle.

From outside the meetinghouse came a high-pitched whinny of terror. Another and another. Then the sound of rearing horses and splintering riggs. The shouting of the congregation wavered, broke off. Half of them were crowding toward the back with the terrible sense of what had happened, before Ed Thatcher yelled through the door, "Git out, evvabody! Soot in the chimney! Roof's afire!"

They went crazy. They went wild, screaming crazy. Tom saw it happen. Ten men—maybe fifteen—got out through the little in-opening door before the hickory chunk that held it open was kicked away and the door pushed solidly shut by the heaving, fighting wall of flesh behind it. Those at the door hammered and clawed in vain; the ones behind fought toward them, jamming the door tighter and tighter. Tom saw Miss Sukey Tolliver go down and heard her scream as a boot heel bit into her flesh. Sara Bell—Sara Bell —. He fought his way to where she clung to the edge of the pulpit. With his body he tried to screen her from the frantic congregation surging for the jammed door.

"Save us, preacher, save us!" a woman shrilled. "We'll be roasted alive!"

Tom saw Brother Calhoun on his knees, his head thrown back, his lips moving; then a wave of thick smoke cut off the sight. Men piled up benches to try to reach the little windows, but they were too high. Men battered at the log walls, but Crooked Elbow was built to stand siege.

"Tom," Sara Bell sobbed, "you shouldn't have done it! You shouldn't have burned the fiddle! I tried to get to you, but I couldn't! Not the fiddle!"

The fiddle! It was like a strong hand had touched him on the shoulder! That was it! The fiddle. "Stay here, Sara Bell; hold tight." He put her arms around the pulpit and started for the fireplace. He pushed and shoved and struck without mercy. On the top log, the fiddle case lay, still smoldering. He jerked it off and beat at the coals with his bare hands. He didn't even feel the metal clasps burn into his flesh as he opened the case. Inside lay the fiddle, calm, serene, unafraid. He put it to his chin and pulled the bow across it in a great surge of joy. Out of tune, but no matter, they were together again.

"Here! Up here!" It was Sara Bell calling over the weeping, praying throng around the pulpit top. He made his way to her and she boosted him up on the pulpit top. He never stopped to wonder how she knew what was in his mind. He felt her hands steady his ankles as he strove to keep his balance and endure the heat and smoke.

Then he swung out with "Lancers." Jingling, teasing, laughing, it poured from the fiddle and caught the crazed people of Crooked Elbow congregation and reminded them of something. Then he went into "Old Dan Tucker," and felt the fear loosen up. Most of 'em had been dandled on their gran'paps' knees to that tune. He began to sing out calls, "Chase the chicken, chase the squirrel, chase that pretty girl 'round the world." He coughed from the smoke, but they heard—heard and remembered. "Take your lady with a grapevine twist!" They were moving back a little. He could tell by the drift of the smoke that the door had opened a crack.

"Look at me, I'm down and busted; in Old Hamilton's bank I trusted!" That got a laugh—it always did in Andy Jackson's country. Tom knew it was all right. If folks can laugh, they can act sensible.

He could hear the crackle of the flames on the roof now, but the door was opening in. As folks came back under the spell of the fiddle it suddenly came full open. They went pouring outside, like sand down a rat hole, but not pushing, not shoving. He hurried them along with "Portland Fancy," a tune he'd picked up from a Maine man selling tinware. As the last ones made it out, he jumped from the pulpit and with Sara Bell under one arm and the fiddle under the other, cleared the threshold as the hot sparks began to shower down.

They reached the clearing with the rest of the congregation, but they weren't much more than there before the roof crashed in and flames shot up to the night sky and dimmed the stars. Crooked Elbow that had been a refuge for more than forty years was gone in less than that many minutes.

Some of the men went to look after their rigs and horses, but, for the most part, folks just stood and stared, with the light of the fire on their faces showing them dazed and not able to take in what had happened. Tom was sure he couldn't. All he was certain of was that he still had Sara Bell and the fiddle, and that Brother Calhoun would see him forever as a backslider, a man who profaned the pulpit with fiddle music. He was right back where he started, only worse off, lots worse.

"Brethren."

Tom turned with the others, Sara Bell's soft curls brushing his chin. The great bell of Brother Calhoun's voice was cracked and hoarse, but it could still turn the scattered folks in the clearing into a congregation. "Hear me, brethren, for I'm here to confess my—sin." A shocked murmur rose, and then shouts of protest, but Brother Calhoun paid them no heed.

"It's true. True as—salvation. When I went down on my knees in there to ask for help, I saw the truth, and it was a bitter sight." He stopped a moment as if to gather strength, and Tom felt Sara Bell's small cold hand creep into his. "They said—folks said—that no man could stand against me when I preached—and I believed them. I was proud—proud that I could break men down. I thought it was for the Lord, but I saw in there that it was my wicked, sinful pride. I lighted that fire to break a man down, to haul Tom Norman over to my way, and—God forgive me—I nearly brought you all to your death." He shuddered and put his hands over his face. Tom stared at the ground, for it's a terrible thing to see a strong man humbled. "And when I asked for deliverance, it came—but it came from the very thing I've preached against for twenty years—the fiddle."

Uneasy silence held them all. No man wished to look at his neighbor, Tom least of all. If he could have said any word to ease Brother Calhoun's burden, he would have, but words seemed weak and foolish things. At last the preacher's head came up and the white plume lifted with a memory of its old pride. "But deliverance did come—no matter where it came from—and I take that as a sign that the Lord means me to go on with my work. There's one thing I can do to make up for my—sin" and he lashed himself with the word—"I can build you a new meetinghouse if it takes the last days of my life."

"We'll all help!" Big Jud Smith shouted. " 'T wasn't all your fault, preacher. We should 'a' kep' that chimney clean." The chorus of "Amens" shook the clearing. Tom saw a sudden shine in the preacher's eyes that might have been tears in a lesser man, but he held up his hand for silence and walked across the clearing to Sara Bell and Tom.

"I ask your forgiveness, Tom Norman," he said clearly, "and if you're not opposed to a narrow-minded, pigheaded old fool in your family, we can have the wedding right now." Tom tried to take the big hand that reached out to him, but Sara Bell got in the way, hugging her pa around the neck and laughing and crying like all get out.

It was a strange wedding, with a burning church for light and the bride with soot on her face and the groom with a fiddle under his arm. It was strange, but Tom wouldn't have had it different, not for anything in the world. When Sara Bell tiptoed for his kiss, he knew he'd been right all the time, and that it was worth what they'd gone through because this was for all the rest of their lives. And maybe afterward. At an ordinary wedding this would have been where he started fiddling for the first quadrille, and he had a flickering wish he could do it now, for he'd like to play out how he felt. It made him lonesome not to, even with Sara Bell beside him.

"Are dance tunes all that fiddle will play—son?" Brother Calhoun asked him, hesitating a little, but trying hard. " 'Gainst the Rules it may be, but I've a fancy tonight to hear it play a hymn."

Like a flash, Tom put the fiddle to his chin and the old hymn tunes he used to play for ma came singing out, sweet as bird song in the morning. Sara Bell began to sing, and all others joined in, and his soul climbed up to the stars with the joy he felt. Then the happiness he'd waited for at the altar swept over him and he played it on his fiddle till the congregation hushed singing for the wonder of the music Tom and the fiddle made.

As the fire burned low and the stars slipped in the sky, it was Brother Calhoun who stood up and with his finger to his lips tiptoed to the black carryall and left Tom and Sara Bell together. One by one, the weary congregation followed him and found their rigs or their pallets. They listened still to the music as it came through the dreaming cedars, but many a one smiled in the darkness as it broke off suddenly and did not start again.

They knew that even such a fiddler as Tom Norman knew that music wasn't all there was to a wedding.

CHAPTER EIGHT

DEVICES

WITHOUT PROFESSIONAL TECHNIQUE, originality has little chance of expressing itself. Would-be writers cannot move freely with even what native skills they possess until they know consciously what they want to achieve within their reader's mind, and what devices will be most effective in achieving it.

Successful writers have learned their craft through long study of writings of established authors in order to isolate and understand the specific principles of content, structure, and treatment. Until the students could see for themselves the principle underlying each device, they were lost, unable to see the story for the words. When, however, they learned *why* the writer used what he did, and learned also to build their stories upon similiar devices, then their stories took shape and began to achieve a needed unity and form. This is what I want for you.

A device may be defined as a special word arrangement of a writer's problem which gives the desired reader reaction. Through the study of individual devices, you put a story or an article under the microscope and see *why* the author did *what* he did, *where* he did it. By taking these devices, changing the subject matter and the words, you can turn them into five-finger writing exercises and develop your own ability to draw forth a similar reaction.

You can break down both fiction and nonfiction into devices. Although the arrangement may be different, the major ones apply to both types of writing.

In both fiction and nonfiction, you have to capture your reader's attention, stir his interest, and gain his reading time. For fiction and nonfiction, you have a beginning, middle, and end.

136

Perhaps for fiction the middle may best be divided into two parts. Nevertheless, a book, article, or story will contain many individual devices which you can study carefully to learn the effective forms for your own use. You must recognize these forms, study them, and practice them.

A scene as studied in the last chapter is a device.

Your next step is to plan your files.

You may do this by using notebooks or a card system. The larger filing folders may be too bulky. From a story which you have chosen to study, jot down the title, the name of the author, and the publication information. Then—if you are not mutilating a treasured volume—cut the clipping of the special device which you plan to use, and paste it to the page or card. Above the clipping jot a heading such as "Scene," "Bait," "Characterization," or whatever the device illustrates.

Below the clipping, write such headings as "Author's problem," "Authors solution," and "Student's comment."[1]

The problem of the author is in relation *to his reader*—how to make the reader see and feel the thing needed at this particular step in writing. As you work these devices, it is best to take an entire story apart, then put it together again. That way you see more than the individual parts. You see the weaving together which achieved the whole. And the whole is more than the sum of its parts.

By the time you have carefully analyzed stories and articles which are typical of the type of work which you yourself would like to do, you will have clarified much of the original author's methods and seen how to take the whole and polish each of its parts.

The main value of collecting devices and rewriting them is that they open your eyes to the methods which have been shown you. Devices give you a pattern to follow that you can see and understand. Also, they make it possible for you to judge your own efforts and correct many of your own mistakes.

[1] Adapted from Walter S. Campbell, *Writing: Advice and Devices* (New York, Doubleday & Company, Inc., 1950).

When you have written the various devices over and over, changing the subject matter and words, each form will become a new skill for you. After you perceive, you must perform.

It is the performance over and over that takes the top-head knowledge of something and sends it drop by drop into the subconscious, where the skill becomes an automatic part of your life. Your knowledge grows as you discover the general truth behind the specific performance and you see why certain things have to be done the way they are.

You must know *how-to* as well as *what*.

Study the following devices based on the stories in this book and see how this form generates knowledge and adds to skill.

Reveal Characters through Other Character's Reactions

CLIPPING: "Heaven Knows," by Ennen Reaves Hall.

While Hebe hitched the team to the wagon, Elvy made a list of the things she wanted from town. Not that she expected Hebe to even look at it. He would get what few necessities he thought he could and they'd manage.

. . . Smiling, her tongue in her cheek, Elvy added other words under it. "A chunk of the world." Then, feeling foolish, she hurriedly tried to erase them. If Hebe saw that, he'd think she was crazy.

AUTHOR'S PROBLEM: To develop this minor character quickly, simply, and definitely, giving the "stuff he is made from." To do this in a way (that is not too obvious) which will not place the reader's sympathy with him—for that must be focused on the VPC (viewpoint character).

AUTHOR'S SOLUTION: To develop this minor character mainly through the reactions (mental and physical) of the VPC.

EFFECT ON THE READER: The contrast of the basic nature of this minor character and the VPC definitely places the sympathy of the reader with the latter.

STUDENT'S COMMENT: The conflict within the VPC is intensified by the contrast of the natures. The author was able to get over to the reader the fact that in this story-setting "life is real, life is earnest" through the characterization of the minor character.

138

Writing exercises:

1. Emily heard her bursts of laughter fill a suddenly silent room. The mood of her guests had in an instant switched from gaiety to a hushed withdrawal. A few managed to fitfully snuff out their cigarettes or deposit their glasses out of sight. Emily instinctively knew what had happened, even before she turned around to face Elliot standing in the doorway. But knowing did not help her. She felt her whole body grow limp under the stare of his smouldering eyes.

2. Marion was looking forward to the few minutes when she would enjoy a cup of coffee before she had to pick up the children. Fumbling through her clutch bag for the car keys, her glove caught on the frames of her broken glasses. Instantly she remembered she must go by Dr. Watt's office and have them fixed. But the thought of seeing him actually made her sick. She was almost certain that it was he who had spoken against Charles at the school board meeting. Her stomach churned now and she had no desire for coffee.

3. The mention of Sister Charity's coming brought smiles and good spirits to the tired patients in the ward. I saw for myself why the staff called her the "miracle medicine."

Introduction of Characters: Refer to Them without Presenting Them

CLIPPING: "Heaven Knows," by Ennen Reaves Hall.

Sugar, Hebe maintained, was one of the things they could do without. Wasn't there plenty of sorghum molasses? Yet there were times when Elvy longed for the luxury of pie or cake or the sugar cookies three-year-old Billy would adore.

AUTHOR'S PROBLEM: To introduce this minor character without interrupting the continuity of thought concerning the problem at hand. Also, to show this character's relationship to the others.

AUTHOR'S SOLUTION: A plausible way to introduce this character was by showing how he also was affected by the problem.

EFFECT ON THE READER: "Three-year-old Billy" is a complete,

simple, and effective introduction. These descriptive words have their own built-in emotional punch so that the reader can quickly form his mental image of the character. Also, the reader's sympathy is placed immediately with the character, for after all, he is three years old and has never had a sugar cookie!

STUDENT'S COMMENT: Introduction of this minor character early augments the description of the other characters concerning age, interests, and needs.

Writing exercises:

1. Charles raised the shade of the upstairs window and there in Carter's driveway was a new black Buick with a Texas license. Their Uncle Will, who owned the place, had come in during the night. Charles remembered that each time he appeared on the scene there was trouble for the Carters.

2. Shuffling through the morning's mail on the table, I came to a thick envelope for Winters. The postmark was from Chicago. Turning it over, I was startled to see the return address was of one "C. A. Winters, Jr."

So, Winters had a son.

3. Dora did the washing for the men of her family on Wednesday. She simply could not boil their overalls with the rest of the wash and have a line full of white clothes. There were times when it was almost impossible to get the grease out of them even with her homemade lye soap. That was all but Tom's. His were not a washing problem but a mending problem where the braces of his legs wore through the heavy denim. Today, as she had done so many times before, she wondered how many patches she had sewed on for him during the years they had been married.

Devices of the Beginning—Show Symptoms of Inner and Outer Problem in Character

CLIPPING: "Heaven Knows," by Ennen Reaves Hall.

. . . But she was puzzled a little at what she heard. "For your Heavenly Father knoweth what things ye have need of before ye ask," Hebe's resonant voice intoned.

Impulsively Elvy asked, "Hebe, if that's true, why do we have to pray? If God knows what we need, He knows the corn has to have rain and yet you pray about it every day and worry so."

The air was heavy with Hebe's disapproval before he answered. "Having doubts like that is sinful,.Elvy. We're told to ask for what we need, and I do."

Like making a list, Elvy thought. *A list you don't expect anyone to see.*

AUTHOR'S PROBLEM: She wants the reader to see both the inner and outer problem of her heroine.

AUTHOR'S SOLUTION: She uses a line of Scripture and two opposing interpretations of it to bring the inner and outer problems into focus.

STUDENT'S COMMENT: The author has chosen to be blunt rather than devious in stating the inner problem and thus has gained clarity. She is wise, however, in questioning immediately the meaning of the Scripture which states the problem. Not for a second is the reader allowed to believe that the problem is solved.

Writing exercises:

1. "As the twig is bent, so grows the tree. . . ."

If Donald had to hear his father say that one more time, he'd run away from home. He might run away, anyway. He was tired of having that willow "twig" bent against him. He didn't mind a whipping so much if he deserved it, but it wasn't fair to take his own whippings, and Danny's, too!

2. Jeb didn't figure himself to be a lightweight, but he figured himself about twenty pounds lighter than Rob Jones. It didn't matter, though. It looked like he'd have to fight Rob. He would if he intended to claim Alice Ledbetter as his girl the rest of this school year.

3. If Mother could just see that the dress didn't matter. Regina would look well in the hand-me-down formal. No one but Mother and her would know it was Aunt Gretchen's castoff. It wasn't the dress that bothered her. If she could just explain to Mother that she mustn't fuss over Bob when he came to pick her up for the dance. All she had to do, really, was open the door and invite

him in. She didn't have to serve him tea and cookies. She didn't have to plump a pillow and make him feel "at home."

Devices of the Beginning—Give a Gimmick in Bait

CLIPPING: "Showdown at San Saba," by Al Dewlen.

The sun held a close beat on our San Saba town, as though it aimed to cook away the whole dead place at one scald, and I wouldn't have cared a Sunday hatful if it had. Yet I kept on running, chancing it my bare feet wouldn't split wide open in that hot yellow sand of South Nevada Street, and I squeezed my hand tighter around the cracked butt of that old .44 frame that my pa had thrown away and which I'd dug out to play with and to practice my lightning-fast draw, which, up to now, I'd figured never to use until I growed to be a man.

AUTHOR'S PROBLEM: He wants to hint at or reveal an inner problem, and chooses here to hint at it.

AUTHOR'S SOLUTION: He uses a gimmick, an old broken-down gun.

STUDENT'S COMMENT: This is real bait as the VPC is made to torture his feet, running to carry the gimmick someplace, with the intention of putting a useless thing (the gimmick) to work.

Writing exercises:

1. My eyes gradually adjusted to the gloom of the cave. I had to push aside cobwebs to find my way to one of the rickety chairs that furnished the hovel. Dragging my crippled leg after me, I half sat and half fell into the chair. A mirthless cackle erupted as the chair creaked under my weight. Across from me I saw an old crone, hunched on her own chair; her gnarled, arthritic fingers held a tattered fan up before her face.

2. The kid—he couldn't have been more than ten years old—rode up the dusty street on the most wretchedly sway-back, big-footed old mule I'd ever seen. We all quit our talking to watch him. He rode up to the jailhouse, just as if he had some mind to do business with the Sheriff. He didn't get down off the mule. He just stepped off him, he swung so low. He hitched the animal—

or what was left of that animal—to the rack. Then he untied a
bullwhip from the saddle. He slung it over his arm and walked
into the Sheriff's office just as big as you please. We all burst out
laughing. We couldn't help it. Even from where we stood, we
could tell the whip was rotted almost plumb through—that besides it was almost three times as long as the kid.

3. Old man Cassidy beckoned. Tommy looked around, to
either side of him and then back to old man Cassidy. The signal
was for him. Mr. Cassidy motioned him over to the side—to the
imaginary bull pen for the little league pitchers. He wanted him,
Tommy Spencer, himself, to warm up! This was his big chance.
He hoped nobody would say anything about the bulge in his
pocket. Maybe they wouldn't notice. He kept his old ball there.
It was tattered. The string had broken. He'd mended it. He knew
it was no good, not really. But he didn't see how he could pitch
a game without that ball—just in case.

Devices of the Beginning—Weave in Setting

CLIPPING: "Comanche Son," by Fred Grove.
    He sighted dusty movement again when the slipping sun seemed
    lodged above the low summits of the rocky Wichitas and the dark
    soil of Medicine Bluff Creek curved ahead. Through bright layers
    of shimmering August heat the trailing horsemen looked dwarfed
    on the sea of yellow prairie swelling higher off north.
    . . . He forded the summer-shallow creek, his mind edged with
    excitement at being so near the end of his journey. He passed Fort
    Sill's orderly cluster of gray limestone buildings erected around a
    central square. He pressed forward through powder-dry grass and
    came to a huddle of sun-punished adobe buildings on the endless
    prairie.

AUTHOR'S PROBLEM: He must locate the story without tying
the reader in long, descriptive passages.

AUTHOR'S SOLUTION: He puts his hero on horseback and has
him move through the locale of the story. By the time he gets
to his destination, the reader is aware of the dry, hot prairie near
an army post.

STUDENT'S COMMENT: Since the hero never stops moving, the reader is willing to move with him through the description.

Writing exercises:

1. Rain pelted her new hat, but Gladys couldn't take shelter now. She had to meet that train. A red light stopped her. A taxi careened around the corner and splattered her coat. Darn! Still, she could have the coat cleaned. She could never make it up if the special from Des Moines were on time and she was late. She crossed the street. She did smile at the apple vendor under the El. She had time for smiles. Out into the rain again, and clip-clop across the wooden bridge. She was almost running as she hurried up the ramp to the station. She heard a train whistle. Then she did run.

2. Ella decided she'd feed the chickens as she went to the barn. That would give her some excuse if Dave asked her what she was doing hanging around the "real" work. Of course, he'd think she was silly anyway, feeding the chickens in the middle of the day when she'd already seen to them a couple of hours before. She took the scraps from the sink, though, and started out the door. At the stoop she paused to stub her toe against Roscoe. The dog was so old now, he didn't much hanker to trail her. Lazily he got up at her command and lumbered along. He looked disgruntled. She had no right to spoil his nap. She took the long way to the chicken yard, out under the shade of the big locust tree. The little shade felt good on the plains farm. Looking out across the field, she felt like maybe she could see next Friday. There was not a house in sight, only the road leading, she supposed, into town. At least that's where it led yesterday. Sometimes out on the farm she wondered if there still were towns . . . or even people. Maybe she and Dave were the only people left in the world. She threw the scraps to the chickens and started for the barn.

"Heaven Knows"

by Ennen Reaves Hall

W<small>HILE</small> Hebe hitched the team to the wagon, Elvy made a list of the things she wanted from town. Not that she expected Hebe to even look at it. He would get what few necessities he thought he could and they'd manage. But it was fun making a list and pretending he would bring it all back with him. At that, she hesitated before writing down sugar.

Sugar, Hebe maintained was one of the things they could do without. Wasn't there plenty of sorghum molasses? Yet there were times when Elvy longed for the luxury of pie or cake or the sugar cookies three-year-old Billy would adore. So she wrote the word down, just to see how it looked on paper. Wonderful!

Smiling, her tongue in her cheek, Elvy added other words under it. "A chunk of the world." Then, feeling foolish, she hurriedly tried to erase them. If Hebe saw that, he'd think she was crazy. Hebe couldn't understand how "out of the world" a woman felt living on a West Texas homestead claim, seeing people only at rare intervals, and with her monotonous days blending together like the endless brown prairies that stretched off toward a world she could only wonder about. Such as the exciting world that Hebe would see today in Santa Anna.

Hebe came in for the morning Scripture-reading before leaving for the long trip to town. Leaving the useless list unfinished, Elvy took up her small son to keep him quiet. She always liked hearing Hebe read the Scriptures aloud. His deep voice was impressive, and, even with Billy trying to make his corncob doll climb up Elvy's long braids, she listened attentively. But she was puzzled a little at what she heard. "For your Heavenly Father

145

knoweth what things ye have need of before ye ask," Hebe's resonant voice intoned.

Impulsively Elvy asked, "Hebe, if that's true, why do we have to pray? If God knows what we need, He knows the corn has to have rain and yet you pray about it every day and worry so."

The air was heavy with Hebe's disapproval before he answered. "Having doubts like that is sinful, Elvy. We're told to ask for what we need, and I do."

Like making a list, Elvy thought. *A list you don't expect anyone to see.* That must be the way Hebe prayed, the way he kept right on worrying after he'd read his list to God. She smiled at the thought that it must sound a little funny in Heaven, hearing Hebe read his list of needs as though God didn't already know.

When Hebe drove away, Elvy stood in the door until the wagon was just a moving speck against the horizon. Her mind was full of rebellious doubts, scampering around like the busy little prairie dogs Hebe hated so. If God knew about people's needs, didn't He know how badly she wanted to go to town with Hebe today? And how tired a woman got of never doing anything different, or seeing people, or having new, exciting foods to eat? Not even sugar for a pound cake, or an annual trip into town for supplies. Of course, the two day's trip in the blistering heat would have been hard on Billy. And there was Hebe's corn to guard against stray cattle.

The corn, of course, was important. Acres and acres of it, stretching away as far as Elvy could see, like a rippling sea of bright green. It was the pride of Hebe's heart. Although only June, the stalks already stood nearly five feet high, the plumed tips about even with Elvy's head. And it meant even more than food for themselves and the stock during the winter to come. The corn was to make Texas history, for it would prove a point Hebe had argued ever since taking up the homestead—that the plains were good for more than just cattlegrazing, that Texas would some day be feeding the world.

146

Elvy understood all that, but the rebellious doubts were still stirring in her as she turned to begin her long, monotonous day.

❋   ❋   ❋

Around mid-morning a startled note in the bark of the prairie dogs brought Elvy back to the door. A man living six miles down the creek sat his horse in front of the house, a sack of flour riding behind him.

"Mornin', Miz Anderson. Hebe around?"

"Howdy, Mister Staton. No, Hebe left early to go to Santa Anna for grub."

"I just come from town but missed him. Quite a lot of excitement in Santa Anna. Had a train robb'ry yesterday. Feller with a handkerchief over his face stopped the Santa Fe, locked up the train crew in the express car and made off with five thousand dollars. Half the county's out hunting him now."

A brief interest stirred Elvy. "You think they'll catch him?"

" 'Most sure to. The engineer says the robber stood right under a leaky valve when he boarded the engine and that there'd ought to be grease spots high up between his shoulder blades. Feller won't know that, of course, but the sheriff'll spot him that way. Well, I'll be ridin' on and git this flour to the old woman."

The news from the county seat town touched Elvy lightly, as news from another world. She had forgotten it by the time she and Billy had finished their noon snack. When a loud "Hello!" sent her running back to the door, her only thought was that this was a memorable day—two callers within a few hours.

A stranger had ridden up this time. Hardly more than a boy, she thought. Or was he? After seeing his eyes—hard and too-bright—she wasn't sure.

"Yore man at home?" the young-old man asked.

"Hebe's in town," Elvy answered. "Just me and Billy here."

"How about some grub? I ain't et today."

Compassion rose in Elvy as she saw the gaunt hunger lines in his face, the evidences of fatigue. She nodded, said hospitably: "Light and 'tend your horse while I fix something."

But something like panic was rising in her as she thought of the bare shelves in her kitchen. What in the world could she give the man to eat? Not just plain corn-meal mush, such as she and Billy had eaten. A man couldn't ride in the hot Texas sun with just corn-meal mush on his stomach. They'd eaten the last of the side meat for breakfast, and it was between seasons for potatoes. There were onions, but corn pone and onions was no sort of meal to offer company. Unless she could find an egg to go with it, and that was doubtful since the hens she had were all molting.

A quick search of the barnyard killed all hope of an egg. As Elvy hurried back to the house, her desperation growing, a long-legged rooster pecked playfully at her toes. A horrifying thought rose to tempt her: *Ebenezer would make fine eating for a hungry man.* He was just right for frying. But Billy had made such a pet of the chicken that Hebe had said not to kill him unless she just had to.

Well, didn't she have to now? There was nothing else to give the hungry stranger and simple hospitality demanded she feed him. Only she couldn't kill Ebenezer. He was like a member of the family.

Elvy started running from temptation, but the rooster followed her. A vision of the man's gaunt face rose to reproach her. Surely a man was worth more than a chicken, she thought desperately, and Billy would soon forget. Setting her lips tightly, she whirled and swooped. Before the luckless Ebenezer could let out a squawk he flopped, headless, on the ground. Feeling like a murderess, Elvy picked up the chicken and ran for the kitchen door.

It didn't take long to prepare the rooster for frying and there was plently of lard. The stranger didn't seem to mind waiting. He had taken out his harmonica and was playing gay tunes for Billy in the other room.

When Elvy called, the man came in eagerly. He ate greedily, with eyes only for the food. Elvy, hungry for conversation, tried to start talk.

"Did you hear about the train robbery in Santa Anna? A man robbed the express car of five thousand dollars! Isn't it awful?"

He looked up, his hard eyes glittering. "What's so awful about it? I reckon the Santa Fe can afford to lose five thousand dollars. And I'd say the feller was smart. All you git in this world is what you take away from somebody."

His harsh words struck a spark of sudden, fierce anger in Elvy. "That's not true!" she cried, hotly. "Haven't you just eaten Ebenezer?" To her horror she felt hot tears sting her eyelids.

The man stared from her angry face to the heaped up bones on his plate. "Just et who, Ma'am?"

"Ebenezer, Billy's pet rooster. I fed him to you because I didn't have anything else. Not that I mind Ebenezer, but you've no right to—to—"

"But why did you do it?" Now he sounded angry himself. "Why did you give me the kid's pet, even if you didn't have anything else. You didn't owe me anything —."

"You were hungry," she said, simply. "That's what I mean. People all have to give to each other and help each other, but they shouldn't steal—."

The man got up, his eyes so hard they frightened Elvy. "So I et Ebenezer," he said, flatly. "Well, I'll pay for him."

Elvy made a quick gesture of repudiation. "I'm sorry. I didn't mean to make you feel like that. Of course I can't take money for a meal. And I don't really mind Ebenezer. It's just your talking like nobody had ever done anything for you —."

"All anybody's ever done for me," he said, harshly, "is to kick me down when I tried to get up. Well, thanks for Ebenezer anyway, Ma'am."

He left the room and Elvy stood staring after him in shocked horror. For high on the man's back, between his shoulder blades, were telltale grease spots! She turned a little sick as she realized she had fed Ebenezer to the Santa Anna train robber!

Her heart pounding, she ran to the window to watch the man mount his sweat-lathered horse. She was glad he was going. He must be mean and cruel and dangerous. Yet he had played such nice tunes for Billy —."

Thought of the child made her whirl in sudden alarm, realizing she hadn't heard him for some time. He wasn't in the house, she quickly discovered.

Running to the door, Elvy called again and again. The child didn't answer, was nowhere in sight. The train robber gave her a curious glance as he rode off, but Elvy hardly noticed him. Alarm was rising in her at the thought that Billy had wandered away from the house, perhaps into the cornfield. Hebe had warned her over and over again about that. "Once let him get lost in there," he'd said, "and it would be like hunting for a needle in a straw stack."

Elvy looked at the tall corn, deceptive in its inviting shade, and shuddered. It wasn't cool in there as it looked to be. The green corn caught and held the hot rays of the sun and the stalks stood so thick and close they formed an airless jungle.

Still calling, Elvy ran along the edge of the field, looking for small tracks. She soon found them, the tiny indentations in the soft earth confirming her fears. Elvy tried following them but quickly discovered the boy wasn't following the rows, but was crossing and recrossing the furrows in a way that indicated panic. Billy was lost and very frightened and running crazily through the corn!

Unless she found him quickly, Elvy knew he could be overcome by the intense heat. Calling constantly, she tried following that crazy pattern of small prints until she finally had to stop, breathless, in the terrifying realization that she too was lost. She could never find Billy that way!

The heat rose in suffocating waves from the dark ground, like hot steam from a kettle. The sun beat down fiercely and Elvy felt light-headed and giddy, staggering now as she ran. The saw-like blades of the corn whipped at her face until it felt raw. Often she stumbled and fell prone on the hot, moist ground. It was at a time like that she remembered the creek that ran through the far end of the field, and fear sent her stumbling on again.

Elvy thought, desperately, that she must pray. But when she tried to form words, her mind envisioned the young shoat that had gotten into the corn just the week before. She had helped

Hebe chase it, but when they had finally found it the animal lay stretched between the rows of whispering corn, dead from heat and exertion. It had run itself to death, just as she and Billy might do unless they had help.

Help? There was only Heaven to help—and Elvy couldn't pray. Hebe had always done the praying for both of them. Stumbling in the loose dirt, she fell again and lay there sobbing, panic like drums inside her.

Then suddenly the panic was gone and Elvy struggled up. It was as though she had heard Hebe's deep voice reading from the Book: "For your Heavenly Father knoweth what things ye have need of before ye ask."

Why, that meant she didn't have to pray! She didn't have to be afraid! God knew all about Billy and He'd help her find him.

It was then she remembered the train robber. Almost calmly she reasoned that if she could get back to the house, catch a horse and overtake him the two of them could find Billy much quicker. Not once did she think that the man might be reluctant to return and help her. Such details she was leaving to Heaven. What she must do was find the house, and suddenly she was confident she could.

Fifteen minutes later she staggered out of the field and there, riding toward her, was the train robber. "I had a feeling something was wrong, Ma'am," he said, hesitantly. "I thought I heard you calling, so I rode back."

Elvy told him, quickly. "You find that creek and patrol it," he ordered. "Keep calling. I'll find the little feller."

❋   ❋   ❋

It was nearly an hour later, just when Elvy thought her throat would close up and refuse to make another sound, that the man came stumbling up with Billy in his arms. A little later they laid the tired child on the bed at home.

The man looked down at him and murmured, gently, "Just plum tuckered out, pore little feller."

Billy aroused and looked up at them. "I losted Ebenezer. I tried to find him and I couldn't."

151

Looking from Billy's tear-streaked face to the strangely gentled one of the outlaw, Elvy was surprised to see how much younger the man looked. Why, he was hardly more than a boy himself!

The man's eyes wavered under her gaze and he ran a grimy sleeve over his face as he looked uneasily at the sun, now little higher than the cabin windows. "I'd better git going," he said, starting for the door.

"Wait a minute," Elvy said softly, "I want to wash your shirt before you go. It won't take long."

"Wash my shirt?" His surprise was almost ludicrous. "Why should you wash my shirt, Ma'am?"

"Because it's got grease spots across the shoulders. And a neighbor said this morning the Santa Anna sheriff was looking for a man with spots like those on his shirt back. He got them when he stood under a leaky valve of a Santa Fe engine."

Without a word he peeled off his shirt, glanced quickly at the dust-filled grease spots, then handed the garment to her. Telling him to build the fire and put on her flat-iron, Elvy hurried out to where her zinc washtub leaned against the house.

She was pressing the clean garment when she felt him watching her from the doorway. He said, slowly, "Thinking about that train robber, Ma'am. Maybe he ain't as bad as you think. Sometimes a man gits desp'rate thinking he ain't got a chance to get anywhere playing it straight."

Elvy said, gently, "He shouldn't feel that way. I guess God knows what a person needs and helps him to get it. I know He turned you around today and sent you back—and maybe it wasn't just to help me and Billy, but so I could wash your shirt and help you keep out of jail."

He laughed at that, but there was no humor in the sound. "I didn't think God would help a train robber escape," he jeered.

Handing him the clean shirt, Elvy said, "I guess God knows your needs the same as mine."

Hebe got home late the next day and at once started telling Elvy about the train robbery. "I know," Elvy said, absently, as she explored the box of groceries. "Mister Staton rode by and told me yesterday morning."

"Staton couldn't have known all of it," Hebe said. "Not that the robber sneaked back into town last night and left the money, every blessed cent of it, on a bench in the depot. The agent found it when he opened up early this morning. Reckon the law was getting close and the fellow got panicky."

Happiness was bubbling up like a spring inside Elvy. "Maybe he just got sorry for what he'd done, Hebe."

"Rats! Those kind of men don't get sorry till they see they're about to get caught. But bringing back the money won't save his hide if the law catches him, and chances are good they will for he's got grease spots —."

"Maybe," Elvy said, dreamily, "God will help him escape."

Hebe looked outraged. "That's plain blasphemy, Elvy. I declare, you do have some of the craziest ideas —."

Elvy wasn't listening. She was staring at a brown paper parcel she held in her hands. Sugar! Hebe had actually brought sugar.

Remembering the list he hadn't even seen, Elvy smiled happily. Sugar—and a chunk of the world! *"For the Heavenly Father knoweth—"* she murmured, softly, and wondered if she dared tell Hebe what had happened to Ebenezer.

CHAPTER NINE

THE BEGINNING

NOT ONLY MUST YOU KNOW your reader and love him, but you must lure him into reading *your* writing. This means that as he leafs through a magazine or a book, his mind upon a thousand or so things, you must reach out and capture his attention. Since he is merely turning pages, not reading, you must do it quickly or you've lost your chance!

1. *You do it with bait.*

The long-anticipated day of escape proved to be Tuesday.

. . . a plain wonder that at twenty-four he was still unwed. It caused talk in the county.

The letter was short, scrawled heavily across the page, so Jim caught the bus immediately.

"Rain should come by afternoon," Martha murmured optimistically, going to the window. "Good Lord!" she exclaimed.

The vague uneasiness he had felt when he had suggested visiting his folks rolled over him now with a desperation close to panic.

You see that each of these examples stirs interest. All suggest that something important is about to happen. In this manner you catch your reader's eye. This is equally true in nonfiction:

I met Minnie ten years after she was dead.

What happened to me was no different from what happened to thousands of others, only I was spared to tell about it.

The most important conflict in the next fifty years will be the fight to win the minds of men; thus far, we've taken a terrible beating.

154

As you build your files, you will discover various ways in which you can catch your reader's attention.

2. Introduce all your important characters—in character.

Your main characters must either appear on the pages of the beginning, or be mentioned, thought about, or discussed there.

Introducing the vpc:	He sighted dusty movement again when the slipping sun seemed lodged above the low summits of the rocky Wichitas .... A spare and unhurried man ... his mind edged with excitement. ("Comanche Son")
Introducing the main character, not the vpc:	Mistletoe Corners was just sitting there in the late May sun, minding its own business the day Charleyhorse came home from school.("The Most Important Man in Town")
If a character is to appear later, he must be thought about or mentioned:	"I've come for my boy." ("Comanche Son") "Feller with a handkerchief over his face stopped the Santa Fe." ("Heaven Knows")

It is not enough, however, merely to show the character in the beginning; he must enter the story in character. By this, I mean that he must do something which will reveal the pattern of his action throughout the story.

This is true with main characters:	He drove all around the square at ten miles an hour more than the law allows and parked in the front of a sign that said not to park there. ("The Most Important Man in Town") ... he reined the big steel dust bay around and pulled a Spencer from his saddle boot below his leg, raised the sights, and sent a futile bullet flying at them. ("Comanche Son")
It is true also with minor characters:	Levi Sawyer looked more Iowa farmer than Indian agent. ... He had a plowman's stocky frame and his heavy mouth, wide and straight and firm, gave him a certain stern look. "Comanche Son")

Each character must enter doing the type of thing which he will also do at the crisis of the story:

"The answer to a prayer!" said my father, who manages the Mistletoe Corners Mudcats and is the Sheriff of Chickamasia County on the side. ("The Most Important Man in Town")

"He hasn't changed much," said my big sister Gloria, frowning. My sister is assistant county attorney, and death on lawlessness. ("The Most Important Man in Town")

Standing by the truck, the big worried-looking man listed all the jobs he wanted Roy to finish while he was gone. Then he stood frowning, not looking at Roy. ("Real Gone Guy")

. . . if there was any honest grit in the whole Lockhart family it had to be in my own belly; it sure wasn't noticeable in pa's. ("Showdown at San Saba")

Each example reveals something about the character. By these indicators, your reader quickly identifies which one is the main character, which the villian, and which the object of desire. This makes for ease of reading and quickens interest. However, you notice that in all of the following examples, the reader is never told, but shown.

3. *Set the emotional tone.* This must be done in the early words of the story. Your reader must know the story's mood.

Western

Knowing them well by now, he sensed an extra doggedness, an added wolfish patience, a clenched hanging on for the gold he carried after selling his herd in Caldwell and paying off the crew. ("Comanche Son")

Religious

Impulsively Elvy asked, "Hebe, if that's true, why do we have to pray?" ("Heaven Knows")

Romantic

"I think you're making a mistake," he had said. "When you find it out, I'll be around and waiting." Well, she'd found it out. ("Violets from Portugal")

4. *Set your stage,* showing time, place, and type of background.

A reader must know where the action is taking place, when it is occurring, and what kind of background there is before he can visualize it within his mind. He must have a stage and time period where he can watch the action of these characters which you cause to perform for him. This is true whether you are writing biography, history, or fiction.

Place	When Roy got to the ranch gate after his long hike from the school-bus stop . . . . ("Real Gone Guy")
Time and place	He sighted dusty movement again when the slipping sun seemed lodged above the low summits of the rocky Wichitas . . . ahead. ("Comanche Son")
Folk story with historical background	It wasn't important playing like he'd do for a wedding or an infare, or like he'd done the time Andy Jackson asked him to the Hermitage. ("The Preacher's Confession")
Action story with western background	He hadn't looked at Roy directly since the day he came to the city jail to arrange about the probation. The cops had rounded up a gang of boys in a stolen car, and Roy had been one of the gang. ("Real Gone Guy")
Idea story with pioneer background	She smiled at the thought that it must sound a little funny in Heaven, hearing Hebe read his list of needs as though God didn't already know. ("Heaven Knows")
Atmosphere—war	"Air reconnaissance hasn't been able to tell us anything. Our ground reconnaissance can't get through. The Germans have eighty-eights dug in and concealed along all roads and passages known to us." The general looked at the four men in front of him. ("Reconnaissance Patrol")

Your background adds clarity to your story. Also, it provides a special setting for the particular type of story which you desire to emphasize. Most westerns are stories of action, and there are historical stories which show how the environment of the times affected the character's thoughts and actions. Stories that show backgrounds of special community groups are often favored by editors. Your background, however, deals with facts. Be sure that these facts are accurate and carefully researched.

5. *State the problem*—the subjective problem and the objective problem.

Of course not all pieces of short copy have two phases of a problem. A how-to article does not; neither does an essay. But fiction adds a study in depth, and in this is a difficulty which may have created the outside problem. A boy, by refusing to stand up to a bully, may have invited the bully's advance upon his own possessions. Whatever it is, it is a problem in life, and rises from a weak character trait that has not yet crossed over to the plus side of growth. In fact, this crossing-over struggle is what makes your story.

The objective problem is the pattern of events which the viewpoint character has to face, and in the facing he either wins or loses.

Subjective problem	Elvy understood all that, but the rebellious doubts were still stirring in her as she turned to begin her long, monotonous day. ("Heaven Knows")
Objective problem	A stranger had ridden up this time. Hardly more than a boy, she thought. Or was he? After seeing his eyes—hard and too-bright—she wasn't sure. ("Heaven Knows")
Subjective problem	Lots of preachers felt that way. That was one reason Tom quit going to meeting after ma died. ("The Preacher's Confession")
Objective problem	The big man looked straight at him, and it gave Tom a fair start to see Sara Bell's brown

eyes in his massive weather-beaten face. "It's not you I mean, young man, when I speak of the Evil One. It's that—that thing you hold, that viper in your bosom." ("The Preacher's Confession")

In "Heaven Knows" it is later that the stranger develops into a problem, but the very warning given by the rider tells the reader that danger is ahead for Elvy. This is the needed element. In "The Preacher's Confession" the story's main problem is not the giving up of the fiddle. It is winning the girl, but the girl has to be won (for the VPC's happiness) with the keeping of the fiddle. Therefore, these elements of the story are written into the beginning, creating the problem which the reader sees immediately.

The subjective problem of Elvy is that of rebellion and distrust. She solves it by showing trust in a thief and thereby stirring the honesty within him.

The subjective problem of Tom was that he loved his fiddle almost beyond reason; but when he could genuinely give it up for the love of another, he received both the fiddle and the girl.

Emotional growth moves an emotion out from being tied to the pettiness of the human self, into a largeness of the welfare of the whole. It is the self-element that weakens the emotion, because the self-element opposes itself against all others. It is always partial, never whole.

Humanity is made up of human beings learning basic fundamental truths. Every problem that you have had and solved is material for your stories—and they are stories that you alone can write, for you have had the experience.

6. *Hint at the solution.*

Plant the idea of the desired solution for your reader. If your reader can agree with your viewpoint character's desire, the pleasure in the end of the story is much more satisfying.

> . . . Scowling fiercely, he climbed the stairs to the small dingy attic room that was his new home, his happy, happy home. Until his dirty old foot slipped and Ed threw him to the wolves! ("Real Gone Guy")

. . . "I'm Ben Wrattan—I've come for my boy," which was all he could get out, so swiftly did the thickness fill his dry throat and smothered feeling seize his chest. ("Comanche Son")

. . . didn't He know how badly she wanted to go to town with Hebe today? And how tired a woman got of never doing anything different, or seeing people. . . ? ("Heaven Knows")

You notice that the hint of the solution comes in the bitter, negative desire, or the fear that chokes (the personal element of the emotion) and the feeling that while there is a solution, something is preventing it.

7. Start the conflict in a complete scene.

The moment a threat appears, interest quickens. Gordon Cooper's flight around the world became almost a normal feat to the TV viewers; then something happened: the machine failed and Gordon Cooper had to take manuel control. The TV viewers began biting their fingernails. Conflict makes both fiction and nonfiction exciting.

Emotional start of conflict	. . . The vague uneasiness he had felt when he had suggested visiting his folks rolled over him now with a desperation close to panic. ("Stubborn Bride")
Action start of conflict	. . . I squeezed my hand tighter around the cracked butt of that old .44 frame that my pa had thrown away . . . which, up to now, I'd figured never to use until I growed to be a man. ("Showdown at San Saba")

You can use either form. Don't stop to explain to the reader all the things he needs to know about the story; start the conflict.

Go through the examples in this book and see how a complete scene always opens the story. Too many writers hint at something in the beginning, and when the scene is forgotten, the writer wonders why his story does not come alive. A beginning is never complete without its opening scene.

8. *Plant essential facts.*

Lead your reader to expect trouble by the fears ahead, and if there is a need for a gun in the last half of the story, be sure that it is seen by the reader in the beginning. Plant the essential facts.

"Studyin' law. . . . With a good, strong minor in history," Charleyhorse said. ("The Most Important Man in Town")

. . . I was supposed to farm next to the old man. He didn't want to let me go. ("Stubborn Bride")

Plants are necessary to make your story creditable. A story must seem reasonable. When a story fails this test the mind throws it out the window and the emotion no longer accepts the situation. But when the necessary ingredients to make a story reasonable are included in the beginning, there is no jarring reaction to stop the reader from enjoying the story.

9. *Point to coming events.*

. . . Nobody was going to hurt mamma! ("Stubborn Bride")

"I take her serious, too," Charleyhorse said. "Only don't tell her I said so." ("The Most Important Man in Town")

Pointers can either be emotional hopes or facts that gain in significance after the story itself is told. In "The Most Important Man in Town" it is not until the end of the story that the reader discovers that Charleyhorse's action was a deliberate and different manner of courting the girl. Pointers add to the art of making fiction plausible, and therefore acceptable to the reader.

10. *Lead into a complication.*

A complication is a new situation that makes the original problem more difficult to solve. Complications can arise out of outside problems, or complications may be due to the vpc's attempt to solve the problem acting from his weak character trait. This always increases the problem.

"Let me see him." Ben said, and when the agent moved uneasily, in silence, Ben stabbed him with a look of raw suspicion. ("Comanche Son")

. . . "I didn't third-degree you about your folks, did I?" ("Stubborn Bride")

It was when John Quincy Winant turned that I knew I was kissing close to a live, gun-fighting man. ("Showdown at San Saba")

In planning your complication, ask yourself: what is the worst thing possible that could happen to my main character right now? That gives you a good idea of a selection for a complication. Never make it easy. In the final action, you are going to have him backed up in a tight corner. Now you start him waltzing in that direction without his being aware of it. The more he struggles to get out of his problem, the deeper he gets in, like a fly stuck upon fly paper.

The samples in this chapter are not all that are in the stories. You have only been given highlights—just enough to help you see which device is which. Now go through the next story and see if you can mark each device of the beginning, and this time mark them all. (Give all about the setting, all the characterization, all the sentences that show the subjective and objective problem.) Take the beginning apart carefully; then practice writing exercises of your own. Watch your perception grow!

"Comanche Son"

by Fred Grove

HE sighted dusty movement again when the slipping sun seemed lodged above the low summits of the rocky Wichitas and the dark coil of Medicine Bluff Creek curved ahead. Through glass-bright layers of shimmering August heat the trailing horse-men looked dwarfed on the sea of yellow prairie swelling higher off north.

A spare and unhurried man, he reined the big steel dust bay around and pulled a Spencer from his saddle boot below his leg, raised the sights, and sent a futile bullet flying at them. They halted as he expected, beyond carbine range, and he rode on, thinking how, in the beginning, four instead of three had jumped him on the Cimarron. Knowing them well by now, he sensed an extra doggedness, an added wolfish patience, a clenched hanging on for the gold he carried after selling his herd in Caldwell and paying off his trail crew.

He forded the summer-shallow creek, his mind edged with excitement at being so near the end of his journey. He passed Fort Sill's orderly cluster of gray limestone buildings erected around a central square. He pressed forward through powder-dry grass and came to a huddle of sun-punished adobe buildings on the endless prairie.

He dismounted slowly, his deliberate movements covering a welling eagerness as he looked around, for a moment affected by the bleakness of this Quaker venture of brotherly love in the loneliness of Indian country. Smoke smell lay on the hot wind. Tepees rose on the nearby dusty flats. Camp dogs barked. Ponies grazed. He went in, then, long steps quickening, stirring the music of jingling spur rowels.

And presently he stood in a dim, still room and he was saying, "I'm Ben Wrattan—I've come for my boy," which was all he could get out, so swiftly did the thickness fill his dry throat and the smothered feeling seize his chest.

Levi Sawyer looked more Iowa farmer than Indian agent. His enormous hands, lump-knuckled and toil-worn, hung like hammers on the sturdy handles of his arms. He had a plowman's stocky frame and his heavy mouth, wide and straight and firm, gave him a certain stern look. But beneath the craggy brows Ben saw the mildest, clearest, friendliest gray eyes of his memory.

After the first cordial greeting, the shape of welcome rounding Sawyer's face gradually retreated. A frown formed.

"He's here?" Ben demanded.

Sawyer had the habit of looking up and working his lips, as if he drew the nub of a thing through his mind, back and forth, reflecting, examining, and sought a higher help before replying.

"Tehan," he said, speaking carefully, "the lad thee read about in the Kansas newspapers, is still here. True. He's been attending our agency school since April, when the Quahadas brought him in."

"I sent word—came as fast as I could," Ben said, eyeing Sawyer for assurance. "Everything tallies. Your description of the boy, where the Indians said they stole him on the Brazos, the year and the time of year. He has to be my son!"

Sympathy stood in Sawyer's eyes. "It is always the same when Texas people come looking for their loved ones. So positive, so hopeful. I cannot be until doubt no longer exists."

"Let me see him," Ben said, and when the agent moved uneasily, in silence, Ben stabbed him with a look of raw suspicion.

Sawyer said, "I only want to remind thee that most captive children have endured terrible experiences. Many hardships. Much of what they remember is confused. Gunshots, yells, fire, horses running. Sometimes I feel they do not wish to recall what happened to their parents or kin."

"There's little for the boy to recollect. He was born in '62, after

164

I left for the war. He was stolen in '65, before I got home. Taken as he played in the yard." Ben was bitter.

"And . . . the boy's mother?" Sawyer asked, hesitating.

"She lived through the raid and she's still hoping. I've been as far as the Apache agencies in New Mexico and Arizona. My wife's told me so much about the boy, I feel I'll know him. I know I will!"

"There is another thing," Sawyer said, neither sharing nor discouraging Ben's enthusiasm. "It is true, Comanches can be very cruel, judged by our standards. Yet, when they adopt a captive, they love him like a Comanche."

Ben's temper flared. "If they loved him, why'd they give him up?"

"I withheld their rations until they did. There are few buffalo to hunt this year."

Sawyer's eyes were wise, gentle with understanding. "The lad was treated with kindness by a Comanche called Two Strikes. Spoiled, in fact. Never a hand laid on him. All that will make it harder for him to become a white boy again."

Ben's voice turned harsh. "My boy wouldn't want to stay with a brute Comanche! Is something wrong? He hurt—crippled? This been too much for his mind?"

"His health is excellent," Sawyer said, quick to reply. "His mind is bright. His marks are high in school."

"In heaven's name what is it, then?"

"I will go get the lad," Sawyer said, in a forbearance that worried Ben.

Sawyer went out and the room fell still again, close with heat. Ben never moved his eyes from the doorway. What if the boy wasn't his? What was Sawyer holding back? After a while, Ben heard steps and voices. His blood was pounding as he got to his feet, fighting a banked impatience.

Just then a slim boy walked in, quietly followed by Sawyer, and paused with the sensitive wariness of a half-grown antelope. Sawyer had dressed him in shoes, gray britches, blue cotton shirt, and a nice dark coat. Ben stared, turned mute by a sense of unreality, content only to watch. Watching the proud, unsmiling face, its trace of suspicion, a face tanned dark as an Indian's, not a muscle moving—a Comanche's wide-open look of country without end, of hot winds and curly grasses and rainy-weather lakes and buffalo making the prairie earth tremble, the Llano Estacado and its mysterious, sobering silence. But the eyes were blue, a deep blue, and the hair, freshly cut, was pale yellow, like that of the big-eyed woman who waited on the Brazos, pale like flax.

Ben's gaze became a tearing thing. A feeling was beating high in his chest, but he forced himself to be calm. "Howdy, boy," he said and waited.

For a little run of time the far-seeing eyes just stared, and then Ben saw the sizing-up arrogance. There was no answer. Ben flinched inwardly. "There should be a scar down the left leg," he said, all hint of command scrubbed from his voice.

Sawyer said, "Show him, lad."

There was a pause while the boy, motionless, chin lifted, threw his insolence at the white man. A Comanche insolence, Ben decided darkly. To his surprise, however the boy obeyed, and when Ben looked down, he wanted to cry out. For it was there, dimly white but unmistakable, the long slash of puckered skin where Ben's first-born had fallen upon the double-edged ax, as Margaret Ann had first described in her letters and then in person, afterward.

Ben glanced happily at Sawyer. The agent had no reply, and Ben asked the unimpressed boy, "Do you remember how you got this?"

The blue eyes only looked at him, the contempt showing.

"You fell on an ax left in a green pecan log on the woodpile," Ben said, coaxing. "Remember?"

No, the eyes said.

Despite that, Ben's confidence was soaring. "There should be a birthmark the size of a thumbprint, shaped like a berry, along

166

your right ribs, here," he said, easy and cheerful, indicating with his left hand.

Again the boy looked to Sawyer and complied, though half-insolent about removing his shirt, and again Ben, looking but never touching, found the telltale blemish. He threw a gleam of triumph at the silent Sawyer, and, his face wreathed in a broad smile, he dropped to his knees. "Son, your name is Jim Travis Wrattan. I'm Ben Wrattan—your father. Your mother is living. Her name is Margaret Ann. I'm going to take you home to her."

Ben was reaching as he finished and he pulled the brown face against his bearded one. That interval held, while the thickness climbed in Ben's throat and his head swam, until a sudden understanding crackled inside him. Why, the boy was like wood in his arms! Ben got up and stood back, silently, *What have they done to him?*

"My name—is Tehan," the boy said, a chopped-off, pushed-out Indian pride to his tone that Ben hated. "My white father dead—white mother dead—."

"That's not true!" Ben snarled.

"My people tell me—the Quahadas."

"Don't call *them* your people! Listen, they wounded your mother and killed your grandfather! They'd have killed her if Rangers hadn't been hot after 'em!" Ben was fighting for clarity, for persuasion, trying to pierce the unblinking copper expression. "Comanches did that—they stole you!"

The boy, unchanged, scornfully pulled down his shirt. "Kiowas make raid—Quahadas buy me. Two Strikes tell me." He slapped his chest. "Two Strikes great warrior—great horse thief."

"He lied! Comanches did it! They even told Mister Sawyer here they took you!" Ben stopped, realizing it was no use now. He spoke with a quiet desperation. "Boy, don't you remember the cabin under the pecan trees? The cool spring . . . the plum thicket?" He gained in eloquence. He called up every animal and incident he could remember from his wife's letters during the war. At mention of a spotted puppy the Indian look in the stern features seemed to lessen, just barely, then to return, set like flint.

"My white people dead," the boy said, almost in monotone. "I am Quahada now." He slipped into the cavernous new coat. A twist of his shoulders said the garment was nothing, it was white man.

Ben lowered his voice. "If I wasn't your father, would I know about the scar and the birthmarks?"

"He see marks," came the immediate skepticism, the boy pointing at Sawyer, accusing. "He tell you. All white men lie." His right hand, in fluid, graceful motion, cut the taunting sign of the forked tongue. "Liars—cowards. Like women. My people—the Quahadas—tell me. So it is true."

Ben looked away in resignation, sick at heart, sending his helplessness across the room to Sawyer. "Might as well take him back. I can't drive these heathen notions out of his head."

Sawyer, expressionless, gestured to leave. Ben didn't look up until the boy reached the doorway. One moment he presented a slim, defiant shape there, lost in the oversize white man's clothes. The next he was gone, silently, like mesquite smoke on warm wind, like a Comanche.

"Won't he run off?" Ben asked in alarm.

"Agency employees are outside," Sawyer said calmly. "Yes, he's tried. Twice soldiers caught him trying to steal a horse from the stone corral at the fort. Another time we found him walking back to Quahada country." Sawyer turned his face upward, in his reflective way, and Ben, still shaken, was not prepared when the agent said simply, "I think thee and the lad should leave tomorrow."

Ben couldn't answer that just now.

"There's a definite family resemblance," Sawyer said, smiling for the first time. "I noticed that at once. In spirit as well. The boy is strong-willed, like his father. I have no doubts."

"But he thinks —."

"He is only a boy, brought up on proud Indian ways. Loyal to

168

the Quahadas. Suspicious of whites. A little frightened, I think, at seeing the strange white man who claims to be his father. Just as you are troubled over his 'heathen notions,' as you call them."

"How can I make him understand?"

"If you mean more evidence, more proof, you have shown me more than enough. The need, I think, is of the spirit, of the heart. Something between thee. Be patient. Give him time."

"Time," Ben said bitterly, "when he hates all white men!"

Sawyer seemed to be thinking ahead. "A mail escort will be going south tomorrow for Fort Richardson."

❆　❆　❆

As eight troopers, escorting a mule-drawn army ambulance, drew up at the agency in the bright sunlight, Ben and the boy came out on the porch with Sawyer.

The agent's eyes swept to the well-muscled bay stallion, standing quietly, fox ears cocked. "What a fine animal! Must be sixteen hands high. Such a head, neck, and shoulders. Yes, and the short back and strong loin."

"He can pick 'em up and lay 'em down," Ben said. "Steel dust blood. He'll weigh close to twelve hundred pounds. Bought him in Kansas to build up my saddle stock."

Several Indians had drifted up, watching handsome horse-flesh as only Comanches do, worshiping, craving, and Ben saw the boy give a start of recognition.

"Quahadas," Sawyer explained. "Camped here to draw rations."

Ben shook hands and motioned the boy toward a blue-roan pony, purchased that morning from the fort sutler. They started to their mounts.

Without warning the boy broke free, running westward, before Ben could grab him. Ben started after him, burdened by his high-heeled boots and heavy Texas-style spurs. He had gone but a few rods when he felt a rowel rake across an instep. His feet tangled and he pitched into the dust. As he hit and rolled, he heard laughter from the cavalrymen and the Comanches, and the latter stung worst of all.

He knew his face was crimson as he sprang up furiously and paced to his horse, swung up, and spurred off at a run. Coming alongside, Ben saw the boy glance back and angle away, surprisingly fleet in the heavy brogans. Ben's mount, as if tailing a cow, cut with the motion, jumping out, and Ben reached down a scooping arm and lifted the squirming figure to the saddle. They started back in that fashion, the captive fighting like a wildcat.

"Boy," said Ben when he halted, "you will ride your pony, else I will tie you to the saddle!"

Drawing painful kicks on the shins, he hauled the boy closer, rump-tilted. Ben's flattened hand rose and fell, whapping, and unexpectedly the struggling ceased. Ben saw the tense mouth hinge down and a startled look spring the blue eyes wider.

"Two Strikes didn't whip me," the boy protested, with an eye on the watching Quahadas.

"He should have," Ben barked. "Made you respect your elders. And that wasn't any whipping. You got spanked." As quickly, he was relenting. He let the boy down. "Now it's a pretty day. Mount up, Jim Travis."

"Tehan!" The reply was tinged with insolence. Nevertheless, the boy went over and untied the pony's reins, and stepped around to the right side, the Indian side.

"Not that way!" Ben yelled. "He'll throw you sky high!"

True, as Levi Sawyer might have said, the pony shied and brushed against the hitching rack, and back, thereby making the mounting somewhat less difficult. But even as Ben saw his warning ignored, he wasn't expecting the catlike swiftness of the boy's climbing leap into the saddle.

Ben ate his chagrin in silence as the escort formed. At the last moment Sawyer held them up while he found a straw hat for the boy, then they rode off.

170

"Look how pony soldiers ride," Ben heard the young, jeering voice as the drab agency buildings fell behind on the sun-faded floor of the plain. "Bunched up—like buffalo calves—like cowards. All white men cowards."

A harsh retort rushed to Ben's lips, but he stifled it, sensing that mere rough words would never work on this wild boy. Too, he understood better now his reluctance of yesterday when Sawyer had said to take the boy. Right of blood, possession, was not enough. It was as if he traveled a strange and broken country, seeking a way through; it was out there somewhere, maybe close, yet it eluded him.

"The pony is yours," he said after a bit, laying no stress on his generosity. "Also the new saddle."

The blond head jerked, off guard, and, for a moment, Ben caught the small gleam of pleasure, rubbed out as the boy stiffened. "No *bueno* for hunting. White man's saddle make his back sore. No horse for Quahadas."

"Maybe so," Ben said, without affront. "But I've never seen a horse that Quahadas wouldn't steal."

"Only the brave steal horses."

"Brave," Ben acknowledged, "if you are Comanche. If you're white man, it is cowardly and you get hanged when caught."

"Me," said the boy, curling his lip, slapping his chest, "I am Quahada Comanche. No white man," and he spat into the brown prairie grass.

Red River lay southward. The day wore on slowly, into late afternoon.

It was then that Ben, looking back again, made out the familiar knot of toiling horsemen, and a feeling tapped, telling him they had never been far behind. Thereafter, they held a measured distance, varying little, biding, dogging, always there.

"You look back," the scornful voice broke in. "You afraid of white men?"

"I fought them once and there will be another fight soon. They want the wohaw gold I carry."

"So the coward pony soldiers will not help us?"

"They are going to Fort Richardson. On south. Tomorrow you and I will take another way—southwest—to our home on the Brazos."

The boy became thoughtful. "When the bad white men come, I will know how brave you are."

"You will need strong medicine—look!" There was an excited westward pointing. "Quahadas!"

It took some eye-burning and squinting for Ben to locate them, riding about parallel with the escort, using the low sun as a shield between them and the troopers. At that long distance it was hard to tell how many.

"Think they're coming for you, boy? Well, I'll fight them!"

He needed no spoken reply, for the blue glare alone told him what to expect.

Toward evening they forded the low, rust-colored river and made camp in a grove of whispering cottonwoods. The boy sat apart and stared his disdain at the pony soldiers performing the camp duties of squaws. During supper he wolfed down bacon and hard-bread like a Comanche, using his fingers, wiping them on his new cotton shirt. Ben flinched at the Indian camp manners and made a mental reminder for the future. Afterward, he saw the lad spread his blanket and turn his back in scorn on the circle of white men.

Light faded to purple darkness. Ben, having leather-hobbled his animals, made a restless turn of the camp and felt the damp breath of the river against his face and inside his soggy clothing. He marked the river bluffs, skylighted dimly, dark, low humps. And thus watching, scouting his gaze far left and right, he spotted something, high up. Sure as shooting, a small fire burned over there.

Indians or whites? *As if it makes any difference,* he thought, and turned back, a bitter twist on his mouth.

He came awake more on old instincts than from any intruding sound, yet not knowing why. It was still night, still quiet. Through the shuffling cottonwood tops he could see stars dappling the great moon-pale sky, feel cool wind rising off the scented Texas prairie. Beyond, hobbled horses and mules cropped the short grass. He stayed reared up on one elbow, vaguely disturbed; then, hearing nothing wrong, he relaxed and automatically looked for the boy. For a breath he went rigid and next he was up, springing, striding across the empty bed for the saddle stock.

Discovering the pony gave him a flash of relief, but the stallion was gone. As he paused, he heard the unevenness of a crow-hopping horse in the fooling darkness. He was off with the sound, his stocking feet noiseless. A moving clump appeared, a horse snorted. He lengthened stride and there he found them. The stallion, the small shape bent down, working at the leather hobbles, now jerking up.

"Boy!"

Ben grabbed and caught the arm-swinging figure and felt a rain of kicks and fists.

A picket ran up, carbine ready. "What's this?"

"Loose hobble," Ben said, not thinking, ashamed to admit what had happened, quieting the struggling boy by main force. "My son ran out and caught the stud. It's all right."

The walk back took the spark from Ben's anger, and he held himself carefully when he spoke. "There will be no more night-hawkin'. This tryin' to sneak off to Quahada country. You savvy that, boy?" he asked, hoping for an indication of obedience.

"My name—is Tehan."

Ben longed to shake him. Slowly an impulse deepened. Why not put him on his honor? "Will you give your word you won't run off again?" A silence took hold, a Comanche's scornful silence, Ben realized with a dull defeat. "Boy, you're plumb contrary. I'll have to tie you up rest of the night."

He looped his lariat around the skinny waist, tensed for a fight. Perversely, the boy sat like a post. Ben made a knot, lay down with the other end wrapped around his right wrist, and tried to think what he had done wrong since the first meeting in Sawyer's office. He thought of a captive deer he had seen as a boy in the

173

settlements, its graceful neck broken when it leaped high for freedom and struck the rail fencing. Was it right to pen a wild thing against its will?

Morning seemed to bring a change in the boys's manner, the night's humiliation forgotten, the arrogance gone. Had a lesson been learned? Ben wondered, the thought lingering after breakfast as he finished saddling.

He saw the boy measure him with a calculating look—and slip to the right side of the pony. It went wall-eyed and Ben shouted, "The other side!" He was surprised and not surprised. Contrariness! But, again, Ben hadn't counted on the boy's lithe quickness. In close, one hand clutching the pony's mane, he was already swinging into the saddle.

It was a pretty piece of riding, Comanche style. Ben read as much in the troopers' amused expressions, and a grudging pride lifted inside him, a feeling he smothered on intercepting the sidelong look of triumph behind the blue eyes.

Around noon they left the escort. For the first time, Ben allowed himself to consider that they were no longer followed. All through the morning he had sighted no pursuit. Had the white men and Quahadas figured he and the boy intended to go on with the troopers? Ben led off southwest, into a sun-blasted vastness of buffalo and grama grasses that rolled in massive folds across the deep country.

The boy looked miserable and a sympathy crept over Ben. When he spoke, he received only a mechanical nod or a grunt or a single word, low-spoken. Between them, now, he recognized a gap that kin blood might never close. The gap between Comanche and Texan, and that was a painful plenty. He gave up making talk. Meanwhile, the puzzle behind him increased. There was no sign. Neither had there been on the Cimarron until almost too late. Except there, he had picked off the lead rider, and the fleet steel dust horse had taken him out of danger. Today the light pony, not conditioned for hard riding, was lagging. Its jaded trot set the pace.

It was far into the afternoon when they entered choppy country, patched with gnarled mesquite, here and there a bony ridge and shallow canyon.

Ben dragged out the Spencer, scowled at the hiding ridges, and rode ahead, the boy trailing. They crossed the dry bed of a small creek. Not many rods on Ben drew rein, every sense keyed high. He turned in the saddle. "Boy, you hear anything?" There was no answer and Ben was about to go ahead, when the boy made a throaty noise. Something ran quickly across his face. "Horses—on rocks —."

Now Ben heard it. Horses running. The ring of metal shoes on stone. Close ahead. He waved the boy back. The pony switched tiredly around, balking, and Ben used his quirt. They went hard until Ben, alongside, motioned up the twisting creek bed. As they turned, he looked back and saw the three white men. Onward, he pulled up in a willow clump and heard the clattering pursuit pause. A bitter knowledge came. No reckless rush. They'd use caution this time. He knew them! Despite that, he had let himself be circled while the pony lagged. So he figured there was time left him. He rode to thicker cover, his decision building as he dismounted and faced around. "Boy, you stay with the horses —."

He saw the slim face, already flushed with excitement, go tense. The questioning eyes fastened on Ben's lariat.

Ben shook his head. "No more of that. Listen, boy. When the shooting starts, you get on my horse. Be careful to mount him on the white man's side. If you see the white men coming, ride fast. Circle around. Find the pony soldiers. Be ready—watch sharp ... It's either that—" Ben left it unspoken, unfinished. "You savvy, boy? he said thickly, rougher than he intended, and saw the jerky nod. Ben kept looking at him, marking the features on his memory. Kin or not, could you cage a wild thing? Without another word he handed the stallion's reins to the boy and swung back, thinking they had come this far and still neither knew the other. Each a stranger, blindfolded.

175

He found concealment in a stand of willows. In the long-running stillness, he missed having the alert boy beside him, and as the uneasy silence hung on he found his mind split between them and concern for the boy.

It was too quiet.

When the first shot slammed, he was caught looking down creek. He jerked at the crack of sound, flattening, in surprise. A patch of powder-smoke rose above the wooded ridge across the creek. He placed a bullet below it and crawled deeper into the willows. As yet, there was no stir along the creek. And now the rifleman commenced a rapid shooting. Ben held his fire. After a time, he decided the marksmanship was more bothersome than dangerous. Did it mean he was being circled again?

He spotted them, then, spaced like infantry skirmishers, bent over, advancing through the scrawny mesquite that studded the slopes rising above the creek channel. He became quite still. The rifle on the ridge crashed again, searching the willows. He ignored it.

Possibly they were too confident, made bold by superior numbers and the covering fire. Ben let them come on until he could see the nondescript faces clearly. Both seemed to locate him at the same instant, in etched astonishment. Ben faced them instead of turning toward the ridge, unsuspecting.

His first bullet knocked the foremost man to the ground. The other, dodging, made a snap shot, a panicky shot, and fell. He jerked up, hurt, shocked eyes bulging fear, and went scrabbling back into the mesquite, pulling one leg after him.

Ben lowered the short gun, aware of an extraordinary stillness. His ears were ringing. He tasted powder-smoke. He waited and presently heard boots slamming down the ridge, and after a while he picked up the shuffle of horses going off north. These sounds faded. He reloaded the tubular magazine in the butt stock of the carbine with fat, copper-cased cartridges, and glanced up. The man lay where he had fallen.

Ben got to his feet, a gray revulsion striking through him. He walked heavily, in dread. It seemed longer to the pony than he remembered. It was there, tied. He had expected that and moved on. Nowhere did he see or hear the steel dust horse, and again he was not surprised. Yet, when he walked ahead and stopped, everything rose up to hurt him. The worn-out, searching years, even the finding.

He was standing still, indecisively, when he sensed he was not alone.

"Look—quick—look!" It was a young voice shrill with alarm.

Ben wheeled to see a coppery shape stepping from behind a mesquite, very near. The Indian's bullet was so close Ben felt the rifle's breath hot on his face just before he fired and the Indian fell.

Ben was no longer interested in the Indian. He was jerking to the sound of horses running down the slope. He saw them through an opening in the mesquite, coming like the wind. Several Quahadas, led by an Indian on a paint horse. Somewhere the steel dust horse was trumpeting.

Ben got ready. At that moment, the boy materialized between him and the Quahadas. Ben checked himself, afraid to fire, expecting the Comanches to scoop up the boy. Instead, they swept past him for the creek-bank willows. In there, Ben saw, moving dimly, whickering, making the branches shake, was the picketed stallion.

Ben could shoot now. One man fell forward abruptly and held on to the neck of his pony. The rest milled in confusion at the firing behind them, whirled, and, hanging low on their horses, dashed to the creek bed and down it as Ben continued to shoot. Something told him they wouldn't come back, for the horse-stealing party was already a failure. One warrior lay here and another was wounded.

Ben eyed the fallen Comanche before he spoke. "Two Strikes?"

"He got away," the boy said, shaking his head. "He was on the paint."

"Why didn't you take the horse, boy?" Ben asked curiously,

his bewilderment growing. "The way was open—clear to Quahada country. Else go with them? You—just a boy—a mighty horse-stealer?"

The blue eyes avoided his. "Quahadas wanted the big horse—not me. You saw them."

"Leastwise they didn't kill you."

"They have thrown me away." The boy seemed more puzzled than angry.

Ben watched him, considering. A thought caught, flashed. "But you warned me *before* they made their rush. You didn't know they wanted the big horse. Why, boy—why?"

Despair and maybe the old arrogance—Ben awaited both. Neither came. The blue eyes fixed him straight and there was the beginning of an expression he couldn't define unless it was pride. Comanche pride.

"You gave me the big horse," the boy said, in an awed tone that was new to Ben. He came in a step, his eyes enlarging. "You went back. You fought brave—so I could get away. My white father is very brave. My heart is glad."

Ben saw the dark face change, saw it twist, crumbling, as the boy ran toward him.

CHAPTER TEN

THE MIDDLE

THE MIDDLE, WELL DONE, is approximately twice the length of the beginning and is divided into two parts. In the first part, the devices of the beginning may be repeated and enlarged. Character is developed. If the gimmick was not introduced before, it must be brought in here. The story behind the story must be told, either in full, or woven in as the natural thoughts of the main character. Your main character attempts to solve his problem, but he does so with the same character flaw which caused it to materialize in the first place. Therefore his attempt merely gets him into deeper water.

The problem, as the main character works toward the solution, gets worse. If he gains one step, he slides back two. If his problem is facing up to a bully, and he solves it with the don't-look-now-and-maybe-it-will-go-away method, the result is greater peril and more obnoxious bullying. A new complication arises—perhaps more than one—and it is always an intensification of the dramatic problem.

If you are creating a sympathetic character, he yearns to do the right thing, but either he has no idea what it is, or the circumstances about him are more than he can manage.

In the second part of the middle, the main crisis arises. Either circumstances or the antagonist gains the upper hand. Your main character is backed into a corner where he must fight for his life. He is narrowed to two choices and can see only illusion. If he is willing to hurt someone he loves, it appears that he can solve the problem he has been struggling with in a way that brings him his wish. If, however, he refuses to hurt the one he loves, the only answer left for him is complete loss.

This is not a conscious thing or an act of the intellect. Remember that in earlier chapters of this book you were told of two levels for readers: the feeling level and the thinking level. Your viewpoint character has these levels, also. When he is caught up high with feeling, his mind is no longer directing his actions. If you have a strong character who chooses right, he automatically chooses death for himself, life for those he loves. He acts selflessly with complete disregard for his personal welfare.

The middle, then, is a series of ups and downs. John Gallishaw called them furtherances and hindrances. Your complications arise. One scene leads into another with increasing conflict and less hope for the main character to solve his problem. You use color, repetition, dialogue at cross-purposes, plausibility devices, implication, and discovery and reversal. Actions reveal true desires of characters while words tend to "cover up" or be used as a mask.

Hold your scenes together with the glue of transitions, incidents, or psychological characterizations. Watch to create a continuity of interest and rising suspense. See that your emotion flows logically, occurring with proper stimulus, rising to its natural peak, and then ebbing unless some logical fact changes its flow.

Remember that both fiction and general nonfiction are a vacation for the reader. If your reader wants to study, he will go to texts. Then you must write so that the feeling carries your reader along and the mind can accept the facts. Build with skill.

Your middle should rise like a flight of stairs. In the beginning, you asked the dramatic question. Heighten and tighten your reader's interest by arranging facts and scenes along the line of ascending tension. Each step of the stairs should intensify the question. Play back and forth with opposites: courage against fear, hope against despair, love against hate or self-centeredness, ambition against indolence, loyalty against pride.

Let us look at some techniques of the middle:

1. *Character.*

The test of your writing is creating the illusion of believable characters. For the purposes of short copy use two traits, a dominant trait and a weak or negative trait (the one which grows, if your story is a forward, positive story, from weakness into strength). In "Comanche Son" the viewpoint character, Ben, shows these traits: dominant trait—strong-willed; negative trait dependence upon force. (This latter characteristic is often good, but in the instance of keeping his son, his victory came when he refused to use it.)

The emotions are tied to the character traits—the happy ones with the strong trait, the fearful ones to the weak trait. Look at Welty Lockhart in "Showdown at San Saba": dominant trait—courage; negative trait—presumption.

Welty is filled with ideals and dreams of the day when he will be a man, and when his father fails—according to his understanding—he presumes to act. Go through the story and mark the emotions, showing which tie to the strong trait and which are the result of the weak trait. Take two colored pencils, and use one color for marking each. It will be easy, then, to see how Welty's presumption brought him into the situation which created trouble.

Or take Gloria in "The Most Important Man in Town": dominant trait—a beauty who uses her brains; negative trait—desires to have her own way. No one, especially a pretty girl, wants to say, "Notice me." Her action must therefore be indirect. She chases out to tell Charleyhorse to get off the grass. Her actions follow negative trait, while she tries to fit her words to the dominant one. Is she serious? Watch her actions:

"Dave reached for his blackjack pocket. But Gloria got there about then and stepped in front of Dave so she could yell . . . ."

The writer does not tell that the womanly instinct in Gloria is protecting the man she is about to scold, but he *shows* it. And because it is correct, our subconscious, feeling mind sees and approves. Remember, we hide behind words, but our actions give us away. Using these things helps to create the life illusion. When you finish a story your main character will have grown up somewhat and learned more about life—his weak trait becoming a new, positive force within him. As a writer you play a dual role: you see the problem and know the remedy, and that it lies not on outside events but within the troubled soul.

Much of your main character's troubles are due to his own inertias, but he does not know this. You, the writer, do. You see him as both weak and strong; you know that he is weak when he follows the minus characteristic that lives out on the periphery of his being and has yet to be looped through the soul of strength in his inner man. The outside circumstances that he sees are frightening and confuse him, and it is his desire to rise above these problems that is the first half of your story.

2. *Gimmick.*

Every story must turn. If the editor tells you that your story is too predictable, it means that you have been traveling in a straight line. And we can always see down the center of the road. But we cannot see around the corners! A gimmick helps your story to pivot. The gimmick is usually an object, although it can be a phrase, a smell, or anything that holds an emotional memory. In his Pulitzer-prize-winning biography *The Raven*, Marquis James used a ring as a gimmick. In "Violets from Portugal," Helene Carpenter's gimmick was an object, the red kitchen curtains. A phrase was the gimmick in Ed Montgomery's story "The Most Important Man in Town"—"For so long as the grass shall grow and the rivers shall flow . . . ."

Identify the gimmicks in the other stories in this book. Follow the author's treatment throughout, and see how it adds clarity and aids the turn.

3. *The flashback.*

This is the trick that beginners usually love—for they write a few lines and then launch into a long discussion of what had happened so that the reader may understand what is going to happen. To use it in this way is sure death to a story. It belongs in the middle of the story, only after the reader's interest is secure, and then it must be handled with skill.

Note the use of the flashback in "The Preacher's Confession":

> That name cleared things up like a lightning flash on a dark night. All over Tennessee, Kentucky, and even as far west as Missoury, Brother Calhoun was known as a powerful preacher. When he stood up in the pulpit, the devil took to the tall timber.
>
> . . . Tom called to mind what gran'pap had said the day he laid the fiddle in his hands.
>
> "It takes an honest man to be a good fiddler, son. She won't answer true to a liar or a thief. She'll keep you straight if you've got the ear to listen." And it was the truth. Whenever he got out of line, the way a young buck will, he couldn't play for sour apples till he'd straightened things out.

Or the flashback can be woven throughout the story. Bill Scott, Mary Agnes Thompson, and Helene Carpenter used it in this way.

4. *The complication.*

Other things being equal, the more difficult your complications, the more interesting your story. As your main character tries to solve his problem, one or more complications should arise. Again consider "The Preacher's Confession":

Tom's main problem was to win the girl. This created the difficulty of winning the father's consent, which meant giving up the fiddle, or what was seemingly impossible, winning the father's approval of the fiddle.

For the complications in your story, ask yourself: what rising out of the weak character trait of my main character could be the worst possible situation for him? This is your complication. To create the next complication, again ask yourself: what is the worst thing that could happen now? This way you back your main character into a corner.

Interest rises as danger increases. It rises with the deepening of emotion, the dread of what may occur. The most exciting events can stir no interest unless they are told in a manner that creates suspense. Fear photographs the danger, stirs a question concerning it. However, you cannot arouse your reader from interest to dread with one jump. You first stir his curiosity, lead his interest upward until it increases to concern. Well handled, concern can lead into anxiety; from there you may lift the reader into apprehension and finally to dread.

The complication must be presented to your reader in those parts of your story which must be told in scenes. The rest of your material may be summed up in incidents, narrative, etc. But that which stirs your reader's emotions must happen before his mind's eye.

Even in your scenes build this tension. That which pulls your main character toward his goal and happiness is a furtherance; that which blocks him is a hindrance. The main character must struggle to attain, the antagonist must strive for his own purpose, and this creates a block.

This playing back and forth creates the conflict. Your scenes become interesting when you set up situations from which your characters tumble from one complication into the next. Notice how it is done in this scene from "Stubborn Bride":

Furtherance	They went inside and slid into a booth. After a while a dark-haired girl sauntered over. She stared at Frank, then tilted her head back and laughed. "Frankie Palcoucek!" She slapped him
Hindrance	on the shoulder with familiar hilarity. "Look at the looie bars! I figured you'd get kicked out and have to come home!"
Hindrance	Frank wished she'd drop that Frankie stuff. He could feel a tinge of color working up over his neck. When he'd been a kid the other boys always made fun of him because he reddened when he got angry. "Hello, Suzy." He made
Furtherance	his voice easy and finally flashed a smile at her. "Nope, I'm not kicked out. I see you're still around driving the fellows crazy."
Hindrance	"Oh, just dancing my head off, sure." Suzy watched him boldly. "I'll bet this is What's-

184

Furtherance

Hindrance

Hindrance

Furtherance

Hindrance

Her-Name. Your old man said you were bringing her home."

"This is Linda Raeburn. Linda, this is Suzy Hrubeck, an old friend of mine."

"Friend is right," Suzy raised her eyebrows coyly. "Say, you got here just in time for the kolach festival. It's tomorrow, remember?"

"Kolach festival!" Frank groaned and rubbed his hand across his forehead. "Well, you'll be up to your ears in Czecks, Linda, that's for sure."

They drank the beers, and Suzy followed them to the door. Linda got into the car. She was nervous to the point of silence. It was at times like this that she retreated so far within herself that Frank hardly knew what to say to her.

Such a pattern as this helps scenes to keep conflict and interest. Name your right foot "furtherance" and your left foot "hindrance," and watch how the use of both of them moves you forward. Use this pattern in your stories and your scenes will leap to life.

5. *Transitions.*

It is impossible to show every detail of a story in scenes. Moreover, if you did, you would lose your story in its clutter of detail. You must move your main character quickly from one scene of action to the next, at the same time showing the proper time element.

In making your time transition, keep the emotional element: "So my father put the warrant back in his pocket and told Charleyhorse he'd come by his rooming house and arrest him in the morning, if that was all right. So we did." Or carry the transition forward on a stream of emotion: " 'But we must wait until morning.' Time dragged by."

Go through the stories in this book and mark the transitions between scenes.

6. *Crisis.*

This is your big scene, the one for which all the rest is merely a build-up. You may have caught a glimpse of this scene idea when you decided upon your story. It is quite possible that you have gone back in your mind—as many writers do—and recalled a time when you were baffled about a problem. You knew you would do the right thing, if you only knew what it was. The difficulty is knowing. One minute one way looked like the right answer, but the next minute there seemed to be just as much reason for moving the opposite way. You felt the age-old cry: if I only knew what to do.

This is the point where your main character finds himself. He has the desire to do the right thing, but he wants to do it the right way. Take Tom in "The Preacher's Confession." He has had complication lead into complication and now is at the bottom of the pit—there is no apparent way out.

> The third night there was the biggest crowd ever seen at Crooked Elbow Meetinghouse. The little old in-opening door was propped back with a hickory chunk long before sundown, and late-comers stood in ranks at the back. Even at that there was plenty of room made for Tom when he came in with his fiddle. He took a seat near the front, and the next man on the bench gave him space for his fiddle by moving clear to the back. Across the aisle and around the massive bulk of the Widow Barton, Tom saw Sara Bell. Her face was white and tired-looking, and the little smile she managed for him hurt worse than tears. The ache he felt to take her in his arms was the ache of swamp fever that works on a man's bone marrow.
>
> Brother Calhoun stood up behind the pulpit and the tension came up the way the turn of a peg tightens a E string. He shook his white hair back like a banner and there was a pride and confidence in the way he gave out the hymns that made Tom uneasy. Palm-leaf fans were waving all around and Tom took out his silk handkerchief to wipe the sweat from his forehead. Folded into it was Sara Bell's little white handkerchief. The smell of the lemon verbena made him feel better, but, still and all, he had a queer sensation in his middle as he used to before a wrestling match or a fiddlers' contest.

186

All of a sudden there came a stir at the back of the room and everybody turned around to look. Through the little in-opening door marched four exhorters, each carrying a load of firewood. They made their way through the crowded aisles and laid a fire on the bed of last winter's ashes that hadn't been cleaned out since Christmas exercises. They laid it from kindling to top log and then Brother Calhoun lighted it from his tinderbox. The tinderbox. The congregation buzzed with questions, but Tom didn't ask a one. He was recollecting the dream he had down by the creek, and the sick feeling in his middle ran all up and down his body and he could have sworn the fiddle moaned in the case beside him.

"I've kindled an altar fire," Brother Calhoun shouted, "an altar fire where you can burn your sins away and start a new life! Are you strong enough to do it? You are if you have love! Love will make you strong! Love —."

And he preached on love. Love that fills a man's life and lets him do the impossible. Love that will not let a man go. As the flames mounted, his voice mounted till it rang like a bell and filled the meetinghouse with sound that matched the fire for intensity. Tom knew it was divine love Brother Calhoun meant, but to him love and Sara Bell were the same. Could he lay his fiddle in those searing, twisting flames for her? Could he?

The struggle in him was so strong he hardly noticed when Lije Johnson stumbled up the aisle and flung a demijohn into the fireplace. The jug cracked and the rank smell of green whisky sizzling on the stones filled the room. Jamey Munger tossed in a deck of cards that whirled up the chimney in the strong updraft in one last gambler's fan. "Glory! Glory!" the exhorters chanted. Amaryllis Bedford, the vainest woman in Greenbrier County, threw in a red satin carriage cloak and screamed in ecstasy as it caught fire. Old Lady Parsons started jerking like she was pulled by strings. The line at the mourners' bench swayed back and forth. Brother Calhoun leaned across the pulpit and pleaded with Tom, sweat pouring down his face, "Give in—now! Do it now! Burn your sins away! Put them on the altar now—now—now!"

Tom didn't hear him. The chant of "Glory, glory, glory!" beat up through the floor and through his body. Over it all, like another chant, he heard Sara Bell's voice saying, " . . . love—I love you, Tom —I love you."

Suddenly he was standing in the aisle. The fiddle weighed like an anvil in his hand. He wanted to hurry, but he moved like a man with his feet hobbled. Somehow he got to the fireplace. The fierce heat smote him and made him wince. Not for himself, but for the fiddle—the fiddle. For an agonized minute he opened the case and looked at the sweet curved brown body that had been his more than any woman would ever be his. Tears scalded his eyes. He snapped the case shut and laid it on the top log.

Brother Calhoun's arm was heavy on his shoulders. The meeting-house rocked with shouting, "Glory, glory, hallelujah! Glory!" This was the moment when happiness should come to him in a great, rushing wave. Numb with the thing he had done, he waited. Nothing happened. All at once he wanted to run and hide. The smell of scorching leather sickened him. He looked for Sara Bell, but the bulk of the Widow Barton cut her off. Men wrung his hands, women hugged him, Brother Calhoun pounded his shoulders joyfully but he never felt so alone in his life. The fiddle—Sara Bell—the fiddle.

At last your main character has nowhere to go. He must face the thing that he does not like: turning back within himself. This is irksome. It brings discipline that the untrained would forever dodge. The child rebels and the wild colt hates the tedium of obedience. In spite of that, as children we have looked up to "men of honor" and those of "good breeding," and now and then we hear talk of men who can be trusted in a crisis. What do we mean by that? Who are men of honor?

As writers, it dawns upon us slowly that when men charge life with a bit in their teeth, they meet with violence. And violence attracts violence; so do weakness and inertia. It is when man retreats within, inviting the discipline of that inward man where there is no ignorance, that he reaches the place of safety. That is where men of honor arise, and the men who can be depended upon in a crisis come forth.

But this process is not a mental one. This inward man lives deep within the feeling zone and acts from the subconscious. The crisis is the moment when "He who loses his life shall save it!" (When you are writing a biography, if you study your characters, you will find it true that your main character rises to new heights during the moments of crisis.)

7. *The sacrifice.*

Your main character is now caught up high in feeling with regard to his personal problem. He is in a corner where he must fight for his life, and there is illusion in what he can see. It must be apparent to him and to the reader that his problem can be solved in a way that gives him his desire, if he is willing to hurt someone he loves, if he is willing to travel roughshod over others. If, however, he refuses to hurt others, the only personal answer which he can hope to attain is complete loss.

When your story is a minus story, it is because your main character is so self-centered that he cannot risk the loss. If, however, he forgets himself in order to help those in need, the story takes another turn. Suppose we again follow Tom in "The Preacher's Confession." He does not act from a conscious level; he is not guided by his thinking mind or his intellect. Your viewpoint character is caught up now in the feeling level. His mind no longer directs his actions, beyond seeing the need and responding to the need of the whole as the situation demands. He forgets that he is automatically choosing death for himself in concern for the life of those he loves. Feeling causes him to act selflessly, with complete disregard for his personal welfare:

> From outside the meetinghouse came a high-pitched whinny of terror. Another and another. Then the sound of rearing horses and splintering riggs. The shouting of the congregation wavered, broke off. Half of them were crowding toward the back with the terrible sense of what had happened, before Ed Thatcher yelled through the door, "Get out evvabody! Soot in the chimney! Roof's afire!"
>
> They went crazy. They went wild, screaming crazy. Tom saw it happen. Ten men—maybe fifteen—got out through the little in-opening door before the hickory chunk that held it open was kicked away and the door pushed solidly shut by the heaving, fighting wall of flesh behind it. Those at the door hammered and clawed in vain. the ones behind fought toward them, jamming the door tighter and tighter. Tom saw Miss Sukey Tolliver go down and heard her

scream as a boot heel bit into her flesh. Sara Bell—Sara Bell—. He fought his way to where she clung to the edge of the pulpit. With his body he tried to screen her from the frantic congregation surging for the jammed door.

"Save us, preacher, save us!" a woman shrilled. "We'll be roasted alive!"

Tom saw Brother Calhoun on his knees, his head thrown back, his lips moving; then a wave of thick smoke cut off the sight. Men piled up benches to try to reach the little windows, but they were too high. Men battered at the log walls, but Crooked Elbow was built to stand siege.

"Tom," Sara Bell sobbed, "you shouldn't have done it! You shouldn't have burned the fiddle! I tried to get to you, but I couldn't! Not the fiddle!"

The fiddle! It was like a strong hand had touched him on the shoulder. That was it! The fiddle. "Stay here, Sara Bell; hold tight." He put her arms around the pulpit and started for the fireplace. He pushed and shoved and struck without mercy. On the top log, the fiddle case lay, still smoldering. He jerked it off and beat at the coals with his bare hands. He didn't even feel the metal clasps burn into his flesh as he opened the case. Inside lay the fiddle, calm, serene, unafraid. He put it to his chin and pulled the bow across it in a great surge of joy. Out of tune, but no matter, they were together again.

"Here! Up here!" It was Sara Bell calling over the weeping, praying throng around the pulpit. He made his way back to her and she boosted him up on the pulpit top. He never stopped to wonder how she knew what was in his mind. He felt her hands steady his ankles as he strove to keep his balance and endure the heat and the smoke.

Then he swung out with "Lancers." Jingling, teasing, laughing, it poured from the fiddle and caught the crazed people of Crooked Elbow congregation and reminded them of something. Then he went into "Old Dan Tucker," and felt the fear loosen up. Most of 'em had been dandled on their gran'paps' knees to that tune. He began to sing out calls, "Chase the chicken, chase the squirrel, chase that pretty girl 'round the world." He coughed from the smoke, but they heard—heard and remembered. "Take your lady with a grapevine twist!" They were moving back a little. He could tell by the drift of the smoke that the door had opencd a crack.

"Look at me, I'm down and busted; in Old Hamilton's bank I trusted!" That got a laugh—it always did in Andy Jackson's country. Tom knew it was all right. If folks can laugh, they can act sensible.

He could hear the crackle of the flames on the roof now, but the door was opening in. As folks came back under the spell of the fiddle, it suddenly came full open. They went pouring outside, like sand down a rat hole, but not pushing, not shoving. He hurried them along with "Portland Fancy," a tune he'd picked up from a Maine man selling tinware. As the last ones made it out, he jumped from the pulpit and with Sara Bell under one arm and the fiddle under the other, cleared the threshold as the hot sparks began to shower down.

They reached the clearing with the rest of the congregation, but they weren't much more than there before the roof crashed in and flames shot up to the night sky and dimmed the stars. Crooked Elbow that had been a refuge for more than forty years was gone in less than that many minutes.

This, then, is the sacrifice—the selfless part. You will find it in the forward-plotted story. It is this power to be selfless in a moment of crisis that turns your main character from an ordinary person into a hero.

Naturally, he does not stop to think, "Now, I am going to be noble." He does not think of himself at all; if he did, he could not be selfless. All he does is see the need and act in the direction in which it leads.

A student expressed the same thing this way: "The self exists; so also does the Self. In the dark moment, if his act is sacrificial, the Self has acted. Leading up to that moment, as the conflict rages, the self is in command.

"The self is the gross flesh that hems us in. The gross flesh, human thought, conflicting emotions; these are the things of which the self is built. The individual self is a composite of all that the individual has ever thought or felt or done. This self looks out at the world. What it sees is colored by its previous experience—how it has met conflict in the past; whether character has been built or destroyed.

"But the Self is that ineffable, a priori wisdom—that which is known without learning. The Self is the divine universal in man. By the exfoliation of i, I appears. Usually this is a slow, gradual process—if it takes place in the individual at all. But in the dark moment many otherwise unextraordinary individuals experience a sudden and blinding break-through of the Self. These are our moments of greatness."

The deeper truth of emotional growth is that emotional knowledge, when correct, demands that one feel from some other standpoint than the personal in one's relationship to the world. Moreover, the greater the circle for which one feels, the deeper the understanding one's emotions can give him. We grow from the small to the large when our feeling is set free from its self-relationship and works for the good of the whole.

You have had your own moments of giving up the personal, small element for the good of the whole, and gained new knowledge through that experience. In these moments you have seen new truths which you alone can share with the world. Out of such clay, you can mold the gems of your stories.

Go through the stories in this book and locate each sacrifice and see how the sacrifice aided the solution of the problem.

by Ed Montgomery

M ISTLETOE CORNERS was just sitting there in the late May sun, minding its own business, the day Charleyhorse came home from school in a 1946 convertible. He drove all around the square at about ten miles an hour more than the law allows and parked in front of a sign that said not to park there. Our whole family happened to be watching him from the second floor of the court-house.

"Gee!" I said. "Charleyhorse Horse!" You see, he hadn't come home at all the summer before, just roughnecked in the oil fields, so this was the first time I'd seen him since before he made two All-American teams as a sophomore and threw three touchdown passes in the Texas game alone.

"The answer to a prayer!" said my father, who manages the Mistletoe Corners Mudcats and is the sheriff of Chickamasia County on the side. He knew that if Charleyhorse would stay around and play shortstop all summer, it would mean a big differ-ence in the final standings of the Cherokee Valley League.

"He hasn't changed much," said my big sister Gloria, frown-ing. My sister is assistant county attorney, and death on lawless-ness.

"Keep your shirt on," said my father. "Parkin' violations are a city problem."

"I know," Gloria said grimly. "But right now he's destroying county property."

Actually, all Charleyhorse was doing was that he'd walked across the street to the courthouse lawn and was sitting on the grass under an elm tree.

193

"He is not destroyin' county property," my father said. "You can't destroy that old Bermuda grass just sittin' on it. Why, you can't destroy it with a grubbin' hoe!"

"At the very least," Gloria said, "he's trespassing."

"Now you leave him alone, Gloria," my father ordered. "We got us a game comin' up with Antelope City this Sunday and I'll need that boy in there. . . . Buster, you run down there and tell him to get that car out of there before he gets in trouble."

Gloria had already stomped out of there, but I skipped past her before she got as far down the hall as the county clerk's office. Only Dave Dolan got to Charleyhorse before I did.

Dave is chief of police. As a matter of fact, he's the whole city police force, except for Arnie Jenkins, who is the night chief of police.

"Charleyhorse," Dave was saying, "you quit that parkin' in my no-parkin' zones."

Charleyhorse was lying back with his hands behind his head, resting. He opened his eyes and looked at Dave, who is so big he has to weigh on the cotton-gin scales, and probably would have been an All-American himself if somebody had caught him twenty years ago and made him go to school.

"Hah!" Charleyhorse said to Dave, and shut his eyes again.

"Now you listen here!" Dave reached for his blackjack pocket. But Gloria got there about then and stepped in front of Dave so she could yell down at Charleyhorse better.

"Charleyhorse Horse!" she yelled. "You get up from there!"

Charleyhorse sat up. He took his shoes off, tied the laces together, and hung them over the sign that said you were supposed to keep off the grass.

"Hah!" he said. Then he eased his shoulders back onto the grass, wiggled his toes, and shut his eyes again.

Now my sister Gloria wasn't used to having criminals talk to her like that. What's more, she wasn't used to having people close their eyes when she was there. I guess you know she was Miss Mistletoe Corners of 1951 and would likely have been Miss

Oklahoma and maybe Miss America if she could have worn the bathing suit she picked out, instead of the one my father picked out.

At first she was so mad she couldn't talk; then, just when she got her tongue working, Dave spoke up.

"Forgot my blackjack," he said. "I'll be right back, Charleyhorse. You stay right there."

"He will not stay right there!" Gloria yelled after him. "He'll get up right this instant and get off the county's grass!"

Charleyhorse put his arms over his eyes to keep the sun out. "Why will I get off the county's grass?"

"Because you're breaking the law every second you stay on it, that's why."

By then my father couldn't stand to watch out the window and not know what was going on any longer. Here he came walking across the lawn in his high-heeled boots.

Charleyhorse sighed and got up. "Young lady," he said, "you are speaking to a practically full-blooded member of the Chickamasia Indian tribe."

"Charleyhorse," my father said hopefully, "how would it be if you found some nice green grass someplace else to rest on?"

"There isn't any," I said. "To speak of." Nobody paid any attention—hardly anybody ever does when you're eleven years old —but I was right. This was the third year of the drought and most all the grass had dried up.

"I don't care if I'm speaking to the last of the Mohicans," Gloria said. "I'm going in right now and draw up the charges."

"Now, Gloria" my father said, "let's wait and reexamine this issue Monday mornin'. That Antelope City game —."

Charleyhorse sat up straighter and crossed his arms. "Not just a member either," he said. "The chief."

"Congratulations," Gloria said.

"Duly elected," Charleyhorse said. "Comin' home I stopped by my uncle's house, out in Okfuskee County, and me and him and my cousin held us a council and I got elected chief. We had a quorum 'cause that's all of us Chickamasias there is left, except my two cousins that went to California to work in an aircraft plant before the war and never came back."

My big sister looked suspicious. "What have you been doing down there at the university," she asked, "besides playing football?"

"Studyin' law."

Gloria pursed her lips thoughtfully.

"With a good, strong minor in history," Charleyhorse said.

Gloria turned away. "I'll be back," she said over her shoulder. My father went after her, talking fast.

Charleyhorse grinned at me. "Hi, Buster," he said. "Some gal!"

"Edgar Ransom's gone fishing in Colorado," I explained. "That makes Gloria acting attorney, and she takes it real serious."

"I take her serious too," Charleyhorse said. "Only don't tell her I said so."

"I won't."

"I saw her at a football game last fall." Charleyhorse reached around and got his shoes and started putting them on. "She was with Ernie Freeman."

"He's still comin' around," I said. Ernie was a state senator and one of these brilliant young lawyers, and people said around the courthouse he'd be governor someday. But if they let you vote on who would be your brother-in-law, he'd never carry my precinct.

"Here comes ol' Dave back with his blackjack," Charleyhorse said. "Let's ease out of here."

We got his car and went down to that big hole on the river below the red bluff and took a couple of channel catfish off a trotline I had there. Then we took a swim, and didn't get back to the courthouse until just about quitting time. Gloria was sitting in the county attorney's office, drawing up a paper charging Charleyhorse with trespassing.

"I've looked up one side of the revised statutes and down the other," she said happily, "and the law makes no exception for members of the Chickamasia tribe."

"What about the Treaty of Horseshoe Bend?" Charleyhorse asked.

Gloria leaned back in her chair and crossed her arms. "What about it?" she asked cautiously.

"I'm not through that law course yet," Charleyhorse said, "but as far as I have gone, it looks to me like no state constitution or state law can run a reverse on a Federal treaty."

"Any nitwit knows that," Ernie Freeman said, behind us. "You'd think even a lady lawyer would know that, wouldn't you, Charley?"

He came on in and shook hands with Charleyhorse. He didn't pay any attention to me. I couldn't vote for another ten years.

Ernie was as big as Charleyhorse, and he'd been pretty near as good a running back when they played together on the Mistletoe Corners High School football team. Ernie and Gloria had finished college ahead of Charleyhorse because Charleyhorse had lost a couple of years fighting with the Forty-fifth Division in Korea.

"What you got against lady lawyers?" Charleyhorse asked him.

"I just don't like 'em. What I like are former lady lawyers."

Gloria took a deep breath and put her pen down. "Some of the finest lawyers in this country —." she started.

"Name one," Ernie said. "Women are wonderful, but they just don't have the legal mind." He turned to Charleyhorse.

"What about the Treaty of Horseshoe Bend?" he asked. "Sounds interesting."

"It is interestin'," Charleyhorse said. He grinned at everybody and went out.

Gloria slowly opened a drawer and put the trespassing charges in it.

"Cold feet?" Ernie asked.

Ernie laughed. Overbearing, that's what he was. I'd just looked that word up in the dictionary the day before, and that's what he was.

Gloria got up and went to look for some lawbooks. "Don't fall down the stairs on your way out," she said.

Ernie laughed again. "I was just about to ask you to drive over to Tulsa to a movie tonight," he said.

"And if you do fall down the steps on your way out," Gloria said, "try to fall quietly."

She didn't come home till late that night. And the next morning she made some calls to Washington and one to the state attorney general and several to lawyers she knew around the state. Just before noon she came into the jail, where I was watching my father play cassino with an armed-robbery suspect and a man awaiting trial on a charge of larceny of domestic animals.

We went into the sheriff's office and she told us about it. Now you never hear much about the Chickamasia tribe, even around here. Seems like they were a real small tribe, and finally they got the Cherokees to adopt them so they'd have somebody to talk for them to the Great White Father and the other Indians.

But the Chickamasias were a going concern in 1854 when Chief Running Horse and the government negotiated the Treaty of Horseshoe Bend. The Indians gave up part of their lands, including all of what is now Chickamasia County and a little bit of the counties north and east of here. Gloria didn't find out what the government needed the land for. She said it was immaterial and not at issue.

The Chickamasia Nation got money and some more land farther west and some conditions. One of the conditions was that the white man's laws would not apply in the tract the Indians were giving up, so long as the rivers should flow and the grass should grow.

"That was because the land the tribe had left was split by what they gave up," Gloria explained to us. "They'd need to be crossing the government tract to visit back and forth."

"Well," my father said, "it looks like he's got you, Gloria. Just as well too. I think Antelope City is goin' to go with that left-hander of theirs Sunday, and Charleyhorse always did hit him like he owned him."

"But this is ridiculous!" Gloria said.

198

"Now don't you worry about it, honey." My father patted Gloria on the shoulder. "You didn't negotiate that treaty. . . . Buster, let's find Charleyhorse and throw 'im some battin' practice. I'll pitch and you can shag 'em."

"Yes," Gloria said, and she had a glint in her eye and her fighting face on. "And when you find him you show him this warrant for his arrest."

"I—will—not."

"You will," Gloria said firmly, "or I'll go right to work this minute drawing ouster charges against you."

"You wouldn't do that," my father said unhappily. "I've got a family to support."

"And you can just start cooking your own supper, too," Gloria said, getting warmed up. "And making your own bed and doing the laundry, and I may get a grand jury petitioned and get you indicted for malfeasance of office, and that's a felony, and how'd you like to be down there in the pen with all the people you've sent down there?"

❀   ❀   ❀

So my father took the warrant and we found Charleyhorse fishing off the railroad bridge with a casting rod for crappie. He had quite a few minnows left, and my father said it would be sinful to let them go to waste. We helped Charleyhorse use up his live bait till almost dark, and by then it was too late to do anything, so my father put the warrant back in his pocket and told Charleyhorse he'd come by his rooming house and arrest him in the morning, if that was all right.

So we did, and they arraigned Charleyhorse in Judge Hunter's J.P. office over the bank. Charleyhorse pleaded not guilty and asked to have his preliminary trial the next day, so he could clear his name and get that out of the way in time to play against Antelope City on Sunday.

"All right," Judge Hunter said, taking out his watch and looking at it impatiently. "She's set for tomorrow. Court's dismissed."

"Judge," Charleyhorse said, "I wish you'd subpoena the Secretary of the Interior for me. I need him for an expert witness in this thing."

The judge said he wasn't sure whether you could subpeona a member of the President's Cabinet in a justice-of-the-peace court.

"I could look it up for you, Charleyhorse," he said, "but I know a place where the fox squirrels are just about to eat up a man's corn crop and I just hate to let 'em get away with it."

"Well, shucks, then," Charleyhorse said, "just skip it." And he went home and got his rifle, and him and the judge went squirrel hunting.

       ❋   ❋   ❋

Word got around town, and there was a pretty good crowd in and around Judge Hunter's office the next afternoon when Charleyhorse and I got there. The judge counted the house, got his gavel and a spare package of chewing tobacco out of his desk, and moved the hearing over to the county judge's office in the courthouse.

"I forgot to ask you yesterday," the judge said. "You got a lawyer, Charleyhorse?"

"Just me," Charleyhorse said. "I'll be a lawyer in about eighteen months. If you can wait that long."

"We hadn't ought to," the judge said. "There's ol' Ernie Freeman sittin' back there. The court'll appoint him to represent you."

"I'd be glad to have Ernie in my corner," Charleyhorse said, "but I'd rather do most of the talkin'."

"Ain't no skin off of my back," Judge Hunter said. "That all right with you, Ernie?"

"Be just fine," Ernie said, grinning at Gloria.

Gloria called me and my father and Dave Dolan, and made us all testify that we'd seen Charleyhorse sit on the courthouse grass and hang his shoes on the sign. Then she said the state rested.

Charleyhorse got up and faced the judge and took some sheets of onionskin paper out of his pocket.

"Judge," he said, "you can read this if you want to. But what it amounts to is that I couldn't break any law in the book if I wanted to. This treaty says the only law I could break around here would be one passed by the Chickamasia Nation. And I'm the one runs the Chickamasia Nation, so even if I did start breakin' the law, it'd be up to me to see I got tried for it, not you. And anyway, I've passed me a law that says I'm supposed to sit on the courthouse grass ever' chance I get."

"H'm-m-m!" said the judge. "Supposin' you was to take it into your head to go down and rob the bank?"

"It wouldn't be any of your business."

"Linin' out as a pretty unusual case," the judge said. "You got any more to present?"

Charleyhorse looked at Ernie Freeman. "Have I got any more to say?"

Ernie smiled and shook his head.

"What you got to say to all that, Gloria?" the judge asked.

Gloria marched up to the bar of justice like a lady on her way to stomp a snake.

"Your honor," she said, "I am prepared to show that the treaty under consideration, if it was ever a legal document in the first place, has long been invalidated by circumstances and the march of progress."

"Got a whole big old stack of proof there, have you?"

"I have, your honor." Gloria took some papers out of a big folder and cleared her throat.

"Now wait a minute, Gloria," the judge said. "Maybe we won't have to go into that. . . . Charleyhorse, what you say now?"

"It suits me," Charleyhorse said. "If you all want me and the government to trade back, that's fine."

Ernie Freeman looked at Gloria and laughed. Gloria glared at Charleyhorse, and I was glad she didn't have anything better than some typing paper to throw at him.

"That'd make me and my kinfolks own Chickamasia County," Charleyhorse said. "We might evict you people out of our county and import us some buffalo and go back into business."

201

The judge shook his head. "Shucks, Charleyhorse," he said, "I don't know. What'd you say if I just bound you over for trial in county court? Passed the buck to the county judge, in other words?"

"Whatever you think, Judge. I kind of like this courtroom work. I wouldn't mind if Judge Newton would find against me, so I could appeal someplace else. No tellin' how long I could keep on appealin'."

"All right," the judge said. "She's did, then. . . . Gloria, I don't believe I'll set any bond. Shucks, you know Charleyhorse ain't goin' to run off."

Charleyhorse didn't. He got his car and drove it up on the courthouse lawn and started washing it with one of the hoses the county used to water the grass, and nobody stopped him. The county and a few others who had private wells were the only ones in town who could still use water for anything except drinking and taking baths and washing dishes and things like that. That was on account of the restrictions the city council put on when water stopped running into the city reservoir. When Charley got through he had about the only clean car in town.

        ✻   ✻   ✻

They had an emergency meeting that night in the county commissioners' room in the courthouse. The school board was there, and the city council, and the county commissioners, and my father and my sister. And me, but, of course, I was ex officio.

"What's bad about this," said Ted Bowman, the county commissioner for the south district, "is that that crazy Indian really could stretch this out forever in the courts."

"That's right," Mayor Arden chimed in. "And we've got that big ol' bond issue we just voted for the fairgrounds and the one for the new grade school, and bond buyers are so skittish I just doubt if we can sell 'em while we're involved in litigation, cock-eyed as it is."

"Look what it could do to our ad valorem tax collection," Mr. Bowman said. "Any skinflint in the county can refuse to pay, it looks to me like. Say he's not payin' taxes on his property till he finds out whether he owns it or the Chickamasia tribe owns it."

"Well, what can we do about it?" my father asked. He was eager to get out of there and check on the condition of our left fielder, who was having domestic and throwing-arm trouble.

"For one thing," Gloria said, "we can get the county judge to set the case ahead of everything else on the docket."

"All right," the mayor said. "We'll do that. Now what else can we do?"

But nobody could think of anything else.

❖   ❖   ❖

Charleyhorse spent a good part of the next day walking around with his hands behind his back, looking at the town as if he owned it.

"Take good care of my city hall," he said to Dave Dolan. "That's where I'm going to keep my bird dogs."

But the meanest thing he did was tell people he was thinking about annexing his county to Texas as soon as he got a clear title to it.

Just to be on the safe side, my father got him off in a corner and made him promise not to deport any first-string members of the Mudcats or pitch any tepees on the ball-park grounds or let any deer and antelope roam on the outfield grass or anything.

After supper Charleyhorse came around to the house. My sister Gloria was sitting on the front steps telling my father what she thought of a county attorney who would go clear to Colorado on his vacation with a crisis about to happen, and not tell a soul where to get in touch with him. Charleyhorse sat down beside her.

"Let's us go for a ride," he said. "Then, if either one of us happens to think of a possible out-of-court settlement—why, we can discuss it."

"I'm supposed to go for a ride with Ernie Freeman," Gloria said.

"Seems like this is a lot more important."

So they went and got in Charleyhorse's convertible. And they parked on top of the red bluff, looking out over the river, which is what people around here use for a lovers' lane. I know, because I went there on my way to look at my trotline. I want to tell you Charleyhorse's car looked a lot better up there to me than Ernie Freeman's big sedan ever did.

✿   ✿   ✿

The next day was Sunday. Charleyhorse went four for five and handled eleven chances perfectly in the field, and we trounced Antelope City 12 to 2. You would have thought that would make people feel good all day Monday, but it didn't.

I don't guess hardly anybody really thought Charleyhorse was going to take their county away from them, but still it made you wonder. And people were afraid it would get in the papers and make us look silly.

I saw Charleyhorse and Gloria heading out toward the red bluff on Sunday night and again on Monday night.

The trial was on Tuesday morning and I don't guess there was hardly anybody in town who wasn't either in the courtroom or out in the hall trying to get into the courtroom or bedridden or in jail.

Old Judge Newton was a lot different from Judge Hunter, being a lawyer by trade instead of a domino-parlor operator. Judge Newton pounded court into session as soon as the clock on the bank started to strike ten. And here we went again.

Me and my father and Dave Dolan testified again, and Charleyhorse got on the stand and Ernie Freeman asked him about the treaty, and Charleyhorse told him, and Ernie inserted the copy of the treaty in the record. Then Gloria said she wanted to cross-examine.

"Mr. Horse," she said, " is it not true that the provisions of the treaty at issue here have now expired?"

"Huh?" Charleyhorse asked.

"Please state in your own words the designation made in the treaty for the duration of the agreement."

Charleyhorse blinked. "Forever," he said.

"Forever?"

"Yes, ma'am. From then on."

"Is that the wording of the treaty?"

"No, ma'am," Charleyhorse said. "What it says is: 'For so long as the grass shall grow and the rivers shall flow.' That's the way us Indians always used to draw 'em up. Sounds better."

I looked around, and there wasn't anybody in the courtroom who wasn't leaning forward and trying not to breathe.

"And how many rivers are there in Chickamasia County and other territory covered by this transaction?" Gloria asked.

"Just the Cherokee River," Charleyhorse said, sounding puzzled. "Course there's some creeks, but the Cherokee's the only river."

"Aha!" said Gloria. "And have you observed the Cherokee River recently?"

Charleyhorse grinned. "Why, Gloria, you know you and me——."

"Answer yes or no, please," Gloria said crisply.

"Yes, ma'am."

"And was the Cherokee flowing?"

Charleyhorse sat back in his chair real sudden, like he'd been shoved. One of those murmurs you always hear about running through crowds ran through the crowd.

"Well —." Charleyhorse said, and looked at his lawyer.

"No, Mr. Horse," Gloria said, "the Cherokee River is not running. It is down to pools, is it not, Mr. Horse? Just a hole here and there. Some of them hardly more than puddles."

Charleyhorse didn't say anything.

"Furthermore, the Cherokee River has not flowed these two years and more, except for a little bit in the spring of the year. I find further that the Cherokee also stopped flowing in 1936 and again in 1937. And the Lord only knows how many other times the Cherokee has not flowed in the years since 1854."

Charleyhorse looked stunned.

Ernie Freeman jumped up. "Wait a minute!" he said. "Now

don't try to tell me the grass doesn't still grow. Some of it, at least."

"Sure," Charleyhorse said. "Else that sign on the courthouse lawn is misleadin' and irrelevant and what am I doin' here anyway?"

"Ah, yes," Gloria said. "But the wording of the treaty signed by Mr. Horse's illustrious forebear is 'and.' 'So long as the grass shall grow and the rivers shall flow.' Not 'or' the grass shall grow."

Charleyhorse looked at his lawyer. "Shucks, Ernie," he said. "She's got us!"

Ernie Freeman wanted to talk some more, but Charleyhorse didn't give him a chance.

"If it's all the same to you, your honor," he said, "I'd just as soon back off and start over. I plead guilty."

The judge glanced at Gloria, and Gloria nodded her head. The judge sentenced Charleyhorse to ten days in jail. He suspended the sentence, but he said Charleyhorse would have to pay $17.25 court costs, which is real reasonable.

✿　　✿　　✿

I happened to be crouched down behind the honeysuckle bush by the steps when Charleyhorse came calling on my big sister that night. He didn't waste a second.

"Now, look," he said. "As long as you've proved you're a smarter lawyer than me and Ernie Freeman put together—why, you don't have to prove it any more, do you?"

"I don't know what you mean."

"I mean by the time I get out of law school you ought to be ready to retire and let your husband have your job and start workin' his way up the ladder to state senator and governor and things like that."

"What husband?" Gloria asked.

Charleyhorse wrapped his arms around her so she could make sure who he was talking about. When he got through kissing her, she put her head on his shoulder and left it there.

"Forever and ever," she murmured.

206

"Sure," Charleyhorse said. "For as long as the grass grows *or* the rivers flow."

"Or even a Jimson weed," Gloria said.

I remember at the time I thought I must have a pretty dumb sister, for Charleyhorse to have to take her out to the red bluff above the river so many times before he could make her see for herself about that treaty being so bad out of date. But I'm some older now, and I guess she wasn't so dumb.

CHAPTER ELEVEN

THE END

Now BRING YOUR WORK to a quick windup. A good ending should satisfy the reader, prove the point, and be brief. You may use many of the earlier devices here—possibly a new setting for the final scene, transitions, characterization, discovery and reversal, the gimmick, and you should tie up all dangling threads, answer all the unanswered questions.

Although we are now going through a style of writing which leaves some strings dangling, the correct way puts everything in its place. Learn the rules first; then you are at liberty. Often the ending starts with:

1. *The Black Moment.*

Your main character has jumped into the fire, put it out by his personal sacrifice, and, as a result, is emotionally drained. When the ability to think about his personal problem flows back within him, he is apt to be stunned at his own behavior. He is likely to feel that he has played the fool. As he realizes what he has done, he might prefer to crawl in a hole and pull it in after him, as in "The Preacher's Confession":

> Some of the men went to look after their rigs and horses, but, for the most part, folks just stood and stared, with the light of the fire on their faces showing them dazed and not able to take in what had happened. Tom was sure he couldn't. All he was certain of was that he still had Sara Bell and the fiddle, and that Brother Calhoun would see him forever as a backslider, a man who profaned the pulpit with fiddle music. He was right back where he started, only worse off, lots worse.

2. Realization.

Following the Black Moment, the changed circumstances assert themselves and things are not nearly so terrible as the main character has thought. In fact the opposite has happened, and a solution rides upon the horizon. What the main character fails to realize, and probably never does, is that in completely forgetting himself in the tenseness of the moment, he also got rid of the self-element of his own emotions. In losing this self-element he was able for the period of action to see through a larger viewpoint; thus he, himself, grew. Consider the realization in "Stubborn Bride":

> "And afterwards"—the quiet eyes had erased their memories and Anna's gentle gaze moved across the girl's head to the barn down the slope where big Bohomil was milking the cows— "afterwards papa he tells everyone how here in America is better for the Czechs. We do that, huh?"
>
> "Yes, mamma," Linda nodded quickly. She clung to Anna.
>
> Frank looked out across the field where the wheat was waving icy-green in the wind, thrumming a soft song like the rippling sounds of the Moldau whispering of yesterday to its banks. From the kitchen came the sweet smell of prune and poppy-seed kolaches, and down at the barn the cows that were waiting their turn lowed impatiently.
>
> Linda raised her face finally and looked at Frank. He smiled at her and laid his hand against her cheek. A feeling of contentment warmed him. There was a oneness between himself and the girl he loved now. It had never been there before. Strange, he thought, how simple things were when mamma took over.

It is like taking a thread which is on the minus side, threading it through the eye of the needle (spirit, if the word suits you) and coming out on the positive side. When the crossover is made, the minus becomes plus and the problem is solved.

Again we prove the law that the total is more than the sum of its parts. When we can dodge being blinded by our self-interests, we can work with power for the benefit of those we would serve.

This discovery and reversal is the basis of your story structure. Its structure is the backbone of story, biography, or any unforgettable character or personality sketch. Aristotle explained that discovery and reversal is the change from ignorance to knowledge. Go through the stories in this book and see just how many of them were built with this foundation. Now, check your own copy. Have you used this technique to lead your main character into his new knowledge?

3. *New view of the gimmick.*

From the beginning the gimmick has been the focal point that the main character has viewed without knowledge. At times it is seen in complete ignorance. For instance, in the beginning of "Showdown at San Saba," the gimmick was of first importance to the main character who felt that weighty matters needed a gun for settlement: "I squeezed my hand tighter around the cracked butt of that old .44 frame that my pa had thrown away and which I'd dug out to play with and to practice my lightning-fast draw, which, up to now, I'd figured never to use until I growed to be a man." But notice how Welty speaks of the gun at the end of the story: "I thought about it some more when I went and got my old .44 with no cylinder in it or hammer on it and put it in the ale keg we use for slop." This mention of the gimmick demonstrates that the vpc has learned that his father's attitude is correct.

4. *Theme.*

If you wish to sum up your theme in your story, here is the place where your character may realize it in his thoughts, or in dialogue, or in the main character's reaction to the new truth which he has discovered.

However, handle this summing-up with a light touch. Too much will weigh down your story and keep it from reaching the heart, where it belongs. Remember, a story is an experience in emotion. Do not ruin it with words!

5. *Character grows.*

Life has been at work; your main character has learned something by his experience. His mind's eye has enlarged his own viewpoint until it is now wide enough to see the viewpoint of another—in the widening process, new knowledge and understanding are apparent.

These three items—the gimmick, the theme, and character growth—may be revealed in your story simultaneously. Consider this example from "Violets From Portugal":

> But Susan saw a bit of goods sticking out from under the flap. She pulled at it.
>
> "Kelly!" she whispered unbelievingly. "You didn't go back—didn't risk your life for kitchen curtains!"
>
> His grim mouth slipped sideways in a ghost of a smile. "You used to say home, for me, was where my hat was. It isn't. It's where my heart is. *You're* my heart, Sue. A man's no good without his heart. The curtains were only part of the pattern. I thought they might prove something to you." The hunger in his voice was unmistakable.
>
> Tears pressed against her lids. The bands snapped, and her heart seemed to break loose from its moorings. He *did* need her! Knowing *that,* a woman could do anything. Through mist-filled eyes she saw men in uniform. One day they'd be back in business suits on Main Street because of men like Kelly; because of wives such as she was going to be. The thought made her humble, yet proud.

This is your dramatic pattern. It began with the storyteller in the beginning of time. You will find it used over and over again in the Bible. The entire book of Esther is based upon this form: Esther risks her life to save her people and gains both. Haman follows the law in reverse; he erected a gallows to use in hanging his enemy and found his own execution there.

Go through the stories in this book and see if you can mark the parts of the end.

by Al Dewlen

Tʜᴇ sun held a close bead on our San Saba town, as though it
aimed to cook away the whole dead place at one scald, and I
wouldn't have cared a Sunday hatful if it had. Yet I kept on running, chancing it my bare feet wouldn't split wide open in that
hot yellow sand of South Nevada Street, and I squeezed my
hand tighter around the cracked butt of that old .44 frame that
my pa had thrown away and which I'd dug out to play with and
to practice my lightning-fast draw, which, up to now, I'd figured
never to use until I growed to be a man.

I ran sort of blind, partly due to my hair hanging down and
flapping the bothersome way it did, and partly on account of
what people were saying about pa. Once I had taken thought,
I saw what it totted up to, which was, if there was any honest
grit in the whole Lockhart family it had to be in my own belly;
it sure wasn't noticeable in pa's. I knew I was going to cry about
that, too, if ever I got the time.

That dirt got hotter than a dry hub as I bent the corner around
Hack Danciger's livery barn, and it sounded like Uncle Hack
who hollered out, "Hold on there, Welty Lockhart! Your ma
feeling any better?" But much as I shine to Uncle Hack, I just
kept fogging till I was square in front of the Blanco Rose, which
is San Saba's main place for selling drinking whisky and flipping
a card, and a place I've been told never to be at, though I guess
if it wasn't for the Blanco Rose, they'd have changed the name of
San Saba to Shady Rest a long time ago.

I slowed and cut towards those double doors, where maybe
a dozen people stood gawking in; mostly men, except Max Gillenwater, who's in the fourth grade too. Max was down on his hands

212

and knees seeing under the doors. Same as everybody else, I reckon he meant to have a look at John Quincy Winant. It was the first time a man who had blowed fifteen other men straight to hell and gone ever came to San Saba, and if pa heard that— that hell, I mean—I'd get skinned plenty. I stopped at the watering trough and sat on the edge and stuck my feet in to cool out some of the sand sting.

"Hey," Cowie Thomas said from where he leaned on the window, "here's Fenton Lockhart's boy. Look here, Welty, ain't the marshal comin' back? With his gun, maybe?"

I got off the trough and scrouged myself a place at the window. I could have told Cowie no, pa wasn't coming back any second time, he was sticking home to cater to ma. But I didn't. "That Lockhart," I heard Cowie say. "First thing that's come up since he got to be the law, and he just speaks a few words to this gun fighter and goes back home."

I let on I didn't hear, and clung to my busted gun. It was up to me now to handle pa's job myself.

Sure enough, when I looked in, yonder was John Quincy Winant. First glance, it was like getting bib overalls for Christmas when you'd counted on a six-gun. He wore a silly store coat binding tight across the back and short at the tail, and a high tall hat, one of those wooly beavers you see sometimes at church or a burying. It didn't figure for a man some said had shot three over at El Paso the same night, with one of those three being Shawnee Kittinger, who'd gunned a few himself in his own good time. But I quit scratching over the clothes when I seen the holster. The sight of it jogged me about pa, and I commenced my move. Max latched onto my arm as I lit for the door.

"Welty, you going in there?"

"Sure am," I said, and squeezed harder on that old .44 sticking up out of my britches. "Gonna have me a showdown here and now."

"Good dern!" Max said. It made me feel better.

I saw Cowie Thomas and bald old Charlie Hess looking at me, and, not giving anybody the chance to spout off, I went inside. I walked straight at the bar where John Quincy Winant was standing. Seemed to be half the town in there sitting and propping around the walls, but the only body close to Mr. Winant was Bonnie Parnell, the apron-wearing man who always resembled a warty old toad. I wished bad my .44 frame had a hammer on it and a cylinder in it and real bullets besides. I thought of pa, though, just sitting up at the house soothing ma, and I kept on walking.

It was when John Quincy Winant turned that I knew that I was kissing close to a live, gun-fighting man. His big old tea-kettle of a face was burnt dark and sort of greasy-looking. His coat swung back and I seen his gun, a whopper, and black and notched all the way down the butt and standing up high out of a cutaway holster laid backwards on his left side.

"Howdy, sonny," John Quincy Winant said and he winked at my gun. "See you got yourself primed for bear." It didn't appear he aimed to kill me right that very minute.

"Welty, you get along home," Bonnie Parnell cut in. "Your dad will give you a hiding if he catches you in here."

"I got business with this here gun fighter," I said, and I squared around to Mr. Winant.

"What's your name, sonny?" He still didn't sound much like killing.

"Welty Lockhart. Except ma calls me Welton when she's mad, which is mostly, any more." Then, to make sure he knew where us two stood, I said: "If it's any of your business."

"Reckon you're the marshal's boy," John Quincy said, and he grinned onesided. "How old are you, sonny?"

"Twelve," I said.

"You ain't neither; you're 'way shy of eleven," Bonnie Parnell stuck in. "Now git!"

"Why, I'd of figured him fourteen, maybe more," Mr. Winant said. "Handles hisself like a growed-up man."

That mixed me up, all right, which might have been one of his gun-fighting tricks, though it did appear he wasn't doing any harm in San Saba and for a minute I wasn't certain he needed running out. But then, I'd already set my mind.

"Me and pa decided you got to ride on," I said, real quick. I hadn't aimed bringing in pa, but since I had it seemed the best I could do for him anyways, so I let it lay.

Mr. Winant risked using his gun hand for emptying his glass.

"See here, you fool kid," Bonnie began, but Mr. Winant broke in.

"Your pa coming to see me again, sonny?" I sure as thunder hated him asking that.

"Not exactly," I said. "Ma's kind of upset and he stayed up at the house. But I'm telling you to haul out of San Saba." It come to me to tack on "afore sundown," so I tacked it on.

Bonnie Parnell whistled, and it lit on me I wasn't exactly practicing my lightning-fast draw with Max, and maybe I wasn't fooling John Quincy Winant. Most anybody could see my old .44 didn't have any cylinder in it or hammer on it to shoot with.

He just looked at me a minute and I decided if he laughed I'd make my draw, which always beat Max a mile, and throw that old .44 smack at his teeth. But he didn't laugh.

"Now, sonny, I reckon you got it wrong," he said. "It's like I told your pa while ago. Rattler hit my horse about two mile down the road. Pore Roany, he's swoll clean from his fetlock to his shoulder, and mighty sore. I don't guess he can travel for a spell. I aimed to sort of rest up and wait for him. That suited the marshal all right, and it'd make me comfortable if you'd agree with him."

Oh, pa, he'd let it go at that, all right. But I'd heard what people were saying, and I could feel Cowie Thomas watching, and Max's black-button eyes bugging at me under the doors. I sucked in my belly so as to loosen my britches and make the .44 clear fast and easy.

"I already told you to ride out of this town," I said, plenty loud. "So you better, that's what. Or —."

Mr. Winant grinned and shook his head. "Your pa didn't say that, sonny."

"Aw, for Pete's sakes, Welty," Bonnie busted in "chase your scrappy little hide home before I burn your bottom!"

There wasn't any more use, not with a broke-down gun. I backed out, trying to feel good about that scrappy part Bonnie had thrown in. When I got outside, I went to running, partly due to that hot sand clawing after my feet, but more because of what Cowie was saying to Charlie Hess about pa.

"Aw, Cowie," I heard Charlie Hess answering back, "why try to set off trouble? The marshal knows what he's doing. Besides, Miz Lockhart's pretty sick just now." I guess Charlie was about the only one talking up for pa. And doing no good. Like me, just spitting into the wind.

I got clean around behind Hack Danciger's main barn, out of the sun and tolerable well hid, before I slowed and sat down, and when I finished blowing and shivering, I let loose and bawled.

❉   ❉   ❉

Things had been pitiful drowsy before John Quincy Winant rode in like any ordinary body that day and checked his limpy horse at Hack's, and walked up Nevada to the Blanco Rose. You see, nobody wore guns in San Saba, and pa never even wore his himself. It hung on a dried-out holster on our hatrack, and pa never took it down except for a cleaning once in a while.

It wasn't a law about guns, but a ruling of Big Choc McCord's while he was being marshal and sort of simmering-down the town. Which was how pa came to be marshal anyway. One day Cowie Thomas went complaining to Mr. McCord about a tight-mouthed little stranger wearing a gun. Mr. McCord didn't pay it much mind, commenting how the stranger had been around a whole week without anybody noticing, and was packed and waiting on the stage at the time. But Cowie was always one to help out the law, and kept after Mr. McCord. Finally the marshal went bulling over and got himself shot through, icy dead, trying to take that man's gun. We heard tales later, how that stranger was Johnny Ringo, and folks said it was too bad what happened

216

to Mr. McCord. Pretty often I hear Cowie telling about the shooting and how he had a better view than anybody else.

Seemed to me pa bit his pipe extra hard when he heard. But he didn't say anything, outside of a word about Cowie he won't ever let me use and which I didn't admire much, since Cowie did put on real noisy dog fights once in a while and was good about letting me watch.

When pa took Mr. McCord's place, he never said anything about that gun rule, either. Wasn't any need, I guess, everybody being out of the gun habit. But I knew, plain where pa stood on shooting. He'd catch me chasing Max around the feed shed with that old .44 and he'd stop me and go over all that about a good man not needing a gun and how killings weren't called for, ever. But one thing I knew, though I never sassed it back to pa; I knew John Quincy Winant didn't get where he was by packing only a hanky on his hip. Ma didn't side with me there. Or with pa, either, since she'd changed.

Only since winter ma had got a worried look to her eyes and her face turned plumb round, not pretty so you could be proud of her the way it used to be. She got so she ate twice as much as me and pa put together ate, and she looked kind of funny in those baggy dresses she took to wearing all the time. She talked sharp to pa, too, about his job not making much money, or respect either.

When she took a spell of crying and yelling, pa didn't rear up on his hind legs and beller back the way I'd heard Max Gillenwater's pa do. Instead, he mainly pulled at that cotton-colored mustache of his and said nothing. Or if he did, he said it soft and easy, and you could tell he was taking it like ma was a mite out of her head, that's all.

It was Cowie brought the news about Mr. Winant, and pa grunted and hardly thanked him for his pains. But directly he told me to stick close home with ma, and he went off to see that gun fighter. In no time at all, pa was back.

"Snake-bit horse," he said to ma. Before I could ask pa how bad he'd banged up John Quincy Winant, Cowie was back with four-five others, Mayor Tuck Ellis among them. They mostly seemed to figure it might be a duty of pa's to see to it that this killer swapped horses and kept on passing through, or else bunked in jail. That's how I learnt pa hadn't banged up Mr. Winant at all.

"He ain't kicking up any fuss," pa told them. "He ain't broke any law, and long as he's peaceful, I guess I'll just stick around Grace."

"You seen he's wearing a handgun," Cowie Thomas said. Pa gave Cowie his put-out look and he rubbed down the ends of his mustache.

"That's sensible for him," pa said. "His kind of man likely wouldn't live long, once he got caught without one."

Cowie sniffed, and it was clear what he and those others thought. Guess I thought it a little myself, and I didn't care much about looking direct at anybody.

Right after Mayor Ellis went out the gate, ma fell into sort of a fit at pa, about how he wasn't tending to the piddling little old job he did have, though before she'd begged him not to leave; which was how ma acted lately. I watched around the kitchen door. Pa talked soft and ma yelled, and all of a sudden she folded down on the floor and started moaning.

Pa gathered her onto the couch and said I was to run for Doc Chester. I'd about decided I wouldn't do anything pa told me any more, but I seen how sickly ma looked and I took off. When I got back with the doc, ma hadn't stirred, though she looked able, and stout enough for another fit. Pa said clear out, but instead I sat on the flour barrel back of the kitchen door and heard what they said.

"Been to town?" Doc Chester asked.

"This morning," pa said. "But I'm sure sticking home now." He was watching ma, and holding her hand between both of his. "I couldn't be drug out of this house."

Oh, pa said it all right. I heard him. I didn't need to stew things over any longer. Fact was plain, John Quincy Winant had scared pa so bad he was holing up. And Doc Chester was laughing.

218

"Best day I know of to stay home," doc said, and pa laughed the least bit also, while he kept looking down at ma. Humiliated at himself, I guess.

The way it hit, I could have fallen in the flour. Then's when I slipped out to the shed and got my old .44 and struck out for the Blanco Rose and faced up to John Quincy Winant.

       ❖   ❖   ❖

Sitting back of Uncle Hack's, I chewed grass and let whatever wanted go busting through my head. Charlie Hess had always told how pa saved a new brown colt once from a whole pack of slobbering wolves, using nothing but a club. Sometimes I told it over to Max. But I hadn't seen pa do it myself, and I knew now Charlie must have made it up.

I watched the sun burn itself a painful red and kind of plop out of sight, and there wasn't much to do but go home. It was a mess, what I walked into.

Doc Chester was still there, besides Mrs. Gillenwater, who is Max's nice ma, and I could hear hurting noises in the bedroom.

"Out of the way, boy!" doc said, after he stepped on me.

He finished rolling his sleeves and went in where the moaning was and shut the door. It was my ma crying, I could tell. The ache of it made me feel worse than already. I guess that ma couldn't stomach what pa had done, either, and had gone clean out of her head.

Then I saw pa coming in off the back porch, his eyes winter gray and that clay color washed out of his face. Cowie was standing on the back stoop, grinning in. Wasn't any need to suppose what he'd been telling pa. I thought of running off for good, right then, and being a gun-fighting marshal forever. But I stood and let pa rake his eyes over me and waited for him to blow sky high and give my hind end the most thorough beating it ever had.

Pa grabbed our smelly old coffeepot off the stove and poured himself a cup. He looked at me again, and put out another cup and filled it too.

"Come here, son," he said, awful soft, and he motioned his hand at the chair ma usually sat in to gorge herself, and at the spare cup of coffee. Plainly he meant me to sit there and drink it, which was confusing, since pa'd always said I could wait till I was man's age to touch man's drink. I left that coffee be, but I sat while pa commenced on his, and some sloshed into his mustache and made it look yellow; first time I ever noticed a thing like that.

"Why'd you do it son?" he said.

At first I aimed to tell him. But I seen those big shoulders and recalled how pa throwed his saddle up in place with one hand, and how he sometimes let me ride behind him sitting on old Speck's broad rump when we went after the mail, and I couldn't.

"You done a fool thing, son," pa said. "You went inside the Blanco Rose, where I told you never to be. And you lied to that gun slinger. How come, Welty?"

"I don't know," I said.

Pa made his regular slupping sound, getting at his coffee, and it was about the only natural part of this whole balled-up day.

"Son," he pointed his finger, "I'm betting you're man enough for that coffee. Same as I'm betting you're one to go back down there and apologize to Mr. Winant." That yanked me to my feet.

"Pa, you're scared of him, that's what!" Guess I was yelling, and squalling with it. "Cowie says, and everybody! But I ain't scared. I got guts in my belly, that's what! I'm going back down there with yore gun and I'll clean him out of town!"

My eyesight was bothered, and my neck choked till I couldn't say any more. But I had some sense left, all right. I got solid on my feet, so as not to fall when he whopped me, if I could help myself. But pa didn't whop me.

"Well dang my buttons," he said. I noticed pa's mustache drooping low at the ends, and the coffee steam or something was pestering his eyes. In a while, he got up.

"All right, son," he said, still real soft. "Let's get down there. I aim for you to apologize. You can't go threatening a man with killing."

Pa stepped out back and filled our leaky old lantern. He lit it in the living room, letting the oil speckle the floor, and he mentioned to Mrs. Gillenwater we'd be gone a spell and to tell ma not to fret herself. When he turned, he caught me stretching for that big gun hanging on the hatrack. He didn't even holler then.

"Forget that thing, Welty," he said. "Let's go."

Dark as it was, I walked a little piece back of pa. He was telling what I ought to say to Mr. Winant, but I didn't hear much. I was thinking how dumb it was, us carrying that old lantern where everybody'd know we'd come out.

When we got to the Blanco Rose, I was hoping Mr. Winant had high-tailed before sundown, like I cautioned him, or leastways moved some other place to take his supper. But he was facing me and pa before we got all the way inside. So were all the others.

Pa walked up near Mr. Winant and set the drippy old lantern on the bar. John Quincy looked somehow a little red in his eyes, and they'd gotten bigger, and I seen the bottle he had was different from the one he'd used this afternoon.

"Brung my boy down to say a thing or two," pa said. He reached back and got my shoulder and put me around in front of him. "Go ahead, son."

Mr. Winant shifted, but nothing sudden, and he grinned down at me. Pa's hand felt heavy, and the coal-oil smell was mixing up my stomach, and I tried. I couldn't remember all the words. I said: "I didn't have no call to trouble you, Mr. Winant. That ole gun I had wouldn't shoot; it ain't got any hammer on it or no cylinder in it either."

Apologizing didn't make me feel good, the way pa'd said. I heard whispering, and seen Cowie Thomas watching pa with disgusted eyes, and I busted out what came to my head.

"But if that ole .44 was a real .44 and I had it right now, I'd run you out of town because I ain't afeared like —."

"That's plenty, son!" Pa cut off quick and flat. "Bring the lantern." He started for the door.

"Hold up, marshal," Mr. Winant said. "I'd be obliged if you'd round up your nosey citizens and herd 'em out of here. They been gawking all day like my head was on backwards, and I'm full up to the neck."

Pa faced back, almost smiling. "Public place," he said.

"They been eying me till it ain't relaxable," Mr. Winant said, and he looked at Cowie Thomas in place of pa. "I'm getting a little drunk, and a little jumpy, and I'm maybe a little het up. Guess it'd be best to clear 'em out."

"Public place," pa said again, not smiling now.

Mr. Winant straightened. "All right, marshal," he said. "I made my appeal to the law. Now I reckon I'm going to reserve this place, private for myself, the rest of the evenin'." He glared at Cowie. "I want all these bug-eyes cleared out, say in the next two minutes."

Bonnie Parnell slacked off in the face and went sliding away down the bar. Mr. Winant's hand somehow got to his gun, and was sort of teasing it. Cowie headed for the door, and the others sidled the same direction, but it stayed quiet, and we all heard what Cowie said. "If we had us a lawman, no dirty murderer would be pushing us decent citizens around like —."

The gun came half out. "Winant!" pa said, and he stepped nearer the bar, so Cowie was behind him. That gun fighter eased his pistol back down, and he took a long look at pa.

"Wait for me outside, Welty," pa said. I didn't go; I hadn't got our lantern yet, the way pa'd told me.

"All right, Winant," I heard pa saying. "I ain't got time for talk, wife's not well just now. You had my leave long as you didn't start trouble. Well, you ain't got my leave any more. You best mount up and ride."

Mr. Winant tensed up somehow, and all at once I got tight myself, and I wondered if I'd heard pa right, and I was shivering and couldn't help it, though I sure wasn't cold this time of the year.

"Marshal," Mr. Winant said, "I don't care none for getting ordered out of somewheres."

Cowie Thomas moved out from behind pa and he gulped, and blued over in the face the way Max had that day a green peach his jaw was soaking slipped ahead of time and went down, and I seen Mr. Winant's coat spread open and the gun sticking up in plain sight. I thought of that oily gun wasting itself on our hat-rack.

"It's maybe a little raw from your side of the fence," pa said. "But you better ride, I reckon, else I'll have to put you up at the jail till you're ready." My pa said that to John Quincy Winant. I heard it right.

That teakettle face poked towards pa then, and Bonnie Parnell fell against a chair and it rattled over, him on top of it. Me, I didn't flop around. I just looked at my pa and saw he wasn't scared, not one thimbleful.

"Don't see a gun on you, marshal," Mr. Winant's voice had a frying crackle now.

"It's the way I tell my boy Welty," pa said. "They's better answers without a gun."

I surveyed around, quick, for a bottle or a rock, anything that'd do. There wasn't a thing handy, and I didn't even have my old gun with no hammer on it or cylinder in it. So I got my fists wadded tight and ready.

"Well, what do you say?" That was my pa talking.

"I'll wait around till Roany gets good and fit," John Quincy Winant said, and he laid his elbow on the bar. My pa walked straight at him.

"I done apologized like you told me, pa," I said. "Let's go home." Pa kept walking.

"Far enough, marshal." You couldn't tell Mr. Winant's mouth moved.

"Let's go home, pa!" I don't guess pa heard. He took another step and that big gun came out with a sharp slapping sound; like lightning, faster than ever I drawed on Max. It leveled at pa's belt buckle.

"I've shot unarmed varmints," John Quincy Winant said, and

blinked towards Cowie, "but never an unarmed man. Don't make me spoil a straight record."

Pa didn't answer, he only took one more step. The gun wavered like it couldn't settle its mind between killing and crippling. I quit drawing breath. Then the snout raised a little. The crash was as though the whole roof of the Blanco Rose had caved in. Pa heeled back, his shoulder banging the bar. Our old lantern jumped a foot as the bullet nicked it, and I heard the slug sing away. Fire and oil and busted glass spattered all over. Pa grabbed the bar and hung on.

"Pa!" I yelled.

He let go his handhold and slewed around. I seen the big torn place high on his coat where the bullet had plowed his shoulder. Snaky strings of burning coal oil were running down his front.

"Good God, man!" John Quincy hollered. "You're on fire!"

Bonnie Parnell came running; I saw him swing his wiping-up rag at pa's chest. The rag flamed, and a bigger blaze shot up alongside pa's face. I smelled powder and burnt hair and oil smoke. I screamed and pa charged, beeline, at John Quincy Winant, as though it didn't matter he was a sizzling ball of fire!

John Quincy jerked back, tried to untrack. Pa's fist drove out of the flame. All of a sudden Mr. Winant limbered in his knees. I heard the gun clatter down. Next, that gun-fighting man was laid out there, dead cold, on the floor.

Pa spun and sort of groaned and beat at the burning places with his hands. "Hurts!" he moaned, kind of crazy, and he ran out the door. He dove into the watering trough and groaned again and wallowed.

People jammed all around. I heard Bonnie Parnell yelling for help with the fire inside. I was crying and sick besides. I fought to get in to pa. They pushed me, but I got there all the same. They'd lifted pa out of the water and laid him on the ground. His eyes rolled back, all white.

"Get Doc Chester!" Charlie Hess yelled. "He's out to Lockhart's now!"

I got down next to my pa. Before I could say I was mighty sorry what I'd done, somebody grabbed me up. "Here Welty, you come with me." It was Uncle Hack, and I couldn't get loose.

"Pa's dying!" I tried to tell him. "Let me loose. Pa's killed and burnt up!"

"No, he ain't, no, he ain't" Uncle Hack said. "But you don't need to be in there looking and smelling."

I heard a groan, that awful shimmying kind. "Lord, somebody, blow on it!" That was pa. I whacked Uncle Hack in the stomach and got away and got back in there.

Pa's legs was shaking. Charlie Hess was scooping big gobs of butter out of a crock and slapping it at pa's face and on his shoulder where they'd shucked back his clothes. Then Uncle Hack caught me again and dragged me off up South Nevada Street. Somebody ran past the other way.

"Doc can't leave Miz Lockhart right now," he yelled. "Says pack the marshal up there!"

When they pushed me into the house, they were toting pa right behind, and they laid him on the couch. Hack let me over there then. I bent down in all that butter and mess and I got me a good hold around my pa.

"Here, here," pa said, sort of trembly, and he patted my back. "I'm all right. That little ole burn hurt for a minute, that's all. The bullet didn't amount to nothing; kind of figure John Quincy didn't aim for it to."

Pa got my arms and held me back and looked at me. "Son, guns didn't settle this, now did they?" Then Uncle Hack was clapping pa on his good shoulder and laughing.

People poured into our living room, not knocking either. Cowie Thomas wasn't among them, and I expect that was just as well, considering what was getting said about him. Cowie was dumb all right, thinking pa was ever scared of anybody.

Doc came out, and while he was wrapping pa's bad places I heard pa ask how ma was. I went to the kitchen and got an eating apple, not the sour kind ma fixes pie with, but the red kind, and I listened to what everybody was saying to my pa. It sounded fine, and I knowed I'd do some talking to pa my own self, if ever they all went home where they belonged anyway.

When Doc Chester came out again, all those blabbering mouths hushed in a hurry. Doc set his black bag on ma's library table and brought a high brown bottle out of it. He waited till Mrs. Gillenwater fetched glasses. Everyone looked at doc, and I thought of ma's sickness and put my eating apple down.

Doc poured two big drinks and walked across and put one in pa's hand, and he raised the other and said, "It's a big husky boy." They all whooped.

Pa rose up halfway on the couch. "Grace, doc," he said. "She all right?"

"Grace is fine," doc said. "Needn't have worried yourself to a frazzle the way she did. I will say, that new boy is a dandy. Real spunky. Kicking and fighting."

That's when I hit on something, I mean something I guess I almost knew before, but not complete. About ma's gripy times lately, and eating the way she'd done, and pa staying so close by and being no hand for hollering back at her. Somehow I knew pa was looking at me, so I looked at him.

"Doc," pa said, "I reckon I got me two real spunky boys now."

Later on, pa took me in there with him and I saw ma with that worry gone out of her eyes, all right, and there was talking and hugging I'm not much interested in telling about. But I recall ma saying, "You done yourself proud tonight," and pa answering back, "You ain't done so bad yourself." Then pa had another look at my brother, who honest to Pete didn't look worth whooping over to me.

It was the next morning before I found out about John Quincy Winant riding on west with his head all bundled up and his Roany horse limping, and they said he let drop he was heading toward Tombstone, which made me fairly sad, thinking what had happened to others who rode off that same direction.

I thought about it some more when I went and got my old .44

226

with no cylinder in it or hammer on it and put it in the ale keg we used for slop, though I can't say why, since it's certain that gun was one thing Uncle Hack's hogs couldn't eat without straining. I knew for sure, though, that it suited me fine about the way pa was tending to being marshal, and to ma and me. Also tending to little John Quincy Lockhart. Him I almost forgot.

CHAPTER TWELVE

ABILITY GROWS

POSSIBLY THE FINEST TRUTH for would-be-writers is that ability does grow. As your eyes open and you discover what you need to know, as you practice to put your knowledge into performance, skill develops.

Many students have told me that they did not have time to wait for skill to come to them. If they were to do anything great, it was necessary to do it *now*. If you can go in a straight line to perfection, certainly I have no objection. In fact, I would like to see you do it; then tell me how it was accomplished!

Every writer I know has had to build a foundation. A good foundation is four-square with four cornerstones holding up the floor. This, as a writer, you must build for yourself. But you may have help with two of the corners.

The first cornerstone is *perception.*

You have to see what you are trying to do before you can do it. There might be some value in stumbling around in the dark, but traveling is much easier if someone switches on the light.

Once a would-be writer picked up a book and read another writer's personal success formula: he had written of the common things around him. Nothing in the book seemed too difficult or beyond the reader's capacities. So he decided to make his own effort in this field. Thus Rudyard Kipling started his career.

Most writers learn by discovering how those who preceded them achieved their effects. Benjamin Franklin taught himself to write by studying the printed page, then closing the book and rewriting what he had read. When he could do well or better, he knew that he was on his way.

Working alone, trying to become a writer, is far from easy.

228

No one knows this better than I do. As the new and would-be writer struggles across the no-man's-land from amateur to professional, he discovers that it is like fighting your way in a blinding snowstorm. Those who know how, who pause from their own skill, showing others the way, in my book, touch the fringe of greatness.

The second cornerstone is *performance.*

Most writers, in considering their own book, believe themselves to be writing subjects of interest. The reader, purchasing a book, thinks that he is buying subject matter. Both are wrong.

Readers do not purchase information; they buy skill. Writers do not write subject matter; they handle it. And the ability to handle it comes with performing.

Without the ability to make yourself work, as a writer you cannot succeed. Yet, fortunately, this ability to perform will take the determined plodder beyond many a talented person who dodges discipline. Walter S. Campbell said, when he started teaching writing, that he expected to find talent rare, and workers plentiful, but he discovered that the reverse was true.

I have found it easy to spot the lazy students—they are always asking, "Is this necessary?" or dodging part of the tedium. Then when time for the foundation to be built comes, they wonder why their own platform is not in order.

Margaret Cousins once said that in her early days her editor told her to have twenty-five article ideas on his desk every Monday morning. This drove her into libraries, museums, movies, and a wild variety of activities. This helped her learn how to perform.

Edna Ferber has no patience for those individuals who ask if she writes when she is in the mood. For her writing is a daily business, seven days a week. She writes at home, on planes, in woodsheds, in bathrooms, aboard ship, in train stations—wherever she is, writing is done daily.

The third cornerstone is *persistence.*

As you work from these centers, knowledge and ability move forward toward the square of your foundation. The constant studying and writing aids in building this third requirement of persistence.

The rule is: The first time a thing is done, it is difficult; the second time, only a fraction easier; but as repetition continues, it is finally done without effort and with skill.

As long as you write with your conscious mind directing your work, the writing will be difficult and may be awkward. It is much the same as driving a car. As long as you are learning how to drive, keeping up with the rules of driving, watching the dashboard, and handling the outside traffic are almost overwhelming chores. But afterwhile, you discover yourself doing these things automatically. This is because the subconscious has taken over.

Persistence is the action that shifts your ability from the conscious mind to the subconscious. Smoothness comes from writing at the deeper levels. This takes time. Many writers have found it so.

Robert Louis Stevenson attempted his first novel before he was fifteen, and thereafter wrote regularly, turning out book after book. But he was thirty-one before he overcame his succession of defeats.

Another would-be writer worked diligently, but developed fame on the platform with his guitar and ballads. Nevertheless, from 1912 to 1926, Carl Sandburg kept plugging away at his dream; then in 1926, he achieved success with his biography of Lincoln. John Steinbeck's first three books were financial failures, and he had to fall back on such jobs as hod-carrying and fruit-picking. *Tortilla Flat,* the book that lifted him into the spotlight, was first rejected by nine publishers.

The editors of *Atlantic Monthly* told Louisa May Alcott to go back to school teaching. Jack London was down to one good meal a week. He ate that one at the home of his sweetheart and dared not eat too much for fear she would discover how hungry he really was. He was to the point of suicide when an editor offered to buy one of his 40,000 word manuscripts for $40 on condition he could cut the manuscript to 20,000 words. The editor wrote: "Too lengthy, not strengthy!" Perhaps, had someone been able to teach Jack London to cut his own work, he could have achieved sales faster.

Ennen Reaves Hall was a grandmother when she began her studies. Since then she has earned over $80,000 in confessions, plus the sales of her books.

Fred Grove began with correspondence studies, and sold his first story within a year. In less than ten years he had sold a novel.

How long it takes you to learn depends upon how-much you know when you start. Nevertheless, if you have the courage to work, constantly to teach yourself by practice as you learn from those who guide you, and the grit to keep on through the dark night of waiting, you will discover something else: You do not have to lay the fourth cornerstone.

It will be laid for you! If your other work is in line and laid true, the fourth cornerstone will appear in place when you approach. And when you arrive, you will see and recognize it with joy.

Its name is *perfection.*

So your foundation is built four-square—perception, performance, persistence, and perfection. It is waiting for you to achieve it through your own concentrated efforts. When you have your foundation secure, you may build what you will.

Of course, I have given you the dramatic form used mainly in fiction. You will find the same form often used in nonfiction, particularly where facts fall in line. Walt Disney uses this pattern in his nature stories as well as in his fantasies. Take it, learn it, make it your own.

Margaret Cousins, whom Kenneth McCormick calls one of our great editors of today, has said:

> There is a steady rumor that fiction, like the theatre, has become a fabulous invalid, and that the tread of death forever sounds upon its stair. I have never been able to give credulity to this gossip, for I believe that people cannot live without stories any more than they can live without bread. I think there will always be fiction, and while the form may undergo transmutations and see changes, stories

will survive as long as there are those to tell and those to listen. It is certainly true that since the war, non-fiction has burgeoned and the demand for fiction has declined. However, in the new dynamism of non-fiction, we find that most of the fictional techniques have been employed, so that it is sometimes difficult to tell the difference.

It is the story that reminds us of the nobility of the spirit; therefore, it will live. Someone has said that God placed His hallmark upon every plant that grew. He had, also, placed it in the tales that have been told since the beginning of time. The great are those who have given themselves for the souls of men.

A nation needs its storytellers.

We need you to see how it is done and to do it well!

Take a look at the following story, study the analysis, and see if it now seems clear to you. Afterwards, best of luck to you with your own work!

"Real Gone Guy"

by William R. Scott

Bait
Setting—day
Viewpoint Character
Place
Antagonist

Opening scene—
Action starts

Hint of emotional
problem

Essential facts

Inner emotional
problem

Promise of conflict

Pointing to future
event

Aid to creating
sympathy for VPC

Hint at solution

Other characters

THE long anticipated day of escape proved to be Tuesday. When Roy got to the ranch gate after his long hike from the school-bus stop, his half-brother Ed was getting ready to leave for Texas on his cattle-buying trip. Standing by the truck, the big worried-looking man listed all the jobs he wanted Roy to finish while he was gone. Then he stood frowning, not looking at Roy. He hadn't looked at Roy directly since the day he came to the city jail to arrange about the probation. The cops had rounded up a gang of boys in a stolen car, and Roy had been one of the gang.

"Makes him sick to look at a dangerous criminal," Roy thought sourly.

Ed pushed his hat back on his curly black hair and said, "I'll be away five days. Six at the most."

"Crazy man," Roy thought. "I'll be real gone in six days." He saw the brooding worry in Ed's face, and felt with an unwanted twist of grief how much Ed resembled their father, who had died six months before. He'd met Ed at the funeral and thought he'd like him. But that was before he came to live with Ed and his wife Marnie and their two kids.

233

Character revelation

Emotional conflict

Pointing to future
events

Setting, time of
year, place

Emotional desire

Inner problem

Promise of conflict

Hindrance

Emotional climate

Now Ed brought his worried scowl around to Roy's shoulder—not quite to his face—and said, in his gruff fashion, "Remember, kid, I don't want Marnie lifting a finger to do something you're supposed to do. She's not well." And as if to himself, "Shouldn't have moved so soon after the baby came, I guess. Should have waited a couple more weeks." He shrugged and sighed. "The point is, kid, no gold-bricking while I'm gone, see?"

Roy sighed wearily, impatiently, shivering in the chill evening air and staring bleakly at the naked trees in the creek bottom. He wished he was back in Tulsa—but he couldn't go back there, man. Anyway, his maternal grandparents were real ancients and didn't want him upsetting the creaky, dreary routine of their lives.

"You hear me, kid?" Ed asked.

"Yeah," Roy said, "I hear you, man."

Suddenly, Ed's face was angry. "Okay, wise guy, hear this, too! You mind Marnie; don't give her any smart talk. And don't cut any classes at school, either."

He got into the truck and turned the key in the switch. "I'll say it again, kid," he growled. "You're on probation. One wrong move and you go back to the juvenile authorities. I'm giving you a chance to grow into a decent man, but it's up to you. So watch your step." He looked at Roy directly then, a grim, warning stare.

He drove away, and Roy watched him go with sullen, resentful eyes before he trudged on toward the house. As he passed the battered old station wagon he saw that the keys were in it. Just like that other time . . . . He thought about his plan briefly. No phone at the ranch yet. Half a mile to the highway where he'd been catching the school bus the past week. If he had a car nobody could stop him.

Private plans for solution

Furtherance

Judy was riding her tricycle on the screened gallery of the house. "Hello, Half-Uncle Roy," she said.

Introducing helping character

Half-Uncle Roy, for Pete's sake! He looked at his niece with jaundiced eyes. Almost six, a scrawny little chick with uncombed taffy-blond hair, a front tooth gone, dirty knees and elbows, a soiled dress and frayed sweater. My gosh! Even if Ed's wife wasn't the healthiest, even if she did have a load with the housework and the baby, couldn't she at least teach this brat to comb her hair and use soap and water once in a while?

Gimmick

Adding to VPC's character, showing his ability to see other's problem through his own bitterness

"Hello, Mouse," he grunted, and went on into the house. He heard the baby fussing in the back bedroom, but didn't see Ed's wife anywhere. Scowling fiercely, he climbed the stairs to the small, dingy attic room that was his new home, his happy, happy home. Until his dirty old foot slipped and Ed threw him to the wolves!

Hinting at inward emotional problem solution

He changed into his work clothes and went downstairs, feeling hungry. In the old days when he and his Pop were batching, he always prowled the refrigerator when he got home from school. But now, famished as he was, he didn't want Ed's wife bawling him out for taking liberties with the left-

Character trait—dependable, refuses to break the rules in spite of temptation

Introduction of character	overs. Marnie was blond and pretty, except for the drawn, kind of haggard look, and mostly she treated him all right, polite-like, but he could tell she had to strain a little. Naturally, she resented him moving in. Natch.
Bitter emotional climate, yet sympathetic for others	

Introduction of character

Bitter emotional climate, yet sympathetic for others

overs. Marnie was blond and pretty, except for the drawn, kind of haggard look, and mostly she treated him all right, polite-like, but he could tell she had to strain a little. Naturally, she resented him moving in. Natch.

On the gallery, Judy said, "Where you goin', Half-Uncle Roy?"

Character trait— gentle to small fry

Say, that was a good question, wasn't it? "Alaska," he said, and she giggled shrilly and shouted, "Oh, you're silly!"

Character trait in action—doing chores
Emotional climate

Emotional climate continued—the sense of not belonging

That makes two of us, he thought as he went down the slope toward the barn and sheds. He looked at the wintry landscape and it made him feel an aching, desolate kind of loneliness. Man, where were all the drugstores? He felt a lacerating homesickness for the old days: the apartment in Tulsa, getting supper for his elderly Pop, maybe the two of them making a movie or ball game afterward. A guy that lived all his life in a city could get the creeping shrieks looking at this empty wilderness. Even a tough guy like Roy Cantrell, Esquire.

Hinting at past harmony, an arrow toward possible future harmony

And the squares at school, he thought. Real gone village types, yokels, and nervous about new transfer students. All except that giddy little chick, Dorene Phipps. Hot dog!

Introduction of important character by thought

"Welcome to the Senior class of Cottonwood High," he mimicked in his mind. "I am Dorene Phipps, Senior Class President. We welcome you and hope you like our school, Roy."

Emotional climate

Oh, mercy me! Well, at least the little ick-chick had held out the hand of friendship,

236

while the male gender just acted uneasy. Like they'd heard about his fabulous career in crime. Well, so what?

He did the chores methodically. He didn't mind the chores. In spite of world-wide opinions to the contrary, he didn't shirk

work. What he shirked was Ed's ways, his pessimistic, suspicious attitude. So today he was walking out. A guy of seventeen who

looked easy nineteen or over could snag onto a job somewhere, and what good was a high-school diploma, anyway?

❂   ❂   ❂

It was dusk when he returned to the

house to wash up for supper. When he came out of the bathroom, Ed's wife was standing in the back bedroom door holding the baby. She looked real pale.

"Supper's cooked," she said listlessly. "Will you fix plates for yourself and Judy? Just stack them when you're finished."

She didn't look at him, either, he noticed. The Edward Cantrells never hardly seldom ever looked at Roy Cantrell, one of Amer-

ica's ten most unwanted criminals, man.

Over her shoulder she said in a kind of

weary voice, "Judy, you go to bed right after you eat, now."

Roy kind of enjoyed that supper, despite

Judy's bright and steady stare. It was the first meal he'd eaten without the uneasy presence of Mr. and Mrs. E. Cantrell, his keepers.

"Half-Uncle Roy," Judy said, "are you married?"

Solemnly, he said, "Not any more, Mouse."
What a weird little chick, he thought.

"Do you miss my daddy?" she inquired curiously.

"Oh, dear me, yes." Roy said.

Character—playing with small fry

She frowned thoughtfully. "Where did we get you, Half-Uncle Roy?"

"Your pappy bought me at a slave auction, Mouse," Roy told her.

Subconscious actions

After supper a funny thing happened, something he couldn't explain to himself. He got soap and a washrag and scoured Judy's face and hands and grimy knees and elbows. Then he combed her hair. "Well, that'll hold you for a couple days, Mouse," he told her, and sent her on to bed.

Subconscious actions (past habits asserting themselves)

After that, he washed all the accumulated dirty dishes and pots and pans, and tidied up the kitchen. He didn't know why. Maybe he felt sorry for Ed's pretty wife—after all, man, look at her plight. She was stuck with old warden Ed.

Furtherance

He packed one suitcase. He could have taken everything, but he only packed one

Executing plan

suitcase. Dungarees, slacks, shirts, socks, T-shirts, loafers, underwear, the picture of

Detail

his father and mother—a middle-aged Ed and the pretty frail girl he'd outlived by ten years. He dressed in slacks, corduroy shirt, windbreaker, topcoat, and his cord-soled Oxfords. Impatiently he watched the small clock and listened to his low-tuned radio, forcing himself to wait. Finally, at ten-thirty, he picked up the suitcase and slipped

Plan in action

down the creaky stairs and out into the night.

The station wagon was parked on the slope; he could coast two hundred yards before he started the motor. He got in and sat there listening to the loud thumping of his heart. He was all set. . . . Good-by dear half-brother Ed.

Unexpected difficulty with his subconscious self

He kept sitting there, shivering a little, his heart hammering like a frantic tom-tom, but he didn't touch the keys or the hand brake. He couldn't do it; he couldn't steal the station wagon.

Hindrance

That other time he'd been just one of a gang, one of five boys prowling the dark city streets. Chug Mooney was the one who had discovered some guy had left his keys in his car; originally, it was Chug's wild idea. "Teach this jerk a lesson," he had said. And it had seemed like a good joke at the time. "Drive this car somewhere and leave it." But then Chug had decided to cruise a while, and Chug had run a red light and decided to race the cops. Chug had put up a battle, resisting the cops. So all five of them had gone to jail.

Flashback explaining the motive above

Roy's grandma and grandpa had been shocked and appalled, and said helplessly that they just couldn't cope with the incorrigible boy. Well, gentlemen of the jury, the incorrigible boy couldn't cope with them, either—those loyal, doddering old squares. But the thing was, Roy hadn't actually ever stolen any automobiles yet, and he hated to start now.

Following the inner man or subconscious

Sighing, Roy got out of the station wagon and started walking, the suitcase banging against his leg, the icy wind bringing tears

239

Furtherance	to his eyes. Great night to break out, man. But it wasn't the weather that made him
Complication	feel so reluctant. It was thinking about Ed's wife having to do the chores for six days.
Hindrance	It seemed hours before he reached the
Emotional change— vpc's surprise	highway, and by then he felt real put down. He wanted to go, but he kept thinking,
Ability to see problems of another conflicting with his personal desire	"They'll be all alone in this crazy never-never land for six whole days." Headlights came down the asphalt, an ancient pickup slowed, stopped; a man's voice asked, "Want
Furtherance	a lift to town, bub?" and Roy took one step.
Opportunity to complete plan	Just one yearning, eager step toward freedom. Then he stopped. "No, thanks," he
Sacrifice (made by subconscious unplanned and unexpected)	groaned. "I just got out here." And he turned and plodded forlornly back to the black ranch house.
Next complication starts	He was halfway up the stairs when he heard the noise. Like a moan, like a cry for
Hindrance	help. "Marnie's having a bad dream," he thought. Then he heard it again, the shuddering moan.
Makes effort to help emotional climate	He went back to the bedroom, turning on lights as he went. He hesitated outside
Furtherance	the door, fearful and ill at ease. "You sick, Mrs. Cantrell?" he asked.
Emotional climate— problem increases	She mumbled, and he got one word that gave him goose bumps. "Hospital," she said.
Hindrance	He'd never met a crisis before. Now he
Character in action— responsibility habit takes over	was suddenly in charge of a frightening emergency. He pushed the door open, peering into the dark bedroom. My gosh! The baby, Judy . . . what should he do first? He turned and bolted out of the house. Station
Furtherance	wagon, he thought. He started the motor, drove it up to the steps, left it there with the

heater going to warm it. That much he had figured out for himself. But when he got inside again and called to her, she didn't answer, and it frightened him stupid. He went into the gloom of the bedroom and touched her arm, her cold, damp arm. "Ma-am!" he pleaded.

She stirred, began to mumble again. "Quilts," she said. "Station wagon . . . baby . . . diapers . . . bottles . . . refrigerator."

He put it together, he got it. Armload of diapers, the kid was in his basket, bottles of formula in the refrigerator. He went into the other bedroom and woke Judy. "Get dressed, Mouse," he said, "we're going to town."

Frantic with haste and alarm, he did all the things, put the bottles and diapers and the baby in his basket into the station wagon. When he checked, Judy was asleep again. He got her dressed, embarrassed but resigned, and wrapped a blanket around her and deposited her on the front seat. And then came the part he felt sick about.

"Can you—walk to the car?" he asked Marnie awkwardly.

She made no answer. He reached for the lamp on the bedside table, turned it on. She was out; she looked awful, kind of pale blue. He wanted to run. Get out, like he'd started to do. . . . Why wasn't there somebody here to tell him what to do? Someone to help him? He thought, "I don't know anybody closer than Tulsa! I got to do it all myself. I *always* got to do everything myself!"

Roy weighed 142 pounds and was 5 feet

Emotion—concern for others

Hindrance

Furtherance—trying to handle the situation

Problem increasing

Hindrance

Emotion—self-pity

9 inches tall. He was not a strong boy. Mrs. Ed Cantrell, normally a tall, slim, healthy woman, still weighed maybe 115 pounds, not counting the cocoon of blankets and quilts Roy managed to tuck around her. But somehow he got the limp, unwieldy bundle of her off the bed, through the door, through two rooms, down the outside steps, and into the back of the station wagon. It was a nightmare trip, but he made it. He closed the back end of the station wagon, drove to the highway, and headed east toward town.

At the first lighted service station he stopped to telephone ahead to the hospital.

"Have a doctor ready," he said tensely. "It's an emergency."

"What sort of emergency?" a woman's voice demanded.

"Well," he said, "she—she had a baby about a month ago, and she's —."

"Bring her in," the nurse interrupted.

He drove to town. He had no driver's license, but he drove to Cottonwood—not daring to go fast, not daring to go slow.

He drove to the hospital, to the lighted side door with its concrete platform. He got out, and saw a nurse coming down a corridor inside, pushing a cart. Just one nurse. One dumpy, hard-faced, bored-acting nurse. So Roy had to get Ed's wife out of the station wagon and carry her up the steps and hoist her onto the cart.

"The doc here yet?" Roy panted anxiously, and the nurse said curtly that he was on his way. "Listen!" Roy said. "He better hurry! Listen —." But she had gone back

Furtherance

Manages to fill
requirements

Hindrance

Transition

Furtherance

Dependability trait
at work

Furtherance

Emotional climate

Hindrance—VPC still
bitter, critical, and
filled with self-pity

Hindrance—trying
to handle things

242

down the corridor with Ed's wife.

Roy stood there a long time shivering, not knowing what he was supposed to do now, and finally he glanced over his shoulder and saw Judy's scared eyes staring at him from the front seat.

He got in the station wagon, looking at her. "Poor little Mouse," he thought. "She's all loused up." He said, "Look, Mouse, why don't you climb over into the back and get some of that Grade-A sleep?"

And with a kind of pathetic eagerness she climbed over the back of the seat and lay down. It hit Roy in some odd way; it made him feel like bawling. She was so grateful for being told what to do. He had taken the strain off her almost-six mind. But nobody was handing out advice to R. Cantrell, boy bad-man. Nobody cared if he lived or died.

When he was sure Judy slept, he went into the building, along the echoing, empty corridor to a desk. He leaned against the antiseptic whiteness of the wall and fretted and worried, until a door down the hall whispered open and the nurse came hurrying out. "How is she?" he croaked, but she only gave him a curt, contemptuous look and shrugged. Like saying, how should she know? He was getting ready to ask about the doctor when a man walked in, looking sleepy and not very much pleased about the situation. The nurse nodded her head toward the whispering door, and she and the man disappeared into the room.

Almost immediately the dumpy, grim woman came trotting out. "You happen to

Marginal notes (left column):

Discovery

Furtherance

Unselfish concern

Action of the scene increases toward uncertain climax

Reversal

Hindrance

Emotional climate— bitterness and self-pity reasserting themselves

Unselfish concern over another character

Hindrance

New complication

243

Hindrance	know her blood type?" she asked Roy harshly.
Emotional concern increased	The question scared him badly. "No," he said.
	"She have her baby here?"
Furtherance	"No," he said. He knew that much.
Outer problem increased	The nurse grabbed the phone and called a number and waited, and in the silence Roy heard a faint wail, a thin crying, mewling
Hindrance	sound. The baby! he thought unhappily. Oh, gosh!
Hindrance—a second problem	"The baby is crying," he said shakily, and the nurse scowled and said, "Babies do, mister. It's probably his feeding time."
Furtherance	"Oh," Roy said. "Well—I've got bottles."
Emotional climate— yearning for help	He hoped she would help him this little bit. She was a woman, wasn't she?
Hindrance	But this tough-eyed old chick said sarcastically, "Goody for you! So you got bot-
Emotional climate— disappointment	tles—so the baby is hungry. Does that suggest anything?"
Hindrance	Roy sighed. "They're supposed to be— well, warmed, aren't they?"
Dialogue at cross— purposes	She shook her head and groaned. "Helpless men! Of course it's supposed to be warm," she snapped.
Emotional response	Roy had had just about enough of her lip, boy. He wanted to slap her silly face, or bawl, or something. But his glare was wasted on her; she spoke urgently into the telephone and hung up and loped into Marnie's
Futherance	room. The door sighed shut behind her.
Character habit— handling the responsibility	Roy got a bottle and found a bathroom, and there was hot water. He wasn't any dope; he could figure things out. He ran a washbowl full of hot water and put the

baby's bottle in it. It took forever to warm the bottle, a million years, but at last it dripped warm onto his arm—he'd seen Ed's wife test it like that—and he hurried out to the station wagon.

Judy was crouching by the basket rocking it and saying, "Don't cry, don't cry, don't cry."

You think that kid paid her any mind? No, he was ripping his lungs out, yelling. But when Roy shoved the nipple into his mouth his wails ran down like an engine out of gas, and he started making gurgling, glugging, contented sounds. Why, man, it was simple.

"Is Mommy coming outside pretty soon, Half-Uncle Roy?" Judy asked.

"Not for a while yet, Mouse," he said. "You go back to sleep, huh?" He wished *he* could wake up and find he'd just dreamed all this. He wished . . . Abruptly the baby stopped being satisfied with things and started fussing again.

"He needs to burk," Judy said softly. "I mean, burt."

Oh, gosh, Roy thought. "Who's stopping him?" he snarled.

"You s'pose to pat on his back so he'll do it." Judy said sleepily.

Grimly, Roy said, "He's *lying* on his back, Mouse. How can I pat it?"

"You s'pose to pick him up an' pat his back," she said.

Pick him up! Pick up a month-old baby? Oh, no! "You know so much about it," he said, "why don't *you* do it, Mouse?"

Self-approval

Sympathy for another's problem (adds to sympathy for vpc)

Furtherance

The lift of successful effort—furtherance

Hindrance

Self-pity

Hindrance

Hindrance—more problems, more confusion

Furtherance

245

Obediently, carefully, she extracted the
yowling infant from the basket, draped him
over her shoulder, and slapped him on the
shoulder blades. And presently the baby
belched! And she gave Roy a triumphant
grin.

So he shoved the bottle at her and said,
"Here, he's all yours, Mouse. You're a better mamma than I am. Take over."

Judy fed the baby, and Roy sat tapping
the steering wheel and worrying. He ought
to get in touch with Ed, but Ed hadn't said
where he could be reached. It wouldn't have
occurred to him they might need to call.

After a while Judy said quietly. "He's
asleep, Half-Uncle Roy."

So he told her to get to sleep herself, and
he wandered restlessly back inside the hospital. The hard-faced nurse was just loping
out of that mysterious room again. "We
typed her blood," she said sternly. "Type A
positive. She needs an immediate transfusion. You'll have to find a donor, mister.
Maybe two or three. No time to waste,
either."

He stared at her aghast. "*I've* got to get
donors?"

"We don't have a donor list," she said
curtly. "We don't have a blood bank. We're
giving her plasma, but she needs whole
blood. You'll have to get friends or relatives
to furnish the blood."

Friends! he thought bitterly. Relatives!
His only real relative was in Texas buying
cattle. Ed's wife's nearest relative was in
California.

Margin notes:
- Helping character
- Emotion of respect
- Hindrance
- Transition
- Transition
- Hindrance
- New problem
- Rise of emotional reaction of unfairness

246

The nurse eyed him balefully. "What type are you, mister?"

The helpless, scared type, he thought. "I don't know," he said.

The nurse sighed that disgusted sigh.

Dialogue at cross-purposes

"Come on, I had to call the lab technician out of bed to type your wife. She'll type you, too."

Understanding of nurse's reactions dawns

He was halfway down the hall before that sentence caught up with him. "Wife?" he said, astonished. "She's my half-sister-in-law."

"Oh," the nurse said, less unfriendly for some odd reason. "I thought you were the big lug who let her work too hard too soon after having a baby. My error, chum. Where is the villain of this drama?"

Furtherance—emotion of appreciation

"Texas," Roy said, understanding the question perfectly.

The lab technician pricked Roy's finger, grimly silent, and ran the test.

Furtherance

"Bingo!" the nurse said. Amazingly, she smiled at Roy. "You're a universal donor, bud," she said. "And the RH factor is right. Hey, you're over eighteen, aren't you?" she asked.

Sacrifice

Her look clued him. "I'm twenty-one," he said, to be safe.

"Well, I broke my glasses," she said. "Let's go, Grandpaw."

Deep concern for another

When Roy went into the room he saw Ed's wife in bed under clean white sheets, looking terribly wan and haggard, but she opened her eyes and recognized him and smiled. "Roy," she murmured. And in a whisper she asked about the baby and Judy.

He told her the baby was okay, had been fed and burted. "That Judy," he said. "That's a smart kid." Ed's wife smiled faintly, closed her eyes. She's pretty, Roy thought. She sure is pretty, even now.

They transferred his blood directly into Ed's wife, him lying on the cart. He kept worrying about the baby, and about how sick Ed's wife might be. My gosh! Judy he could handle, but a month-old kid! . . . When the doctor finished with him he went out of the room, holding the alcohol-soaked cotton on the stinging puncture, and he said nervously to the nurse, "When will she be able to go home?"

"That's up to the doctor, chum," she said crisply.

She got the big ledger on the desk and started asking him questions. Mrs. Ed Cantrell, he stated; twenty-five maybe; he didn't know if there was hospitalization insurance. Ed's occupation? Well, until a month ago he was a construction foreman, but now he was a rancher, only he didn't have any cattle yet. That's why he was in Texas, to buy cattle. Angus cattle. Or Grangus. Some kind of special Texas cattle.

The nurse eyed him intently. "You feel all right?" she asked, and he laughed a giddy laugh and said, "You kidding?" Then the doctor came out to the desk, and Roy said worriedly, "When can she go home?"

Gravely, the doctor said: "It depends, of course. I'd say two days, but it depends. She'll need another transfusion; then we'll see."

Furtherance

Forgets self, wants to measure up but realizes it is beyond him

Hindrance

Crisis

Furtherance

Plant

Hindrance

Crisis deepens

The baby was crying out there in the dark station wagon. Roy thought helplessly, going out to see about the baby, "So I'm in charge of the transfusion department. I got to get donors. Great! What do I do—run an ad in the paper?"

"Don't cry, don't cry, don't cry, don't cry," Judy was saying to the baby.

Self-pity increases

Roy looked helplessly at his niece. "Is he hungry again already, or what?"

"I guess he's wet," she said shyly. "He needs to be changed."

Hindrance

"Can you handle it, Mouse?" he asked hopefully, but she shook her head. "I don't know about that part yet," she murmured.

That's what did it. He'd been operating mechanically, in a kind of trance, but this

Black Moment

was the end. This was the bitter end. He couldn't swing it alone any more. He needed help. Desperately he needed a friend. And he didn't know a soul in Cottonwood. Ed's wife didn't know a soul in Cottonwood. They were all strangers in an alien land.

Beginning of the end

Twist

Then, abruptly, in the night of his defeat he remembered a voice saying, "Welcome to Cottonwood High. I am Dorene Phipps."

He hurried into the hospital. He found a phone book on the desk and checked it. Only one Phipps. He memorized the address and went out to the station wagon and the crying baby. The Mouse had been great, but she was a rookie. Dorene would have a mother.

Furtherance

It took him a while in the strange and deserted town to locate Elm Street and find number 709. It was a big, dark, shabby, two-story house in a fenced yard. Roy went up

the steps and banged on the door. "Oh,
man!" he thought desperately. "All I want
is one little break now. Just one."

After a while a light went on inside, the
porch light flicked on, the door opened, and
a gray-haired, plump man in a bathrobe
looked at him through the screen door.
"Yes?" he said.

"Dorene," Roy stammered. "I got to see
Dorene Phipps. I'm a senior. It's real vital.
I mean she's president. She's the only —."

"At three o'clock in the morning?" the
man said. "Now, see here, young fellow! Are
you drunk, or just out of your mind?"

Shivering, Roy said desperately, "I got to
see her. She's the only one I know. It's an
emergency. It's —."

A woman came up behind the man. A
plump, motherly-looking chick. "What is
it, Fred?" she asked with alarm. And Fred
Phipps told her some crazy nut wanted him
to get Dorene out of bed at three in the
morning. "What for?" she asked, sensibly;
and then she said, "Listen! Is that a baby
crying?"

That's what I got to see Dorene about,"
Roy said forlornly.

"No!" Fred Phipps said, "It can't be —."

A kid about Judy's age inserted her head
between the man and the door, goggling at
Roy. "Who is it, Papa?" she asked. Suddenly
it seemed there were kids all over the place,
staring at him, and the woman said, "Run
get Dorene, one of you children." And another voice called, "I'm coming, for Pete's
sake! What's up?"

Hindrance

Black Moment
increases

"A fellow to see you," her father said. "About a—a baby."

Dorene pushed between her father and the screen door. Her dark hair was tied up in a funny bunch, she wore a fadded wrapper, and she looked like an angel to groggy Roy. She said, "Oh, it's the new boy at school. My goodness!"

"Look," Roy croaked, "I don't know anybody but you, not a soul. Ed's in Texas. They have a baby not quite a month old, and Marnie's in the hospital and needs blood and they won't let her come home for a million years. Judy is okay, but she's only five and a half, she can't do *every*thing. . . . You got to help me, President. I'm a senior, you got to help me!" He broke up, then. "Man, it's the craziest!" he sobbed. "I can't make it."

The light was going around and around, then, and he keeled over.

Somebody was slopping a wet rag on his face, and Judy was saying, "He's my half-uncle. Daddy bought him at a slave auction, and he isn't married any more. He's going to Alaska." The mamma-chick was saying, "It's a precious sweetie-pie; just needed some dry britches. What's the darling's name?" And Judy said, "He's only named R. E., 'cause Mamma wants to name him Ralph Edward, an' Daddy wants to name him Raymond Everett, so they give him 'nishuls till they decide."

Roy figured it was time to cut back in again.

*   *   *

Furtherance

Characterization— trying for help

Emotional reaction— VPC is in over his head (Notice, lack of orange juice earlier after transfusion makes this logical.)

Helping character

Plant

251

Ed came home Sunday before sundown. Roy was in the kitchen fixing supper, and Ed gave him a dumfounded stare. "Didn't know you were a cook," he said. Roy said he used to do most of the cooking for his Pop when they were batching. Ed rubbed his chin. "I noticed you got all the work done, Roy. Corral and the shed roofs."

"The senior class helped me," Roy said. "Yesterday. Painted the kitchen, too. I guess you didn't notice."

"By golly," Ed murmured. "Where's Marnie?" In the living room, Roy told him, and Ed said wonderingly, "You bake those pies, Roy?"

"No," Roy said, "The senior class president baked 'em."

"By golly," Ed said, and went to find his wife. He was gone a long time, and when he came back he looked kind of white and stunned. "Look, kid—Roy," he said huskily. "Let's take a walk, huh?"

Outside in the chill dusk, they walked in silence all the way to the corral where the truck was.

"Roy," Ed said at last, "when I was a couple of years older than you are now, I ran away when my father got married again. Ever since then I've been nursing a childish grudge against that marriage and anything connected with it. See what I mean?"

Roy didn't, exactly, but he nodded.

"Marnie told me all about everything," Ed said self-consciously, and chuckled. "Said if it came to choosing between the Cantrells, she'd run me off. Don't blame

Conclusion

Reversal

New treatment

Different attitude of antagonist

Implication— belonging to the classgroup

Theme—a man earns his respect

Respect increases

Reversal

Explanation of character's reaction

Explanation of motivation

With vpc's bitterness healed, another healing of another character results

Helped character's new attitude

her. I can't tell you how much I—well —."
Wordlessly, he put his arm around Roy's
shoulders and squeezed. "I got us a couple
saddle horses, Roy," he said. "You'll like
this life once you get used to it. I'm gonna
need you—we all need you here. This is
your home, see? Permanently."

"I never rode a horse," Roy said, embarrassed.

"You'll learn. You'll pick it up in no time,"
Ed said.

"Ed," Roy said stiffly, "I started to run off.
I *started* to."

"I know," Ed said. "Marnie—she heard
you leave, heard you come back. You *came*
back, Roy. And I'll never forget it." Then
he said, "Hey, we just agreed on a name
for the baby. Roy Edward Cantrell. Okay?"

"That's a real crazy name, man," Roy said
gruffly.

Theme implied—a
man earns his own
respect

Offer of
comradeship

Emotional
satisfaction—VPC
now belongs

Causes unexpected
realization and
confession

Complete proof
given that VPC again
has a family

The text of *Basic Story Techniques* has been set on the Linotype machine in Caledonia, a face partly inspired by Scotch Modern, which though popular from the early nineteenth century, had grown too wooden and mechanical for twentieth-century taste. By combining some elements from an English design by William Martin, of about 1790, and adding a restrained calligraphic stroke, the late W. A. Dwiggins created Caledonia for present-day book use. It holds obvious promise for continued popularity in the future.

University of Oklahoma Press

Norman